Criminological Research

INTRODUCING QUALITATIVE METHODS provides a series of volumes which introduce qualitative research to the student and beginning researcher. The approach is interdisciplinary and international. A distinctive feature of these volumes is the helpful student exercises.

One stream of the series provides texts on the key methodologies used in qualitative research. The other stream contains books on qualitative research for different disciplines or occupations. Both streams cover the basic literature in a clear and accessible style, but also cover the 'cutting edge' issues in the area.

SERIES EDITOR

David Silverman (Goldsmiths College)

EDITORIAL BOARD

Michael Bloor (University of Wales, Cardiff)
Barbara Czarniawska (University of Gothenburg)
Norman Denzin (University of Illinois, Champaign)
Barry Glassner (University of Southern California)
Jaber Gubrium (University of Missouri)
Anne Murcott (South Bank University)
Jonathan Potter (Loughborough University)

TITLES IN SERIES

Doing Conversational Analysis
Paul ten Have

Using Foucault's Methods
Gavin Kendall and Gary Wickham

The Quality of Qualitative Research
Clive Seale

Qualitative Evaluation
Ian Shaw

Researching Life Stories and Family Histories
Robert L. Miller

Categories in Text and Talk
Georgia Lepper

Focus Groups in Social Research
Michael Bloor, Jane Frankland, Michelle Thomas, Kate Robson

Qualitative Research Through Case Studies
Max Travers

Gender and Qualitative Methods
Helmi Jarviluoma, Pirkko Moisala and Anni Vilkko

Doing Qualitative Health Research
Judith Green and Nicki Thorogood

Methods of Critical Discourse Analysis
Ruth Wodak and Michael Meyer

Qualitative Research in Social Work
Ian Shaw and Nick Gould

Qualitative Research in Information Systems
Michael D. Myers and David Avison

Researching the Visual
Michael Emmison and Philip Smith

Qualitative Research in Education
Peter Freebody

Using Documents in Social Research
Lindsay Prior

Doing Research in Cultural Studies
Paula Saukko

Qualitative Research in Sociology: An Introduction
Amir B. Marvasti

Narratives in Social Science
Barbara Czarniawska

Criminological Research: Understanding Qualitative Methods
Lesley Noaks and Emma Wincup

Criminological Research

Understanding Qualitative Methods

Lesley Noaks and Emma Wincup

SAGE Publications
Los Angeles • London • New Delhi • Singapore
www.sagepublications.com

First published 2004
Reprinted 2006, 2007

 SAGE Publications Ltd
1 Oliver's Yard
55 City Road
London EC1Y 1SP

SAGE Publications Inc
2455 Teller Road
Thousand Oaks
California 91320

SAGE Publications India Pvt. Ltd
B1/I 1 Mohan Cooperative Industrial Area
Mathura Road, New Delhi 110 044
India

SAGE Publications Asia-Pacific Pte Ltd
33 Pekin Street #02/01
Far East Square
Singapore 048763

British Library Cataloguing in Publication Data

A catalogue record for this book is available
from the British Library

ISBN-10 0-7619-7406-7   ISBN-13 978-0-7619-7406-2
ISBN-10 0-7619-7407-5 (pbk)   ISBN-13 978-0-7619-7407-9 (pbk)

Library of Congress Control Number 2003115325

Typeset by C&M Digitals (P) Ltd, Chennai, India
Printed in Great Britain by Cpod, Trowbridge, Wiltshire

Contents

Preface and Acknowledgements

Qualitative research in criminology has a long-established history dating back to the ethnographic studies of crime and deviance carried out by the Chicago School in the 1920s and 1930s. Despite the fact that qualitative techniques have been employed for almost a century, there has been little systematic attention to the use of different types of qualitative methods in criminological research, or consideration of the particular issues surrounding their usage. Consequently we were particularly pleased to be asked to write this contribution to the *Introducing Qualitative Methods* series. Having agreed to take up the challenge, our first task was to prepare a proposal for the publishers. This included an assessment of the likely market for the book. There are now a vast number of books on qualitative research. It is no longer possible to read everything published on the topic, and it is sometimes barely possible to keep up with even a narrowly defined area of interest within it. The question as to whether another text on qualitative research was needed had to be asked. Unsurprisingly our answer to this question was yes. Despite the growing literature, we felt that criminologists interested in qualitative research still struggle to find suitable texts.

Criminologists do not have their own set of methods but conducting criminological research raises numerous difficulties and dilemmas. Those embarking on a criminological study are more likely than not to have chosen a sensitive topic, particularly a politically sensitive one. Undoubtedly, they will face a whole range of ethical dilemmas, not least through being party to knowledge about illegal acts. Principally for those who choose an ethnographic approach, conducting fieldwork often means having to cope with the ongoing presence of risk and danger. Of course, other qualitative researchers face such difficulties and dilemmas but there are some important differences because the subject matter of criminology gives them a particular accent.

Having examined available texts we felt that criminologists could make good use of either the numerous generic texts available on qualitative research or specialist volumes that provide reflexive accounts of the research process (see for example, Jupp et al., 2000; King and Wincup, 2000). However what was missing from the literature was an authoritative text that provided an introduction to qualitative methods and methodological debates, which was grounded in the realities of conducting criminological research. The book fulfils this role and is intended to complement those referred to above. In many respects a book along these lines is long overdue. However, it is also timely because problems of law and order have received unprecedented political attention since the final decade of the twentieth century, at least in England and Wales (see Chapter 2), and this has led to increased government funding for criminological research. At the time of writing such research funding appears not to be so readily available, but law and order issues continue to dominate political debates.

The growth of political interest in crime and criminal justice is mirrored by an ever-expanding range of courses on offer at all levels in universities. More people than ever before are involved in criminological research or are trained in its methods. King and Wincup (2000) argue that if criminological problems are to be properly understood and appropriately addressed, they must be effectively researched in ways that are theoretically grounded, methodologically secure and practically based. Our aim in this book is to support this task through offering comprehensive coverage of the qualitative approaches used by criminologists, and the issues they face when they attempt to put these principles into practice. Throughout the book, we make extensive use of illustrative examples and include both classic and contemporary studies. By drawing upon the research experiences of established criminologists we hope that new generations of criminologists can learn from what has gone on before.

This book is also informed by our own teaching and research experience. Both of us have considerable experience of conducting research on a range of criminological concerns. We have worked together on studies of remand prisoners and the risk management of sex offenders, and separately on projects concerned with female offenders, probation practice and drug use (Wincup) and fear of crime, policing and crime prevention (Noaks). We have always used qualitative approaches, although have sometimes combined these with the use of quantitative techniques. These research experiences inform our teaching of research methods at undergraduate and postgraduate level, including the supervision of doctoral students. Teaching these courses has made us aware that most students struggle when they have to put their learning of qualitative research methods into practice by developing a workable research design. More often than not, students are too ambitious and suggest studies with ill-focused research questions and/or unrealistic data collection plans. Consequently, we have always tried to convey to our students some sense of the reality of conducting criminological research. In so doing we take care to point out that research is always more difficult than anyone envisages but at the same time it offers enjoyment and intellectual challenges. We also inform our students that it is not sufficient to read about how to do interviews or analyse documents in one of the many 'cook book' style research textbooks that are now available and then go off and collect their data. Instead they should try to prepare themselves by building up familiarity with the debates that surround the use of the method, and by reading criminological studies that have used the same method. This book follows in the same vein.

We wrote this book with undergraduate and postgraduate criminology students in mind but it will also be relevant to students studying related disciplines such as forensic psychology, sociology, social policy and socio-legal studies. The book will also be of interest to a wider range of groups. These include researchers at different stages in their careers, lecturers with responsibility for research methods courses, practitioners involved in research and those who fund criminological research.

Structure of the book

The contents of this book are set out in three sections. In Part One we begin by offering an account of the development of the qualitative research tradition within criminology. Two chapters are then devoted to issues which are pertinent to criminological research: the ways in which the political context shapes the research process and the ethical issues which arise when researchers choose to focus on crime and criminal justice. Collectively they provide a backdrop for understanding the discussions which follow in the remainder of the book. In Part Two are a series of chapters that explore the different elements of the research process. We begin with negotiating and sustaining access, move on to consider the main data collection techniques used by qualitative researchers and end with a discussion of qualitative data analysis. Finally, in Part Three we present two case studies which draw upon our own experiences as criminological researchers. The first (written by Emma Wincup) discussess research conducted for the Home Office, and the second (written by Lesley Noaks) is an example of doctoral research.

Each chapter contains references to both methodological and criminological literature and an annotated guide to further reading with full publication details given in the References. Exercises that can be used to form the basis of seminars or workshops on research methods courses also accompany each chapter.

During the course of writing this book we are grateful for the support and advice from a large number of people. Paul Atkinson, Ros Beck, Fiona Brookman, Amanda Coffey, Sara Delamont and a number of anonymous reviewers read the proposal and offered helpful suggestions. We would also like to thank David Silverman for being a supportive and encouraging series editor and Patrick Brindle, Zoë Elliott and Michael Carmichael at Sage for their enthusiasm, encouragement and advice.

Part I

Qualitative Research in Criminology: History, Politics and Ethics

1

The Development of Qualitative Approaches to Criminological Research

Introduction

Qualitative research has a long and distinguished history in the social sciences, arising in part from dissatisfaction with quantitative approaches. The ethnographic studies conducted by the Chicago School in the 1920s and 1930s established the importance of qualitative research for the study of crime and deviance. In this chapter, a brief history is given of the origins of criminology and the development of the empirical research tradition within it. This provides a backdrop for exploring the growth of qualitative approaches to criminological research, and for pinpointing the pragmatic utility and methodological desirability of qualitative approaches for researching crime and criminal justice.

The origins of criminology and criminological research

There is considerable debate about how best to define criminology. For Garland (2002: 7) criminology is 'a specific genre of discourse and inquiry about crime that has developed in the modern period and that can be distinguished from other ways of talking and thinking about criminal conduct'. Criminologists will no doubt be aware that virtually everyone has common sense knowledge about crime, and correspondingly many ideas about the causes of crime and the best ways to tackle it. However, what characterizes criminologists is that they subject these ideas to rigorous enquiry by conducting either quantitative or qualitative research. Defining criminology as a discipline with an emphasis on empirically grounded, scientific study, Garland proposes that criminology grew out of a convergence between a governmental project and a Lombrosian project. The former signifies a series of empirical studies beginning in the eighteenth century that have sought to map patterns of crime and monitor the workings of the criminal justice system. Such work aims to ensure that justice is delivered effectively, efficiently and fairly. The latter project denotes a contrasting project, one based on the notion that it is possible to 'spot the difference' (Coleman and Norris, 2000: 26) between those who offend and those who do not using scientific means. This paved the way for a tradition of inquiry seeking to identify the causes of crime through empirical research, beginning with the use of quantitative methods but later supplemented by qualitative ones.

The legacy of this historical development can still be felt and produces continued tension within the discipline between policy-oriented criminological research, with its emphasis on the management and control of crime, and a theoretically-oriented search for the causes of crime. For Garland (2002) the combination of the two projects is sufficient if criminology is to continue to claim to be a useful and scientific state-sponsored academic discipline. While this aspect of his view is not widely challenged, the implication that classicism 'becomes the criminology that never was' (Coleman and Norris, 2000: 16), in the sense that it does fit Garland's definition of criminology has been disputed. Others, for instance Hughes (1998), would argue that with the benefit of hindsight the Classical School is the first clearly identifiable school of criminology, distinctive because it marks a shift away from explaining crime in terms of religion or superstition. Even a cursory glance through the main texts available on criminological theory, both classic and contemporary, indicate at least implicit support for this view (Lilly et al., 2002; Taylor et al., 1973). The Classical School, a term used retrospectively to describe the work of philosophers such as Beccaria and Bentham, refers to late eighteenth century theorizing about crime which grew out of the Enlightenment project with its focus on reason. The classical approach to the study of crime was underpinned by the notion of rational action and free will. These notions were neither subjected to empirical testing nor had they been developed from exploratory research. Hence, they do not meet Garland's definition of criminology. The debate presented here relates to the question: 'is criminology a science?'; a question that has also plagued closely related disciplines such as sociology. In relation to criminology, Coleman and Norris (2000:176) argue this is a 'difficult question that has taken up a lot of energy over the years, often to little effect'. Given our focus in this text on empirical research, we offer support for Garland's position but note the earlier influences.

The debate outlined above is one of many that criminologists continue to have on fundamental issues. This is unsurprising in many respects. Criminology, as an academic subject, is held together by a substantive concern: crime (Walklate, 1998). Consequently, it is multi-disciplinary in character rather than being dominated by one discipline. For this reason, it is helpful to view criminology as a 'meeting place' for a wide range of disciplines including sociology, social policy, psychology and law among others. Individual criminologists frequently adhere more closely to one social science discipline than others. Hence, to understand fully what they are attempting to articulate, it is important to note the conceptual apparatus they are utilizing (Walklate, 1998). For instance, our own work draws heavily upon sociological concepts and theories, however, we have worked with colleagues from other disciplines. We would argue that this enriches our work but often after considerable discussion has taken place. As a consequence of the diverse theoretical frameworks upon which criminologists can draw, they frequently disagree with one another. Walklate (1998) argues that despite such disagreements there is some consensus (although we would suggest that it is a tenuous one) in that criminologists aspire to influence crime control policy. However, there is much less consensus around features of what constitutes the crime problem.

We will now explore the development of both quantitative and qualitative traditions within criminology, focusing predominantly on the latter but including the former because it provides a backdrop to understanding the emergence of qualitative techniques. We will attempt to locate the emergence and development of these traditions within their social and political context. Before moving on it is important to note that not all criminological research is empirical but takes a theoretical form. Both forms require different skills and training but it is not appropriate for a 'pragmatic division of labour' (Bottoms, 2000: 15) to be fully adopted. All empirical researchers need to acknowledge that theory is an essential element of the data collection and analysis process (see Chapter 8). Similarly theorists need to draw upon, and understand, empirical research as one means of testing the ability of their theoretical account to explain the social world.

The quantitative tradition

The quantitative tradition is closely allied to a theoretical perspective known as positivism, which has been adopted to study a wide range of social phenomenon. Researchers who adhere to this approach aim to explain crime and predict future patterns of criminal behaviour. Emulating the analysis by natural scientists of causal relationships, positivists are concerned with developing objective knowledge about how criminal behaviour was determined by either individual or social pathology. As Muncie (2001) notes, identifying the exact moment when positivist criminology became apparent is difficult but it is typically associated with the work of French and Belgian 'moral' statisticians in the 1820s. The publication of national crime statistics, beginning in France in 1827, provided these scholars with a dataset to be analysed. Quetelet's (1842) work is well known. He was concerned with the propensity to commit crime, which he used to refer to the greater or lesser probability of committing a crime. The potential causes of crime he concerned himself with were the influence of season, climate, sex and age. Based on his analysis of these variables, he concluded that crime patterns are regular and predictable, reaffirming his view that the methods of the natural sciences are wholly appropriate for understanding the causes of crime. For positivists such as Quetelet, the search for the causes of crime emphasized the role of social contexts external to the individual, thus the role of social, economic and environmental factors. Other important sociological positivist work includes Durkheim's (1895) analysis of crime rates and the Chicago School studies of crime patterns within the city of Chicago (Shaw and McKay, 1942). All these studies made use of official crime data in the form of police statistics or court records.

Both positivism and the quantitative tradition have been subjected to fierce criticism, particularly since the 1960s. Critics have argued that it is highly dubious to translate statistical association into causality. Quantitative work in criminology continues to be conducted but no longer adheres to a narrow positivist research tradition. Instead, quantitative work seeks to understand the complexity of social behaviour through examining a wide range of factors (see for example, Hale, 1999). In addition, quantitative research techniques have also been used to explore the workings of the criminal justice system; for example, to identify whether there is evidence of discrimination in the courtroom (Hood, 1992). In the next chapter, we will discuss briefly how quantitative approaches have been widely used since 1997 to evaluate a battery of new criminal justice interventions under the Crime Reduction Programme.

The qualitative tradition

The qualitative tradition in criminology developed in the United States. It owes a great deal to the work of the Chicago School. This school made important contributions to criminological theory, namely through developing 'social disorganisation' theory and their 'ecological model' of the development of cities and patterns of crime within them (see Downes and Rock, 2003). While many aspects of their work, particularly, the 'ecological model' have been discredited, they left behind a tradition of linking urban social problems to crime and provided the inspiration for the development of environmental criminology. Some of this work was based on quantitative research but the Chicago School also bequeathed a tradition of conducting criminological research which was distinctive in that they used ethnographic techniques to explore groups on the margins of urban industrial society in the United States in the 1920s and 1930s. They focused, in particular, on the 'dispossessed, marginal and the strange' (Brewer, 2000: 12), and included in the long list of Chicago School ethnographies (see Deegan, 2001) are studies of gangs, prostitution and homelessness.

Drawing their inspiration from developments within sociological theory, Chicago School researchers pursued innovative qualitative work making use of participant observation, life histories and documents. This work began to influence British criminologists in the 1960s (see Chapter 6 for a more detailed discussion). The qualitative tradition is now firmly established in criminology. Part of the explanation for this is the growth of new theoretical perspectives, which are broadly compatible with qualitative approaches to criminological research. Positivism has been subjected to fierce criticism by advocates of symbolic interactionism. As a result, they turned their attention away from the causes of crime to explore the process by which crimes are created and social reactions to crime. Advocates of the interactionist position see the social world as a product of social interactions, emphasizing the socially constructed nature of crime and deviance. The basic principles of positivism were called into question as symbolic interactionists emphasized the importance of human agency, consciousness and meaning in social activity, and highlighted the plurality of norms and values relating to 'normal' and 'deviant' behaviour. Symbolic interactionism inspired the development of the labelling perspective and the work of 'deviancy theorists' in the UK (discussed further in Chapter 6). Criminologists working within these theoretical frameworks were anti-statistical. While their work has been subjected to vehement criticism for paying insufficient attention to the exercise of power by feminists, Marxists and critical criminologists, these latter theoretical approaches have continued to support the use of qualitative methods.

Further chapters in this text will exemplify that the qualitative tradition is alive and well but continually faces threats to its health. We return to this discussion in the concluding chapter. For now we note that qualitative methods are used by researchers who are influenced by a wide range of theoretical perspectives. While we have demonstrated linkages between different theoretical traditions and the use of either qualitative and quantitative approaches, we hope to demonstrate in the remainder of this chapter that the relationship between theory and research is not a straightforward one.

Combining traditions

While we have just presented quantitative and qualitative traditions within criminology separately, we are mindful of the dangers of too sharp a distinction between the two traditions. As Silverman (1998) argues, it is absurd to push too far the qualitative/quantitative distinction. For Silverman (1998), the qualitative/quantitative research dichotomy is acceptable as a pedagogical device to aid understanding of a complex topic but such dichotomies are dangerous because they tend to locate researchers in oppositional groups. For some criminological researchers this is not problematic because they adhere strictly to either qualitative or quantitative methodology. Our own position is that while we would identify ourselves as qualitative researchers we make use of quantitative measures where appropriate. This might take many forms. Firstly, it is possible to derive some quantitative data from techniques typically associated with the generation of qualitative data. It is feasible that a study involving qualitative interviews will produce some basic quantitative data such as counts of interviewees who identified the same issues as important. Secondly, we might use the same data collection method such as the face-to-face interview to generate both qualitative and quantitative data by including a range of questions, some open-ended, others fixed-choice. Thirdly, we might use two different methods, one that will produce qualitative data (for example, focus groups) and another quantitative data (for example, structured observation).

The process of combining both qualitative and quantitative methodologies is one aspect of triangulation. Triangulation can be defined simply as 'the use of different methods of research, sources of data or types of data to address the same research question' (Jupp, 2001: 308). For Hoyle (2000), the term shrouds in mystery straightforward and sensible means of looking at the social world and obfuscates the role of the social researcher. However the concept is widely used in a number of ways and these are defined in Table 1.1

TABLE 1.1   *Forms of triangulation*

Form of triangulation	Alternative names (if any)	Definition
Data triangulation		Collection of different types of data on the same topic (Jupp, 2001), using the same method or different methods
Investigator triangulation	Researcher triangulation, team triangulation	Collection of data by more than one researcher (Jupp, 2001)
Method triangulation	Technique triangulation	Collection of data by different methods (Jupp, 2001)
Theoretical triangulation		Approaching data with multiple perspectives and hypotheses in mind (Hammersley and Atkinson, 1995)

The term 'triangulation' was first used in the context of social research by Campbell and Fiske (1959) but was used more frequently following the publication of Webb et al.'s text on unobtrusive measures and social research in 1966. While Webb et al. are keen to point out that single measures are not 'scientifically useless' (1966: 174), they propound that 'the most fertile search for validity comes from a combined set of different measures' (1966: 174). Triangulation as a social science concept derives from a loose analogy with navigation and surveying (Hammersley and Atkinson, 1995). The term was used in these professional fields to refer to the use of two or more landmarks to pinpoint a position more accurately than if one were used.

Applied to social research, arguments have been advanced for combining methods. The use of different methods can be an implicit or explicit decision. It may also be built in to the research strategy adopted. Brewer (2000) argues that combining methods is a routine feature of ethnographic research (see also

Chapter 6). Most research projects in the social sciences are in a general sense multi-method because alongside the main method of choice, subsidiary techniques are used. For example, conducting interviews in a prison will always involve some degree of observation of the social setting, which may impact on the research even if the data are not formally recorded or analysed. Similarly, a study relying mainly on participant observation within a youth centre for children at risk of offending is likely to begin with reading published documents about the centre, for instance bids for funding, annual reports and newspaper cuttings.

Numerous advantages are advanced in the literature to persuade researchers to adopt a multi-method approach, and the overarching theme is that combining methods increases the validity of the findings. Reflecting on his own criminological research career, Maguire (2000) argues for utilizing as many diverse sources of evidence as feasible to answer a research question. His rationale is that criminological research often involves working with information that is unreliable to varying extents. By bringing together different methods with their own blend of strengths and weaknesses, it is hoped that the weaknesses of one method can be countered by the strengths of the others. If the data gathered using the different methods offer similar conclusions, criminologists can be more confident that the conclusions offered are valid in the sense that they are plausible and credible. Similar arguments have been advanced by other criminologists (see for example King, 2000).

Denzin (1970) also advocates a strong case for triangulation, suggesting that this is the basic theme of his book entitled *The Research Act in Sociology*. He argues that his definition of each method implies a triangulated perspective. Denzin notes that the shifting nature of the social world and the biases that arise from the sociologist's choice of theories, methods and observers provide difficulties that a researcher working in the natural sciences does not face. For Denzin, the solution is to recognize these difficulties and to use multiple strategies of triangulation (data, investigator, methodological and theoretical) as the preferred line of action. He suggests that triangulation is the key to overcoming intrinsic bias that stems from single method, single observer and single theory studies. Despite Denzin's claim in the preface that he subscribes to a symbolic interactionist perspective, Silverman (1985) and May (2001) both highlight that Denzin's prescriptions can be seen to mesh with the positivist desire to seek an ultimate 'truth' about the social world through cross-validation. In his later writings, Denzin (1990, 1994) no longer subscribes to his earlier view, favouring a more postmodern approach, which gives precedence to the subjective world-view of research subjects as the only reliable vantage point (O'Connell Davidson and Layder, 1993). Between the two extremes are calls for 'reflexive triangulation' (Hammersely and Atkinson, 1995; O'Connell Davidson and Layder, 1993). This position encourages researchers to reflect upon the fact that social research is not conducted neutrally because researchers are part of the social world they are examining. It also reminds us that data should not be treated at face value. This position is supportive of triangulation but adopts a healthy cynicism about its potential to increase validity and overcome bias.

Substantial support can be found for Hammersley and Atkinson's (1995) argument that triangulation is not a simple test. Even if the findings do accord, this cannot be interpreted as 'fact'. It is plausible that the results tally due to systematic or random error. For this reason, Hammersley and Atkinson suggest researchers need to avoid naïve optimism, and resist the temptation to assume that the aggregation of data from different sources will produce a more complete picture. For the majority of qualitative research studies, the goal of establishing 'truth' is actively rejected and multiple versions of reality are acknowledged. Consequently, differences between data are as significant and enlightening as similarities. As King (2000: 306) argues, it is incumbent on the researcher to report the conflicts as far as possible so that the reader may also try to form a judgement. We can add here that the role of the researcher is also to explain different findings.

Jupp's (2001) suggestion that a much less bold and precise claim for triangulation can be made is helpful. He argues that different methods can be used to examine different aspects or dimensions of the same problem. Deliberately avoiding the term 'triangulation' and replacing it with 'methodological pluralism', Walklate advances a similar view:

> Methodological pluralism ... reflects a view of the research process which privileges neither quantitative nor qualitative techniques. It is a position which recognizes that different research techniques can uncover different layers of social reality and the role of the researcher is to look for confirmation and contradictions between those different layers of information (2000: 193).

We would like to advocate that researchers adopt a pragmatic and theoretically coherent approach to data collection, using appropriate methods to answer their research questions. The latter is important because researchers need to guard against the tendency to keep adding research techniques to their research design in an eclectic manner with the blind hope that it will produce a better thesis, report or other publication. A multi-method approach should only be pursued if it adds value to the study by enhancing understanding of the criminological issue of interest. Sometimes there may be little to be achieved by using different methods. As Jupp (2001) argues, some combinations of methods do not work well because they are founded on different assumptions about the nature of the social world and how it can be explained. Hence, combining methods does not automatically enhance validity. There are often pragmatic reasons for considering carefully whether a number of methods should be utilized. Maguire (2000: 138) shares the useful advice he received as a novice researcher: 'the best tip is to imagine the final report and work backwards'. This should not be interpreted as a rigid approach to criminological research.

Instead it requires the researcher to consider what they have been asked to produce both in terms of focus and also length.

Why conduct qualitative research on criminological topics?

In the remainder of this chapter we provide some of the more common responses to the question above in order to persuade the reader to employ qualitative methods for future research projects.

Because it provides a means of researching the 'dark figure of crime'

The 'dark figure of crime' can be defined as 'the figure for unrecorded crime or undetected offenders, that is to say those not included in official statistics' (Coleman and Moynihan, 1996: 146). There are other ways of collecting information on offences which do not appear in official crime statistics using quantitative techniques. Examples include the British Crime Survey, a victimization study involving interviews with 40,000 individuals aged 16 and over, and the Youth Lifestyles Survey, a self-report study of offending by almost 5,000 people aged between twelve and thirty (Flood-Page et al., 2000). Both datasets are collected from individuals living in private households in England and Wales. Maguire (2002: 322) suggests that a 'data explosion' took place at the end of the twentieth century, and he goes further to argue that there is no longer a strong demand in late-modern societies for a crude general 'barometer' (2002: 361) of crime; a role traditionally fulfilled by official crime statistics. Criminologists are streetwise enough to realize that combining the different data sources will never reveal the full extent of the 'dark figure of crime'. More realistically the hope is that combining different sets of quantitative data will build up a more complete understanding of the nature and extent of crime. However, as Coleman and Moynihan (1996) argue, there are some areas of criminological enquiry that are difficult to investigate using official data and survey methods. Hence, they suggest qualitative techniques could be used as a means of researching these areas. While these techniques need to be subjected to critical assessment, they should not be seen as a second best or a kind of fall-back to be employed where there is no quantitative data available. The use of qualitative techniques offer the opportunity to make a distinct contribution by elucidating the contexts in which offending takes place and the meanings attached to such behaviour.

One example of a form of crime, which is difficult to research using quantitative approaches, is white-collar crime. The definition of white-collar crime has been contentious since it was first coined by Sutherland (1949), and it remains a contested concept. We will not attempt to open up this debate here but instead direct the reader to Croall (2001) for an accessible introduction to this complex area of crime. As our working definition, we will adopt the following 'a heterogeneous group of offences committed by people of relatively high status or enjoying relatively high levels of trust, and made possible by their legitimate employment (Tombs and Whyte, 2001: 319–20)'.

It would be misleading to suggest that qualitative research on white-collar crime is unproblematic. Explanations as to why it is rarely detected, reported and prosecuted also serve as explanations for the lack of research in this area. They include the invisibility of such offences, their complex nature, the difficulties of identifying victims and the limited number of convicted individuals (Croall, 2001). Offences are hidden in occupational routines, and for this reason, often the only strategy researchers can employ is to conduct covert participant observation (see Chapters 3 and 4 for a discussion of the difficulties of covert research). One example of this form of research is Ditton's (1977) study, which he describes as an ethnography of fiddling and pilferage. His setting was a medium-sized factory-production bakery. Croall (1998) remarks that researchers are rarely in a position to conduct overt research on the more serious forms of white-collar crime, especially within financial and commercial enterprises. There are, however, some notable exceptions. Levi's (1981) study of long-firm fraud is described by Hobbs (2000: 171) as 'as close to an ethnography of fraud as we are ever likely to get'. Levi conducted an intensive study of court records from the Old Bailey and Manchester Crown Court, interviewed credit controllers and businessmen, criminal justice and legal professionals, observed four trials at the Old Bailey and interviewed offenders within prison and the community. The latter aspect of the research was limited due to lack of time but also because the places frequented by white-collar offenders were beyond the budget of a doctoral student! Where access to the extent enjoyed by Levi has not been possible, qualitative researchers have been creative in their use of data sources. In addition to the sources of data used by Levi, qualitative researchers have also made use of individual case studies, investigative journalism, court reports, media report of cases and interviews with enforcers (Croall, 1998). For Hobbs (2000) multiple methods have become the norm, and researchers inevitably have to compromise. Given the difficulties of pursuing this line of research, as long as researchers remain cognizant of the limits of their data, they can help to illuminate the 'dark figure of crime'.

We could have selected many other forms of crime as illustrative examples. The 'dark figure of crime' includes a wide range of behaviours including corporate, professional and organized crime. Only qualitative research has the potential to provide some insight into these crimes. This argument is advanced powerfully by Hobbs.

> The covert, non-institutionalized base from which professional and organized crime operates favours the use of a range of largely interpretive approaches. Until gangsters, armed robbers, fraudsters and their ilk indicate their enthusiasm for questionnaires or large-scale social surveys, ethnographic research, life histories, oral histories, biographies, autobiographies and journalistic accounts will be at a premium. (1994: 442)

Because it leads to an 'appreciation' of the social world from the point of view of the offender, victim or criminal justice professional

Matza (1969) first used the term 'appreciative studies' to refer to specific studies of deviant subcultures. This work was based on observation, sometimes involving participation, of the social world of deviants. In this respect the influence of symbolic interactionism is apparent. Criminologists now talk about appreciative criminology, referring to 'an approach that seeks to understand and appreciate the social world from the point of view of the individual or category of individual, with particular reference to crime and deviance' (Jupp, 2001: 12). In subsequent chapters of this volume we explore the ways in which different qualitative techniques can be employed to 'appreciate' the social world from the point of view of the offender, victim or criminal justice professional. We provide one example here as an illustration. We hope to demonstrate why the choice of a qualitative approach was appropriate, and in so doing explore why a reliance on quantitative techniques was rejected.

There are numerous examples of criminological studies which have attempted to 'appreciate' the social world from the point of the view of the criminal justice professional. Some of the more recent examples include studies by Silvestri (2003) and Crawley (2003) of police and prison officers respectively. It would be fair to say that some criminal justice professions have attracted more attention than others, with studies of police officers receiving the greatest consideration. There are a number of explanations for this imbalance, and the more obvious ones relate to the ease at which access can be negotiated, the appeal of the professional group and its work to criminological researchers and the priorities of funding bodies. Below is an example of a study that focused on probation practice, and is one of the few studies, which are concerned with the day-to-day work of practitioners in the Probation Service.

In *Residential Work with Offenders*, Wincup (2002) presents reflexive accounts of practice gathered from qualitative research in four bail hostels across England and Wales. The data gathered, predominantly from semi-structured interviews and ethnographic observation, are used to argue that the combination of working with a diverse, often needy and frequently risky, client group in a residential setting creates a unique blend of professional and personal anxieties. Wincup explores, solely from the viewpoint of hostel staff, the dilemmas which stem from working in an environment created to 'advise, assist and befriend' but progressively called upon to 'confront, control and monitor' (see Worrall, 1997 for a discussion of the changing nature of probation practice). Residential workers often experience a sense of isolation, receiving little training and perceive themselves as working on the periphery of the Probation Service. These reflexive accounts are located within their broader criminal justice context to allow discussion of the development of the 'new penology' (Feeley and Simon, 1992) with its emphasis on risk management, as well as ongoing concerns with diversity and the rise of the 'what works?' agenda. The accounts are also analysed in relation to contemporary criminological and sociological debates, particularly those relating to risk and gender. The text provides an insight into the everyday world of bail hostels, attempting to capture the rich and dynamic nature of residential work with offenders. It portrays a collective picture of the everyday, the banal and the commonplace, as well as the unique and the extraordinary. This could not have been achieved using quantitative approaches, although quantitative approaches might have been used to enhance the research (for example, to measure levels of stress).

Before moving on, a few brief comments need to be offered about appreciative research with offenders and victims. Zedner (2002) argues that victims now attract an unprecedented level of interest as a subject of criminology enquiry, and as a result, they are now a central focus of academic research. This is undoubtedly true but quantitative research on victims has been strongest, although some important qualitative work has been undertaken. This form of research has been largely done by feminists concerned with domestic violence, sexual violence and child abuse. Alongside the growing interest with victims, research on offenders continues. However, as Maguire (2002: 369) contends, too little recent research has focused on what he terms the 'reality' of criminal behaviour. This refers to 'knowledge about offending behaviour itself, about how offenders understand and exploit criminal opportunities, about the interactions between offenders and how they perceive and respond to risk' (2002: 369). This discussion is developed further in Chapter 6 in relation to ethnographic research.

Because it can complement quantitative research

Qualitative research can complement quantitative research in a number of ways. Firstly, using qualitative approaches can help to inform the design of research instruments for the collection of quantitative data. King (2000) has used this strategy to conduct research in prisons. He suggests beginning with observation and records, then moving on to interviews and ending with questionnaires. The latter can be used to test the generality of the findings in the wider population. By administering questionnaires at the end of the fieldwork the response rate is also boosted as the researcher has established rapport with the research participants.

Secondly, qualitative studies can contribute to our understanding of the context in which crime occurs and criminal justice is administered through providing rich and detailed data to flesh out the bare skeleton provided by quantitative data (Coleman and Moynihan, 1996). Regardless of the size of the dataset or the number of variables contained within it, quantitative data can only represent abstractions from complex interactions, and as Bottomley and Pease (1986: 170) remind us 'we should not allow statistics to make us forget the people behind the numbers'. A burglary offence, which appears in official crime statistics, is the outcome of negotiation processes between the victim and/or witness and the police. It tells us nothing about decisions to report and record the crime. These decision-making processes can be researched using qualitative techniques such as semi-structured interviews with victims, witnesses and police officers or observation within a police station.

Thirdly, Mhlanga (2000) argues that statistical correlations in quantitative research require further explication using qualitative research techniques. Mhlanga's study of the role of ethnic factors in decisions made by the Crown Prosecution Service (CPS) to prosecute young offenders (Mhlanga, 1999) included an examination of case files of just over 6,000 offenders. These files were used to collect statistical data on a number of key variables including ethnic origin, gender, age and previous convictions. The data gathered were analysed using multivariate techniques, which control for other variables in order to identify the actual impact of ethnic factors. Noting that it is 'always hazardous to move from correlation to explanation' (Mhlanga, 2000: 414), and even more so when the topic of interest is a sensitive one, Mhlanga made a decision to present preliminary findings to CPS lawyers and managers to gain feedback. This took the form of a discussion group (he does not describe it as a focus group). The finding that the CPS were more likely to discontinue cases involving ethnic minority defendants was explored. The discussion group came up with two explanations for this: firstly, the police were 'getting it wrong' by charging ethnic minority defendants without sufficient evidence, and secondly, the CPS 'could be using positive discrimination' in favour of ethnic minority defendants (2000: 415). Mhlanga suggests that in any further research on this topic, it would be highly desirable to conduct individual face-to-face interviews with CPS lawyers.

Because it helps to inform the development of policies of crime control

There are multiple ways in which qualitative research, conducted either by researchers or practitioners, can assist the policy development process. Research can fulfil the role of evaluating current policy. It may also serve as an instrument for generating ideas for policy development. Finally, research may take the form of action research, which integrates the processes of research and action. In so doing, the typical model of academics or other researchers generating knowledge to be applied by practitioners is rejected. We will deal with these issues in turn.

In a chapter on qualitative programme evaluation, Greene (1994) notes that programme evaluations are typically oriented around macro policy issues of effectiveness and cost efficiency. Primary emphasis is placed on effectiveness in terms of quantifiable outcomes. Typical evaluation questions are thus: are desired outcomes attained and attributable to the programme? and is this programme the most efficient alternative? Where possible, quasi-experimental methods are utilized. However, there is growing interest in qualitative approaches to evaluation. Greene argues that the interpretive turn in the social sciences has allowed approaches to develop, that promote pluralism in evaluation contexts, and a case study methodological orientation with an accompanying reliance on qualitative methods. These approaches seek to enhance contextualized understanding for stakeholders closest to the programme. For example, an intepretivist evaluation of an offending behaviour programme would focus on the perspectives of offenders, probation staff delivering the programme and assistant chief officers with responsibility for managing such programmes. The methods of choice would most likely be observation, interviews and documentary research.

Qualitative researchers vary in their attempts to influence crime policies but almost all research produces policy implications, even if they are not made explicit by the researcher. The extent to which the policy suggestions are taken on board by policy-makers has been the subject of considerable debate. We will not pursue this discussion now – apart from a short introduction to action research – but return to it in the next chapter, which focuses on the politics of criminological research. Action research first developed in the US and the UK in the late 1940s by social scientists who advocated closer ties between social theory and solving immediate social problems (Denscombe, 1998). It is typically associated with small-scale research studies. Action research can be perceived as a cyclical process. To begin the process, critical reflection on professional practice is required to identify a problem, which is then researched and the findings are translated into a plan for change. The plan is then implemented and evaluated. The ideal is that the process is ongoing with a rolling programme of research. The reality is that action research often involves discrete, one-off pieces of research (Denscombe, 1998). Action researchers are not limited to qualitative techniques but can use different techniques for data collection. However, qualitative methods are particularly suited to exploratory, small-scale studies.

Concluding comments

In this chapter we have explored, albeit briefly, the maturation of criminology as an academic discipline and we have drawn the reader's attention to competing interpretations of the past. As Coleman and Norris (2000: 24) note in relation to criminology, 'there has been some confusion over both its birthday and parentage'. Exploring this debate included an analysis of the emergence of both qualitative and quantitative research traditions within criminology. We focused predominantly, but not exclusively, on the growth of qualitative approaches to researching crime and criminal justice. While it may at first glance appear out of place to reflect on quantitative approaches in a text on qualitative research, we felt such reflections were needed for two reasons. Firstly, by exploring the strengths and weakness of quantitative approaches we can elucidate the reasons why qualitative approaches developed. Secondly, researchers frequently use both quantitative and qualitative methods in their studies.

By combining both qualitative and quantitative approaches, criminological researchers are avoiding 'methodological pigeonholing' (Bottoms, 2000: 21). This can be defined as 'the tendency to assume that certain sorts of research methods 'go with' particular kinds of theoretical approach, to the exclusion of other kinds of data' (2000: 21). Bottoms suggests that some qualitative researchers have set up mental barriers against the use of qualitative data, and similarly some quantitative researchers have been reluctant to make use of qualitative data. For Bottoms, these unjustifiable mental barriers have been some of the most unhelpful features of the British criminological landscape in the last quarter of the twentieth century. He proposes that these barriers are now being overcome, leading to a healthier approach to criminological research. We fully support his views.

The chapter ended with advancing arguments for using qualitative research techniques, and this includes relying solely on one qualitative method, combining different qualitative methods and utilizing both qualitative and quantitative approaches. This list of arguments is not exhaustive and undoubtedly counter arguments can be made. Completing the activities at the end of the chapter will help to add further arguments and develop responses to potential criticisms of qualitative approaches.

Exercises

1 Select a criminological study that uses both qualitative and quantitative methods. Explore the advantages and disadvantages of combining such methods. Examples include Parker, H. et al. (1998) *Illegal Leisure: The Normalization of Adolescent Recreational Drug Use*, London: Routledge and Newburn, T. et al. (2002) *The Introduction of Referral Orders into the Youth Justice System*, Home Office Research Study 242, London: Home Office.

2 Identify a piece of criminological research that relies solely on quantitative methods. How might including qualitative approaches as well as quantitative ones enhance it? Examples include Hood, R. (1992) *Race and Sentencing*, Oxford: Clarendon Press and Flood-Page, C. et al. (2000) *Youth Crime: Findings from the 1998/99 Youth Lifestyles Survey*, Home Office Research Study 209, London: Home Office.

3 Choose a qualitative study on any criminological topic and put yourself in the position of the author of the study. How would you justify the choice of a qualitative approach to the following: a potential funding body, a researcher with a reputation for being unsympathetic to qualitative approaches or a policy-maker?

FURTHER READING

Garland notes the history of criminology is probably too complex to be captured in a single text. Despite his concerns, his own essay (2002) provides an excellent and comprehensive overview:

- Garland, D. (2002) 'Of crimes and criminals: the development of criminology in Britain'.

In a chapter entitled 'Crime, the criminal and criminology', Coleman and Norris (2000) cover similar ground but in a far less detailed way. Nonetheless they give a flavour of the complex nature of the origins of criminology and its basic subject matter.

Triangulation is discussed, typically very briefly, in most of the introductory social research methods texts. For a more detailed discussion we recommend:

- Brannen, J. (ed.) (1992) *Mixing Methods: Qualitative and Quantitative Research*. The chapters by Brannen, Hammersley and Bryman are particularly useful.

There are an abundance of texts on social research that outline clearly the perceived advantages of qualitative research:

- Bryman's (1988a) *Quantity and Quality in Social Research*. This has become a classic text which offers a balanced discussion.

2

Doing Research on Crime and Justice: A Political Endeavour?

Introduction

Our starting point for this chapter is that all forms of criminological research are inherently bound up with wider political contexts that, ultimately, shape the research process. Most criminological researchers are willing to acknowledge, sometimes reluctantly, the inevitability that their research can never be free from political influences. For some criminologists, the political nature of crime and justice is their starting point, and their research is a form of politics. In this chapter we begin by exploring the different meanings attached to the term 'political'. We then move on to offer a brief account of the increasing politicization of research on crime and criminal justice (particularly from 1979 onwards), and alongside this present a chronological account of the politicization of criminological theory (especially in the 1960s and 1970s). Developing our argument that the political context influences the conduct of criminological research in multiple ways, we reflect upon these influences throughout the research process and beyond. Within the chapter we draw upon our own research experiences, as well as the accounts available in which researchers have shared their own views of conducting criminological research in a highly politicized world.

Towards a definition of 'political'

The term 'political' has multiple meanings attached to it in both lay and academic discourse, and this is apparent by exploring dictionary definitions. For example,

1 (a) Of or concerning the State or its government, or public affairs generally. (b) of, relating to, or engaged in politics. (c) belonging to or forming part of a civil administration.
2 Having an organized form of society of government.
3 Taking or belonging to a side in politics.
4 Relating to or affecting interests of status or authority in an organization rather than matters of principle (*a political decision*).

(*The Concise Oxford Dictionary*, 1990; italics in original)

In academic discourse, the term 'political' is traditionally compared against the term 'civil' (Tonkiss, 1998). The former is conceived as concerned with public affairs and the formal process of government. In contrast, the latter is understood as related to essentially private and freely chosen activity. Together they make up what is commonly understood by sociologists, and other social scientists, as 'society'. However, this dichotomy can be rendered problematic by exploring the interface between the civil and the political. Some of the most influential voices in this respect have been feminist ones. Summarized in the slogan 'the personal is political', feminists have drawn political attention to crimes within the home, encouraging state incursion into the private sphere (see Delamont, 2003 for a more detailed discussion of feminist work). Tonkiss' definition captures feminist and other debates surrounding the civil/political dualism:

> The political realm is that which brings together social relations into focus but specifically in terms of their direction, control, management and adjustment to the demands of the state. The social is rarely, if at all, ever apolitical but the politics are not always those mediated by state and party. (1998: 259)

Reviewing debates in the methodological literature about competing definitions of 'political' (see for example, Hammersley, 1995; Hughes, 2000), it becomes apparent that definitions vary tremendously in terms of how all encompassing they are. Narrow definitions tend to focus on 'explicit political ideologies and organized coercive institutional power of the modern nation state' (Hughes, 2000: 235) while others are much broader and note that all human interactions are micro-political processes (Hammersley, 1995). Helpfully, Hammersley identifies two distinct, but closely related, ways in which research may be seen as political. The first acknowledges that research is implicated in power relations. The key questions here are the extent to which researchers are autonomous from the state or other powerful interests in society, and the extent to which researchers exercise power? The second way relates to the question of whether value judgements are implicated in the research process. We are at risk of devoting the whole chapter to the debate about the meaning of the term 'political', and rather than continuing in detail we recommend that interested readers consult Hammersley's (1995) text. Cognizant of the difficulties of reaching an authoritative definition, we convey our understanding of the term 'political' in the box below.

Criminological research is a political endeavour in two senses. Firstly, the political context inevitably shapes, to varying extents, all stages of the research process because criminologists are researching a social problem, which politicians seek to explain and control. Secondly, criminological researchers inevitably become embroiled in micro-political processes because research often seeks to understand the standpoints of different, sometimes opposing, groups.

The politicization of law and order

Through being explicit about the ways in which criminological research can be perceived as a political endeavour, we have already drawn attention to the politicization of the problem of crime. We develop this discussion briefly here, focusing on England and Wales. Surprisingly law and order has only become contested by different political parties since the mid-1960s, gaining dominance in the 1979 election campaign (Downes and Morgan, 2002). Public spending, according to the Conservatives, needed to be reduced. The only exception to this was in the law and order sphere. The approach adopted during the Thatcher (1979–90) and Major (1990–97) governments varied. It began with a highly punitive approach, embodying 'law and order ideology' (Cavadino and Dignan, 2002: 5) and during the four years leading up to the 1991 Criminal Justice Act this rhetoric continued to colour policy but a 'less dogmatic and more pragmatic' (2002: 6) approach was taken. The 1991 Criminal Justice Act was a radical piece of legislation but some of its central provisions were hastily repealed in 'the law and order counter-reformation' (2002: 6). They were replaced by measures which marked the revival of the highly punitive approach. For example, the pledge to reduce the prison population through the use of community sanctions was overridden by a commitment to the use of custodial sentences. The Conservative government portrayed themselves as *the* party of law and order, leaving the opposition with the task of challenging them.

Following their victory in the 1997 General Election, Labour (now packaged as New Labour) sought to live up to its manifesto promise to be 'tough on crime, tough on the causes of crime'. This promise was an attempt to assure voters that they could be successful on law and order issues. These had been successfully portrayed by previous Conservative governments as Labour's Achilles Heel (Morgan, 2000). Labour passed a deluge of legislation through Parliament, including some measures initially put in place by the Conservatives. Reflecting on the current state of affairs in 2001, Downes and Morgan (2002) suggest that a new and uneasy consensus has been reached by the major political parties, and this has resulted in persistent jostling for political advantage.

The politicization of criminological theory

In this section we offer a loose chronological account of the politicization of criminological theory. The term 'loose' in this context should not be taken to imply that we will present it in a careless way. Rather we simply wish to draw the reader's attention to some of the difficulties of following a strictly chronological and linear account. Attempts to periodize the development of criminological theory are superficially attractive. Such simplification is inherent in the abundance of texts that outline the range of criminological perspectives. These texts tend to introduce the dominant perspective at a particular point in time, note how it was subjected to intense criticism by an emerging perspective, report its decline and then move on to discuss the new perspective which they now treat as the dominant one. The pattern continues. The best texts note that adopting this structure is a pedagogic device, and attempt to convey some sense of the complexities that lie beneath the development of criminological theory. For instance, noting that seemingly 'new' perspectives often draw upon the influences of earlier ones.

Bottoms (2000: 35) distinguishes between five approaches to criminology: classicism, natural-science positivism, active-subject socially-oriented criminologies, active subject individually-oriented criminologies and political-activist criminologies. Here we will focus on the latter approach. For Bottoms, political-activist criminologies include Marxist-oriented criminologies, feminist criminologies and the theoretical movement known as 'left-realism'. Gaining dominance within British criminology since 1970, these perspectives have been somewhat openly political. The combination of political activism and theorizing challenges traditional conceptions of the relationship between theory and research. As Bottoms suggests, the legacy of positivism has left criminology suspicious about political engagement for fear that their research may be perceived as unscientific. Political-activist criminology makes explicit that criminological theory and research are inseparable from the political landscape. However, there is a danger that political goals can override the pursuit of knowledge. We provide a necessarily brief, and hopefully not too crude, summary of the main political-activist criminologies below.

Marx himself wrote little about crime but his theoretical framework has been applied by others to the study of it. One of the key elements of Marxism is that all social phenomena, including crime, can be explained in terms of each society's economic relations. In capitalist society, the private ownership of the means of production allows the bourgeoisie to exploit the proletariat, and thus crime can be seen as part of the struggle in which the economically powerless proletariat attempt to cope with the exploitation and poverty imposed on them. Bonger (1916) was the first to apply Marxist principles to crime but the Marxist tradition had little impact on criminology until the 1970s. At that time, a growing number of criminologists offered Marxist-inspired analyses of the problem of crime (see for example, Chambliss, 1975). They also went further to suggest that the solution to the crime problem lies in revolution, bringing about major social, economic and political change. Other criminologists were reluctant to adopt a pure form of Marxism, and instead attempted to fuse elements of interactionism with the fundamentals of Marxism. The result was the publication of *The New Criminology* by Taylor et al. (1973). With the benefit of hindsight, this text is widely cited as the genesis of critical criminology. Taylor et al. endeavoured to develop a criminological theoretical framework and to endorse a variety of radical politics through their insistence that a society based on principles of socialist diversity and tolerance would be free of crime.

By the mid-1970s criminology was highly politicized. A growing concern with the process of criminalization provided the backdrop for critical criminologists to explore the ways in which power associated with the capitalist state asserts itself in relation to crime. The influence of Marx was joined by that of Foucault and Gramsci. In simple terms, critical criminology seeks to explore the ways in which the variables of class, ethnicity and gender are played out in relation to crime and criminal justice. The concern of critical criminologists is not only with discriminatory practices but the ways in which structural inequalities are perpetuated. For instance, critical criminologists seek to understand the ways in which state practices seek to marginalize, and consequently criminalize, certain groups. The influence of feminism is apparent in critical criminological work. The second wave of the women's movement in the late 1960s and early 1970s introduced a new dimension to criminological debates. It began by noting the misrepresentation, or more commonly neglect, of women in criminological theory, and attempted to redress the balance by focusing their attention on women as victims, offenders and criminal justice professionals. An important dimension to their work is the blurring of the boundary between theory and practice. Feminist criminologists have been active in campaigning for law reform, changes to criminal justice policy and providing a range of support services for female victims of crime.

In the mid-1980s, Left realism emerged in the UK as a response to both the utopianism of earlier Marxist-inspired criminologies and the punitive and exclusionary character of right realist policies in the US. Left realism still claimed to be radical in its criminology but combined this with a commitment to offer effective solutions to the crime problem. Rather than seeking to challenge the state, criminologists on the political left now sought to work with the state as part of an attempt to take crime seriously. We make no attempt to reflect on the current state of criminological theory here or to debate its future. Reviewing the final chapters of the many available texts on criminological theory will provide divergent views on this topic. Suffice to say here that contemporary criminology is characterized by multiple perspectives, and some might describe it as 'fragmented' (Ericson and Carriere, 1994). Supporters of these different perspectives vary in terms of how explicitly political their views on crime are. They also differ in the type of research strategies they generate, hence look to different sources of funding. We develop this issue below.

Pipers and paymasters: shaping criminological research

The key question which preoccupies us in this section of the chapter is whether he (or she) who pays the piper calls the tune? Before attempting to answer this question we need to consider the available 'pipers' or criminological researchers and potential 'paymasters'.

Researchers working in any of the following organizations may conduct criminological research:

- higher education institutions;
- central government departments, sometimes in dedicated research units;
- criminal justice organizations, particularly large police forces and probation areas;
- private sector research organizations, for example, National Centre for Social Research; and
- voluntary sector organizations, for example National Association for Care and Resettlement of Offenders.

Criminological research may also be carried out by practitioners working in the criminal justice sphere. Reiner (2000a: 220) terms this group 'inside insiders'. Research may be done as part of a postgraduate degree or as part of a programme of work. Criminal justice professionals are also eligible to apply for a small number of awards including the Cropwood programme of short-term fellowship awards (based at the Institute of Criminology, University of Cambridge) and the Police Research Award Scheme (funded by the Home Office). The growth of practitioner research is not peculiar to criminology, and there is a growing literature on the subject (see for example, Fuller and Petch, 1995; Robson, 2001).

There are multiple sources of funding available to criminological researchers. The organization which employs the researcher will determine the sources of funding they are eligible to compete for, and consequently the type of research that they can undertake. The main types of funders are listed in Table 2.1 below.

TABLE 2.1   *Funding available for criminological research*

Type of funder	Key funders
Government departments	Home Office; Youth Justice Board; Lord Chancellor's Department
Research councils (funded by Government)	Economic and Social Research Council
Charitable foundations	Joseph Rowntree Foundation; Nuffield Foundation; Leverhulme Trust
Local multi-agency partnerships	Crime and disorder partnerships; drug actions teams; youth offending teams
Criminal justice agencies	Police forces; probation areas; prisons

It might be helpful for readers to be familiar with the diverse sources of funding we have received to conduct criminological research. We have obtained grants, either together or separately, from the Home Office (see Chapter 9 for more information on a Home Office funded project), Department of Environment, Transport and the Regions the National Assembly for Wales, the Nuffield Foundation, Drugscope, and a drug action team. We have also been employed as researchers on projects funded by the Economic and Social Research Council and a local council. The CVs of many criminologists will also have an eclectic mix of funding sources (see for example, Morgan, 2000). We elaborate on the main types of funding for criminological research below, focusing on their research priorities and the procedures for obtaining research funding.

Government funding

A major source of government funding for criminological research is the Home Office. The Home Office funds research in different ways. It has a dedicated research unit, the Home Office Research Development and Statistics directorate (HORDS) but also issues contracts to external research organizations. HORDS has appeared in different guises but dates back to 1956. It has always been a major locus of criminological research but has not always enjoyed an easy relationship with politicians. The Conservative governments of 1979–90 were deeply phobic about criminological research. Michael Howard carefully scrutinized research during his term as Home Secretary (1993–97) and his junior minister (David Maclean) went as far as proposing closure of the research section of the Home Office. Even before that date Home Office research was shifting towards an 'administrative criminology' agenda. This term, coined by Jock Young in the 1980s, refers to criminological research which abandons the search for the causes of crime and focuses its efforts on strategies and policies to prevent and deter crime. The inclusion of the word 'planning' to create the Home Office Research and Planning Unit (HORPU) in 1981 was more than symbolic. As Maguire (2000) notes, the Home Office moved towards a position where funding decisions were almost exclusively driven by narrow short-term policy concerns, and where the research questions, methods and timescale were ever more tightly established in advance by civil servants. This has the effect of losing sight of the broader academic debates, and runs the risk of neglecting more fruitful and innovative ideas. Increased Home Office control over the research agenda has been described as the inevitable corollary of the party politicization of law and order (Morgan, 2000).

When the Labour government came to power in 1997 they seemed committed to the information economy and were willing to invest substantial sums of money to develop it. In April 1999, the Crime Reduction Programme was launched. It ran for three years, with an overall budget of £250 million (£25 million of this was dedicated to research). The programme comprised a series of diverse initiatives, dealing with a wide range of offences and every aspect of the criminal justice process. The aim of the programme was to establish *what works* in reducing crime as part of a commitment to evidence-based policy and practice. As a result, funding was made available for independent evaluation, always leading to the collection of quantitative data. Described by Morgan (2000: 61) as 'the largest programme of criminological research ever undertaken in the United Kingdom', criminological researchers were divided in their response to the increased funding. Some sought to avoid involvement, suggesting that the work was theoretically impoverished and too closely allied to the interests of the state. Others welcomed the opportunity to have some degree of involvement with the development of crime policy but were streetwise enough to recognize the political nature of the work. No doubt others were more pragmatic and opportunistic, unable to resist the large sums of money on offer.

Research opportunities under the Crime Reduction Programme were only offered in response to invitation to tender. The majority of Home Office funding is allocated in this way, and concerns about the process have been aired elsewhere (Crace and Plomin, 2001; Morgan, 2000). Sometimes tenders are issued to a shortlist of applicants who have been requested previously to submit an expression of interest. Typically researchers are sent a detailed document which is fairly prescriptive about the work to be undertaken. There are exceptions to this, and one example is described in Chapter 9. A further example is the Innovative Research Challenge Programme. This takes the form of an open competition, and its aims are described in the HORDS business plan 2001–02 as to enhance 'contact with the wider research community and building on its contribution to Home Office aims, but also to ensure that RDS research retains a *long-term focus*' (emphasis in original).

As other criminologists have noted, policy-oriented research can be innovative and intellectually challenging (Maguire, 2000). It is possible to produce both a concise report devoted to answering the research questions asked by the funder, and to use the knowledge required to produce publications for an academic audience. For instance, a research study we were both involved in or the risk management of sex offenders led to a Home Office report (Maguire, et al., 2001) and the findings also informed a journal article on risk penality (Kemshall and Maguire, 2000). A colleague once used the metaphor of a 'Trojan horse' to describe Home Office contracts, implying that more academically interesting questions can be asked at the same time as conducting government research but researchers often feel they need to be secretive about it.

Research council funding

Criminological research comes largely under the remit of Economic and Social Research Council (ESRC). The ESRC was established in 1965 by Royal Charter as an independent organization. However, its £92 million budget (for 2003–04) for both research and postgraduate training comes mainly from the Government. In the 1990s, thematic priorities were developed in order to focus research on scientific priorities. There are seven in total, and criminological research can be related to all of them. However, the two most important thematic priorities in relation to criminological research are 'Governance and Citizenship' and 'Social Stability and Exclusion'. They provide a focus for some, but not all, ESRC research activities. These include provision of funds for centres, programmes and grants. Since 1990, two programmes have been directly related to crime ('Violence' 1997–2002) and 'Crime and Social Order' (1993–97). In addition, funding has been made available for two research networks on pathways into and out of crime (one running from 2001–05 and the other from 2002–07). Although the ESRC is widely regarded by the criminological community as the most prestigious source of funding, its strategies for allocating funds have been contested. The ESRC make explicit their commitment to funding 'blue-skies' or curiosity-driven research alongside applied and strategic research. However, the incorporation of users' needs into various aspects of the research process has caused concern. The oft-perceived shift to only funding applied research and the subsequent loss of rigour are the most common causes of disquiet (Rappert, 1997). Users in this context include industry, charities, universities, local authorities and other public bodies, government departments and independent policy bodies. Users are involved in a wide range of practices including setting thematic priorities for funding, evaluating research and shaping programmes.

Charitable foundations

There are a number of charitable foundations that are willing to fund criminological research, although none of them have crime as their exclusive focus. In the UK, the major players are the Leverhulme Trust (dating back to 1933), the Nuffield Foundation (founded in 1943) and the Joseph Rowntree Foundation (which has funded research from 1959). The Leverhulme Trust has an annual budget of £25 million, and places emphasis on allowing applicants to choose the topic they wish to research.This form of responsive support is open to researchers from all disciplines. In contrast, the Joseph Rowntree Foundation focuses solely on social policy research, and the £7 million budget funds both ongoing and time-limited research programmes.The Nuffield Foundation runs 14 different grant programmes including an 'open door' one, and gave out £6.4 million in the form of research grants in 2002. While the programmes run by the Joseph Rowntree Foundation and Nuffield Foundation do not concentrate solely on aspects of crime and criminal justice, they do offer opportunities for research in areas of interest to criminologists including programmes, for example the Joseph Rowntree Foundation Drug and Alcohol Research Programme and the Nuffield Foundation's programmes on child protection and access to justice.

Does who pays the piper call the tune?

Having described the various sources of funding available to criminological researchers, we will now attempt to answer the question above. Research agendas are created by funders who have their own preferences for both the research topics and research approaches they wish to support. This applies to all three major sources of funding outlined above. The research programmes which emerge are the end product of a series of interactions between groups. For government departments such as the Home Office, the key players are ministers, civil servants and HORSD. For research councils such as the ESRC, research priorities and programmes are developed by Council, which includes representatives from academia, business and the public sector. For charitable bodies, the trustees are influential in determining the research they are able to fund. All these players will have to work within the parameters of their organization's role, and in the case of charitable trusts the original wishes of the benefactor.

The extent to which funding bodies influence the actual conduct of research varies considerably.Those who enter in a 'customer-contract' relationship with the Home Office experience the greatest level of interest.This can take many forms including the submission of regular progress report (linked to payments) and steering group meetings. Critics might interpret them as compromising the independent nature of the research that has been commissioned. A more balanced view is to recognize the need to be cautious when public money is being invested in research, and to appreciate the support that can be offered, even if the level of involvement feels intrusive at times. Other funding bodies may not operate in the same way but do not give researchers a free rein.They may, for instance, require changes to be made to the research design and to be notified if the research differs from that laid out in the proposal. Even those university researchers whose research is unfunded are not free from the political agendas of government.The context in which they work is highly significant. Since 1989 a research assessment exercise has taken place periodically. The stated purpose of this exercise 'is to enable the higher education funding bodies to distribute public funds for research selectively on the basis of quality' (www.hero.ac.uk), and one of the criteria on which decisions are made is the amount of external research funding received.

We return to the debate about the ways in which conducting funded research, especially for the state, impinges upon academic autonomy when we discuss the politics of publication and dissemination.

The politics of postgraduate research: a brief note

The discussion above may seem removed from readers who are postgraduate research students. Postgraduate students, if they have any funding at all, are likely to be in receipt of studentships from their own academic institution or from the ESRC. Postgraduate students still need to work within the broad parameters of ESRC funding but these researchers are likely to enjoy academic freedom to a far greater extent than their supervisors. This may only be appreciated after the event.

One of us (Smith and Wincup, 2000) has explored elsewhere how the political context can still be important for postgraduate researchers. Reflecting on doctoral research on prisons and bail hostels for women at a time of increasingly punitive responses to offenders, we made the following comment.

> Although not financially sponsored by the state (both of us were awarded university studentships), our research was inevitably influenced by … [the] political context in various ways. Explicitly, we were dependent upon the state for access to the criminal justice agencies we wanted to research. Implicitly, the political context impacted upon our relationships in 'the field'. We had to tread carefully. (2000: 355)

In the same chapter we explored the politics of conducting postgraduate research. We drew attention to the relatively powerless position that postgraduates occupy within academic institutions even though they count considerably towards the rating their department receives in the Research Assessment Exercise. Retaining their academic freedom is one of the challenges postgraduates face. This became apparent at a session one of us (Wincup) ran on 'managing your supervisor' at the 2002 British Society of Criminology Conference. It was rather dispiriting, although not unexpected, to hear students suggesting that their supervisor had 'written' their thesis for them by driving the research in a direction most suited to their theoretical concerns.

The micro-politics of criminological research: taking sides, trying to please everyone and other strategies

In the above discussion we drew attention to the impact on the political context on field relations. As Downes and Morgan (1994) argue, the micro-politics of law and order are articulated in a wide range of settings in both the public and private sphere through the generation of talk about crime and how best to solve it. This influences research but also provides data for analysis. We focus here on the settings in which criminologists conduct research, and in particular explore whether it is possible to be neutral at the data collection stage.

Howard Becker's 1967 essay entitled *Whose side are you on?* continues to offer a major contribution to the debate. Described by Delamont (2002: 149) as a 'manifesto on values and methods', his starting point is that neutrality is a myth shattered by the reality that personal and political sympathies inform research. This does not mean that the goal of research is the pursuit of political goals, although as we noted earlier in this chapter some researchers might argue that it is. Instead, it challenges the aim of positivists and naturalists to strive as far as possible to limit the influences of values on the research process. Qualitative research has little in common with positivist principles but qualitative researchers have been proponents of naturalism. This perspective attempts to study the social world in its 'natural state', undisturbed by the researcher, and offer a detailed description of some aspect of social life ('to tell it how it is'). This perspective has been subjected to criticism by qualitative researchers (see Chapter 6).

The focus of Becker's essay was on research with deviant groups, chosen because researchers who focus on this group frequently have to answer to the charge that siding with deviant groups leads to distortion and bias. Becker suggests that a 'hierarchy of credibility' (1967: 241) operates in deviancy research (and in other areas such as education), and credibility and the right to be heard are distributed differentially throughout the hierarchy. Researchers interested in deviant groups concentrate on those whose voices are normally unheard, and hence challenge what Becker (1967: 243) terms the 'established status order'. According to Becker, accusations of bias are levelled only at researchers who focus on deviants rather those concerned with criminal justice professionals. For Becker, researchers always have to take sides, and their challenge is to ensure that unavoidable sympathies with our research participants do not render our work invalid.

Becker's essay received criticism shortly after it was published by Gouldner (1975) who insisted that value-neutrality was possible and desirable. Remarkably, over 35 years after its publication, Becker's essay continues to be revisited by social researchers (see Delamont (2002) and Liebling (2001) for recent examples). In her article on prisons research, Liebling argues that 'it *is* possible to take more than one side seriously, to find merit in more than one perspective, and to do this without causing outrage on the side of officials or prisoners (2001: 473; emphasis in original). She does note, however, that this is a precarious business and risks encountering the wrath of criminologists who are sceptical of any attempt to understand officialdom. For Liebling, taking more than one side seriously does not lead to impartiality, and is therefore not a form of closet positivism. Instead, attempts to synthesize different or competing perspectives within the prison world at the analysis stage help to sharpen our focus, and consequently this is a valuable analytic task.

For many criminological researchers, regardless of whether they adopt Becker's position, they find themselves in the precarious position of trying to keep everyone happy. This is particularly true for those conducting research within criminal justice agencies who have to strive to avoid alienating opposing groups. For example, Carter's (1994) study of the occupational socialization of prison officers involved forging positive relationships with staff and prisoners within the organizational hierarchy. The groups have the potential to be mutually antagonistic, leading him to describe the research process as a 'nerve-racking experience and a difficult road to walk for the researcher' (1994: 34). For Carter, the researcher has to be seen to be everyone's friend, attempting to understand their different points of view and appearing not to favour any one group or individual.

The politics of publication and dissemination: confidentiality, censorship and controversy

There are numerous ways in which criminologists can publish their findings. Journal articles, research monographs, book chapters and research reports continue to have the greatest kudos in academic circles. The demands of the Research Assessment Exercise in the UK have placed particular importance on the production of peer-reviewed articles. There are, of course, other opportunities to publish work. Potential outlets include practitioner journals (for example, *Prison Service Journal*), professional magazines (for example, *Police Review, The Magistrate*), newspapers (particularly broadsheets), political magazines (for example, *New Statesman and Society*) and journals produced by voluntary sector organizations (for example, *Criminal Justice Matters*). Technological developments have increased opportunities further, and it is now possible to find criminological research reported on websites and in electronic journals. Academic criminologists have yet to experiment with theatrical scripts as a means of conveying their research findings. They have been employed by other qualitative researchers (Mienczakowski, 2001), and this reminds us that dissemination does not have to be confined to the written word.

Submission of a research report of some kind is a requirement of all funders of criminological research. What happens next varies but all require a final report, which may be sent to academics with specialist expertise in the area to review. This happens for Home Office funded research, and the draft is also scrutinized by HORDS researchers and by policy-makers in different areas of the Home Office and in other government departments. Researchers are then asked to respond to the comments, and sometimes this process is repeated. It would be unfair to suggest that this practice is unhelpful. Receiving constructive comments on a draft often leads to a more polished report, even if the feedback is a little painful to read at first. Similarly, observations from policy-makers can produce a more user-friendly, policy-relevant publication. However, the whole process can also be frustrating, not least because it can lead to immoderate delays. It can also produce contradictory feedback and suggested changes to the research design, which are of little use once the data have been collected. Until the final report has been accepted, researchers working on Home Office projects need to ask permission to publish findings. A 'publish and be damned' attitude is unwise if researchers seek to receive future government funding, not least because researchers are expressively forbidden in their legal contracts to make public any findings prior to the publication of the final report without permission.

At the extreme, state funded research may be subjected to censorship. Drawing on his considerable experience as a Home Office researcher (now working in a university), Mair (2000) reveals that he felt his work was never subjected to censorship. Anticipating his critics, he is keen to defend himself against the charge that his work was self-censored through gradual acceptance of repressive practices. However, he does concede that he felt under indirect pressure to produce the 'right' results from his study of electronic monitoring. This illustrates that political pressures may not be explicit but form part of the social milieu in which the researcher works. There are, however, some examples of censorship. We present two examples here, which might be described as infamous.

The first is Baldwin and McConville's Home Office funded study on the outcome of jury trials in Birmingham Crown Court. This was conducted in the mid-1970s. Drawing on the data gathered from over 100 interviews with defendants, they found repeated evidence of plea-bargaining. Since little had been written on the topic in the UK, the researchers hoped to publish a book in the area. The reaction to the findings has been presented in-depth elsewhere (Baldwin, 2000), and we will summarize it here. A confidential draft of the report was leaked to the media. The controversy caused led the Senate of the Bar to contact the Home Secretary urging him to discourage publication. The university put in place an inquiry after being warned by the Home Secretary about possible implications should the book be published. The book was eventually published in 1977. The same year, Cohen and Taylor published an account of their attempts to publish research on long-term imprisonment, going as far as to suggest that their research was 'sabotaged' (1977: 68) by the Home Office. The study employed qualitative methodology, an approach for which they receive a great deal of critical comment, and focused on how prisoners talked about their experiences of coping with lengthy custodial sentences. Despite their protests that the study was 'not particularly radical' (1977: 85) and constituted an important piece of independent sociological inquiry, they found themselves 'trapped in a complex web of social and political restrictions' (1977: 76). They note that official bodies such as the Home Office are able to exercise a high degree of control of research through five forces which they term as the 'centralization of power', 'legalisation of secrecy', 'standardization of research', 'mystifying the decision structure' and 'appealing to the public interest' (1977: 77). Ultimately these forces led to the decision to abandon the research rather than collude with the Home Office agenda.

Even if research is not funded by the state, publishing research findings can have political consequences. Whyte (2000) notes that presenting a paper on the findings of his critical criminological research on the oil industry to an industrial audience led to an abrupt end to his access to the Health and Safety Executive Offshore Safety Division. Hoyle (2000) shares her experience of publishing a book based on her PhD on policing domestic violence. She experienced extensive media publicity because of her unwillingness to support right-wing feminist calls for blanket arrest and prosecution policies and custodial sentences for all convicted abusers. For Hoyle, the criticisms (described as politically driven denunciation) stemmed from her failure to support political orthodoxy on domestic violence.

Making use of criminological research: understanding the linkages between criminological research and crime policy

The relationship between research and policy had been subjected to ongoing academic debate by social scientists (see Hammersley, 1995 for an overview), often leading to the establishment of typologies of the different forms the relationship can take. We concern ourselves here specifically with criminological research and crime policy, which leads us to the depressing conclusion that criminological research has little direct, immediate impact on crime control policy or practice. Of course research need not always have a direct recompense in this way. Travers (2001: 13) argues that research might be done 'entirely for its own sake!'. In contrast, King (2000) implies that it is not sufficient for research to attempt to address challenging intellectual questions. Instead, researchers should aim to have at least some modest impact on society. This may not be immediate. As Hughes (2000) notes, research may have a long-term influence on both the policy and political process. Criminological research over time has the potential to challenge political discourses on law and order through generating debate. One study alone is unlikely to change policy but a coherent and cumulative body of knowledge on a criminological issue might have an impact. This body of knowledge might consist of what has been termed 'basic' (concerned with producing theory) and 'applied' research (Janowitz, 1972).

Criminologists are understandably impatient. There are plentiful examples of missed opportunities to influence policy, and criminologists must accept some of the blame for this. In a paper on young adult offenders and alcohol, Parker

(1996) argues that British criminologists are ill-equipped to respond to, or moderate the power of, the law and order discourse. For Parker, the dominant law and order discourse is 'alcohol plus young men equals violent crime'. British criminologists have largely retreated from qualitative, ethnographic community-based studies of subculture and deviant lifestyles (a point developed further in Chapter 6). Hence, there is a lack of authoritative explanations available to challenge the simplistic, blaming style of political discourse. There are also copious instances of developing policies which run counter to research findings. Frequently cited in this respect is the insistence by Michael Howard, when he was Home Secretary in 1993, that 'prison works' despite the wealth of research findings which suggested the contrary. This was his rationalization for pursuing a highly punitive approach to offending (Cavadino and Dignan, 2002).

As we write this chapter the debate about the relationship between research and policy has received political attention. The National Audit Office (NAO) published a report in April 2003 suggesting that the gulf between academics and policy-makers means that much of the £1.4 billion the government spends on research each year is wasted. To be clear, the report entitled *Getting the Evidence: Using Research in Policy-Making* focused on research commissioned by the Department of International Development, Office of the Deputy Prime Minister, and the Department for Environment, Food and Rural Affairs. University academics are the most common recipients of these research contracts. Only a minority of these research budgets are likely to be concerned with areas of criminological interest. Nonetheless, it is worth considering their findings in more detail because the issues raised are likely to resonate with criminological researchers and policy-makers concerned with crime and criminal justice. Indeed similar arguments are advanced by Mair (2000). Some of the difficulties raised are practical ones, and included poor understanding of research results by policy-makers, inadequate communication of the research results by researchers, and too little being done to propagate findings. These can be resolved by developing research training courses for policy-makers, furthering the report writing skills of researchers, and enhanced dissemination activities. The latter requires increased funding, exploration of more imaginative forms of dissemination to reach the widest audience possible, and clarification of whether the researcher or the funder is responsible for disseminating research findings. Bridging the gap between academics and policy-makers is more challenging. The NAO reported that the grasp of policy questions by researchers was inadequate but are careful to avoid blaming researchers. They note that those commissioning the research are not always clear about what their needs are. The solution of NAO is to involve users throughout the research process, a model already adopted by the ESRC.

Concluding comments

In this chapter we hope we have demonstrated the different ways in which criminological research can be perceived as political. The nature and extent of political influences will vary from project to project, and are dependent on a wide range of factors including the subject matter, the theoretical framework adopted, funding arrangements and the timing of the research. How one defines the term 'political' is crucial and we have opened up this debate for readers to explore further. We adopted an inclusive and catholic definition. Like Hughes (2000: 235) we argued that 'criminological research does not take place in a political and moral vacuum but is a deeply *political* process' (emphasis in original). We also supported Hughes' view that criminological research can never be anything put political.

> We need to be wary of the talk of the end of politics and the rise of non-political technical fixes for research. Such talk is likely to usher in very restrictive research agendas for criminology. Furthermore, it is impossible to envisage a time when criminological research will not generate ... political controversies. (2000: 247)

We are keen proponents of reflexivity, and therefore feel it is important to be aware of the ways in which the political context shapes our research. While this will add incalculable value to our understanding of the development of knowledge, criminologists often seem reluctant to do this, perhaps fearing that it will detract from the credibility of their findings.

Exercises

1 Select a criminological research topic. This may be an area where you are currently conducting research or plan to do so in the future. Consider the political influences that might shape the data collection process.
2 Extend your thinking to cover the process of disseminating your findings to a wide audience. You should think here about the different ways this can be achieved.
3 Look at a recent example of criminological research which has received funding from the government. You will find plentiful examples of research on England and Wales on the Home Office website (www.homeoffice.gov.uk). What impact do you think the source of funding had on the research?
4 Repeat the above but focus on research which has been funded by either a research council or a charitable body.

FURTHER READING

There is a growing literature on the politics of social research but Martyn Hammersley's (1995) text entitled *The Politics of Social Research* still provides the best overview of the debate about whether social research is, or indeed should be, political.

Specifically on the politics of criminological research, the following are recommended.

* Hughes (2000) 'Understanding the politics of criminological research'.
* Morgan, R. (2000) 'The politics of criminological research'.

The former takes the reader through the different stages of the criminological research process, exploring the implications of researching a political world at every stage. The latter muses on the development of the criminological enterprise and the infrastructure of criminological research. Both authors argue that all criminological research is conducted within a political context, which exerts some influence on the research. To understand fully the political context to which they refer, readers are strongly advised to read the series of essays by Downes and Morgan on the politics of law and order from 1945 to 2002.

* Downes, D. and Morgan, R. (2002) 'The skeletons in the cupboard: the politics of law and order at the turn of the millennium'.
* Downes, D. and Morgan, R. (1997) 'Dumping the hostages to fortune? The politics of law and order in post-war Britain'.
* Downes, D. and Morgan, R. (1994) 'Hostages to fortune? The politics of law and order in post-war Britain'.

Useful websites

Home Office	www.homeoffice.gov.uk
Youth Justice Board	www.yjb.gov.uk
Lord Chancellor's Department	www.lcd.gov.uk
Economic and Social Research Council	www.esrc.ac.uk
Joseph Rowntree Foundation	www.jrf.org.uk
Nuffield Foundation	www.nuffieldfoundation.org.uk
Leverhulme Trust	www.leverhulme.org.uk

3

Ethical Dimensions of Qualitative Research in Criminology

Introduction

This chapter reviews the ethical issues that can arise when undertaking qualitative research on crime, criminals, victims and the criminal justice process. In promoting ways of protecting respondents from harm and exploitation we give attention to informed consent, overt and covert research and issues of privacy. We consider the difficulties of researching the sensitive topics commonly encountered in criminological research. We critically review the ethical codes pertinent to researchers in the criminological and criminal justice field, including the codes adopted by the British Society of Criminology, the Socio-Legal Studies Association, the British Sociological Association and the British Psychological Society. The chapter concludes by inviting readers to consider scenarios which exemplify the ethical dilemmas discussed in this chapter.

Definitions

It is important that we begin this chapter by defining what we mean by the ethical dimensions to criminological research. Various definitions are available to us. For Jupp et al. (2000: 171) 'ethics is about the standards to be adopted towards others in carrying out research'. The British Sociological Association (BSA) highlights researchers' 'responsibility both to safeguard the proper interests of those involved in or affected by their work, and to report their findings accurately and truthfully' (2002: 1). In its Code of Research Ethics the British Society of Criminology (BSC) suggests that the 'guidelines do not provide a prescription for the resolution of choices or dilemmas surrounding professional conduct in specific circumstances' (2003: 1). They provide a framework of principles to assist the choices and decisions which have to be made. Fundamentally ethical dimensions are pertinent to how researchers conduct their work through all stages of the research process from project planning to dissemination. As Shaw (2003) emphasises the importance of attention to ethical issues is as pertinent to qualitative as quantitative approaches, although as he acknowledges, and this chapter will discuss, the nature of qualitative research techniques and their application to criminological topics makes for some distinctive ethical challenges.

Ethical issues brought to the fore

A series of recent factors have led to a refocusing on the ethics of social research, including those that apply to criminological studies. The Data Protection Act 1998 and the Human Rights Act 1998 have both had direct impact on social research. While methods texts and academic classes in social research methods have routinely given attention to the ethics of research activity, both of these pieces of legislation have served to put the rights of those involved in research on a statutory footing. In the light of such changes bodies such as the Socio-Legal Studies Association are reviewing their guidelines for ethical research, and the BSA and BSC have recently completed reviews.

Such reviews are not only driven by recent legislative changes and an increasingly rights based climate but also by some of the changing technical context in which research is undertaken. The relatively recent emergence of the internet as a vehicle for research activity highlights a range of ethical issues on access and consent. Similarly the enhanced opportunities for observation made available by the routinization of the CCTV camera raises further questions. Linked to such developments, the consequent enhanced governance and monitoring being applied to social research is reflected in the increased attention that universities and research organizations are giving to vetting work that is undertaken. Researchers are increasingly required to have their proposed work scrutinized by ethical review committees, with some academics expressing fears on the potential impact of this on academic freedoms. Furedi (2002: 20) points to the potential dangers for research in what he describes as universities increasing 'obsession with ethics', and argues that an overly restrictive approach will have 'a corrosive impact on the exercise of academic freedom'.

Producing codes of practice that seek to protect the individual rights of those participating in research is inevitably a delicate balancing act. As May

(2001) suggests the most effective means of not impinging on individual rights and freedoms is not to undertake research or to have research topics of such a sanitized and neutral type they cannot breach individual principles. There is a real danger that too close a scrutiny on research activity will produce an inflexible, overly constrained process. Furedi (2002) comments that such an approach has particularly negative ramifications for qualitative research that is premised on interviewer discretion and responsiveness to interviewee accounts. Any requirement to have predetermined questions agreed in advance would directly cut across the open ended nature of much qualitative work. In contrast, as May suggests:

> a loose and flexible system involving 'anything goes' opens the research door to the unscrupulous ... If research is to be viewed as credible endeavour, then perhaps the relations that are established with all those party to the research must utilize some ethical basis which provides guidelines for, but not ethical constraints on, the researcher? (2001: 62)

Faced with identifying an appropriate balance between these positions those with management or supervisory responsibility for research activity are increasingly turning to risk assessment strategies to assess the potential impact of work undertaken. From an academic perspective it will be important that a continuing commitment to avoiding an overly constrained approach is retained.

Organizational and political constraints

Despite the recent increase in attention to the issue, ethical dilemmas are not a wholly new challenge for criminologists. The nature of the topic and the potential vulnerability of many of the subjects with whom research is undertaken means that this chapter can draw on a valuable archive of previous work wherein researchers have grappled with ethical problems and dilemmas. It is important, however, not to oversimplify the issue and to acknowledge that the ethical issues faced by criminologists and criminal justice researchers can be multi-faceted, relating to individuals, organizations, communities or nation states. As discussed above most of the research undertaken will have a political context. Typically the challenge of producing objective research will be faced by those undertaking funded research where the sponsor might be a government or private organization or company with a vested interest in the outcomes. This can result in pressure to bury unwelcome messages that emerge from the research findings, and the consequent ethical dilemmas that presents.

Empirical research, including qualitative work, cannot be divorced from national and international events. Shifts in the political climate will routinely provide a contextual backdrop for qualitative work. Wardhaugh (2000: 327) in her work with street homeless people describes the contemporary demonization and criminalization of such groups by politicians and the media as a significant 'social and political context' to her work. Quinn (2001) found similar attitudes to asylum seekers to be influential in his access to key policy and political figures.

At an organizational level, qualitative research can produce findings that entail uncomfortable messages for the setting and lack fit with the institutional agenda. Levi and Noaks (1999) report how in their study of violence against the police (officially termed 'assault police') the police force in which the research was undertaken was ill at ease with, and sought to suppress, some of the findings. The research took a unique approach in combining victim and perpetrator accounts of violent incidents with the brief that it should extend beyond official accounts of the problem of assaults on police officers. The account that follows demonstrates how organizations might threaten the independence of research. In this case the research was undertaken within a police force but similar outcomes can occur when researching other criminal justice agencies (see Carter 1995 for a prison-based account). This type of threat to producing valid accounts of events is a major motivation for the type of covert research (discussed later in this chapter) described by Holdaway (1983).

Researching police targeted violence in 'Aggro Force'

'Aggro force' commissioned an independent research study in the light of their placement at the top of a national league table for assaults on their police officers. The research was undertaken by two university-based academics and a seconded police officer. The research was funded by the Home Office and aimed to construct profiles of the offenders and police officers involved in assaults and review the dynamics that led up to the point of aggression. Police officers completed a pro-forma as soon as possible after the assault against them, and face-to-face semi-structured interviews were undertaken with a sample of assailants. The research followed Toch's (1969) approach that violence is an interpersonal phenomenon which is oversimplified by making a sharp distinction between the role of victim and perpetrator. The findings confirmed Toch's analysis revealing that the attitude and approach adopted by police officers frequently contributed to how events were played out and whether violence occurred. Only a minority of assaulted officers experienced 'out of the blue' attacks with no prior interaction with assailants. In the majority of cases the assaults were embedded in ongoing contact, and in some cases assailants provided accounts of how overly assertive and aggressive attitudes on the part of officers had led to an escalation of tension and contributed to the violent outcome. Such findings contributed to the researchers' conclusion that an understanding of the problem of 'assault police' needed to draw on the behaviour of both victims and assailants. This conclusion failed to equate with some senior officers' investment in the project who had hoped it would depict the police as unambiguous victims. For them the public relations function was dependent on a sanitized image of the police, which was fundamentally contradicted by accounts which proposed any active contribution by the police to the violence committed against them. Accounts of 'assault police' could only serve functional ends for organizational purposes if they depicted the police in a totally positive light. Victim precipitation did not fit with the organizational agenda leading some influential senior officers to discredit the project. As the sponsors, the police force sought adaptations to the report in order to downplay their officers' contributions to violent outcomes. They accused the seconded police officer of 'going native' because he was perceived as prepared to criticize his colleagues. Furthermore, while officers acknowledged informally that the researchers had 'got it right', the report's recommendations were not adopted for use in police training even though this was one of the aims of the research project. We adopted an ethical stance and remained true to our findings but were aware that in doing so, limited use would be made of the report as a means of reducing police targeted violence.

Some organizational sites will pre-empt possible research related difficulties and have their own review committees in place to scrutinize research proposals. Martin (2000: 220) describes how the Prison Service 'examines all research proposals that might give rise to ethical concerns'. In spite of this scrutiny, the eventual findings that emerge from studies can be discomforting for institutional settings and groups, and can lead to consequent actions on their part to seek to influence reporting. Baldwin (2000: 250) describes such a scenario in his early court-based research. He graphically describes how certain members of the legal profession sought to suppress the publication of his and Michael McConville's work on plea bargaining. His account highlights the ethical dilemma that can be faced by researchers in whether to publish and be damned. In Chapter 2 we discussed some of the implications of following such a course of action for what might be termed 'repeat player' researchers who seek to make a career in criminal justice research. Baldwin argues for negotiation with interested parties but only so far as this does not compromise the independence of the researcher. His conclusion is that 'it is vital, even axiomatic, that the content of any final report should be the researcher's responsibility and no one else's and that all pressure to discourage the publication of results be firmly resisted' (Baldwin: 2000: 253).

Community concerns

Researchers may also encounter ethical issues at a community level. Residents can become concerned about representations of their community as experiencing significant crime and disorder and a consequent targeting of their area as a site for research. Residents can have understandable concerns about how the image of their area is negatively affected by subsequent research attention. Those, mostly inner city, areas of the UK which experienced riots in the 1990s are an example of locations which received disproportionate attention from both the media and social researchers. While important work has been produced as a result of such attention, some seeking to give an active voice to residents (Campbell, 1993), community concerns about representations of their locale as 'run down', 'violent' or 'sink estates' are understandable. In response to such concerns, Noaks (2000) gave assurances to a community expressing such anxiety that she would maintain confidentiality in relation to where her research was undertaken and use a pseudonym to describe the area. While others have argued 'that work which is grounded in a sense of place cannot credibly anonymise place-names without special and compelling reason to do so' (Loader et al., 1998: 391), in this case it was felt to be justified in directly taking account of the concern expressed by residents.

Hancock (2000: 378), in her writings on conducting research in high crime areas, also highlights a need for researchers 'to be mindful of the sensibilities that exist in a community and consider their implications'. As well as being alert to attitudes to the research she also calls for an awareness of neighbourhood networks and sensitivity on the part of researchers to how those might cut across the willingness of particular groups to be involved with the research.

There is also an issue regarding the need for qualitative research to be responsive with regard to cultural diversity and put in place means of ensuring that full understandings are facilitated between researcher and researched. It is universally important that the language used by researchers is clear and unambiguous. Without this, informed consent cannot be achieved. The need for clarity applies to the spoken word and any written materials that are used.

Qualitative research is premised on reflecting individuals' conceptions of social reality and begins from where they are at. Use of language is a crucial component with qualitative accounts seeking to represent the actual words used by the research participants. Maher (1995) provides a good example of this in her ethnographic fieldwork with New York based women drug users, a majority of whom were drawn from racial/ethnic minorities. She describes how tape recorded interviews were undertaken with more than 200 women with unstructured interviews lasting anything from half an hour to three hours. The research produced a substantial data set which Maher (1995: 139) describes as including 'more than 5000 pages of transcribed interview narrative, several hundred pages of typed fieldnotes, a field diary and photographs ... personal letters, poems and drawings provided by individual women'. Having gathered such a substantial set of data Maher is committed to having the women tell their own story through the research. Her accounts of the work draw on the women's' own accounts of their lives and actions:

> Dey were called coolies. Coke cigarettes. I decided to come back up here to live. Thas when I got on welfare. I learned it from a friend o'mine ... we used to sit aroun' and I used to see her jus' take coke ... An thas how I learned. (1995: 144)

I jus' started bein' aroun' – seein' people do dat like since I came to New York. I mean, they're so open down here. Where I'm from you don' see – you don' walk pass an' see people smokin' outside or stickin' needles and stuff in their arms ... I saw somebody in tha' res'room across the street smokin' crack. (1995: 150–1)

Particular issues also arise when the language used by those participating in research is even more distinct from that of the researcher. On occasions it may be necessary for researchers to make use of a language interpreter in gathering material. Where this proves necessary it is vital that the researcher continues to be alert to the rights and sensitivities of the person being interviewed. There needs to be a check made that the person being interviewed is completely comfortable with how the interpretation is organized and in particular who is undertaking it. Noaks (Noaks and Butler, 1995) has written about the inappropriateness of using intimates, including family members, to undertake interpretation on potentially sensitive topics. It is important that social researchers also take account of the issue and be aware that when researching such topics, the interviewees may not be wholly comfortable with the interpreter. For example when interviewing in relation to domestic or sexual violence, there may need to be a discussion as to whether a professional interpreter or person known to the interviewee provides the interpretation.

Individual rights

As well as the national, organizational and community factors reviewed above, criminological research typically has to take account of individual rights. This is not to suggest that attention to the position of individuals is something separate and outside of the other types of research discussed. Researchers will routinely have to protect the identity of potential whistle blowers and research informants. Gomez-Cespedes (1999) describes the sensitivity of the issues encountered in her qualitative study of organized crime in Mexico. In particular she relates the importance of guaranteeing anonymity to the key actors (including politicians, government officials and police officers) who informed her exploration of an increasingly politically sensitive topic.

Beyond research undertaken in such settings criminologists undertaking work at a one-to-one level also need to be alert to the potential vulnerability of their research participants and in response develop an ethically informed approach. May (2001: 46) reinforces this requirement suggesting that 'ethics are a central part of maintaining the integrity and legitimacy of research practice'. All research participants should experience an approach that gives attention to protecting their rights, seeks to achieve informed consent and respects promises of confidentiality. While such requirements are an imperative for all those involving themselves with research, particular attention is required in the case of the potentially vulnerable participant. Vulnerabilities in relation to criminological research can relate to victim status, offender status or a combination of both. It is also the case that research with official players in the criminal justice process, whether they be magistrates, judges, police, prison or probation officers also requires an ethically thought through approach. In developing such approaches we now proceed to review the support and advice that researchers can acquire from the ethical statements of academic associations.

Review of ethical statements

> The development and application of research ethics is required not only to maintain public confidence and to try and protect individuals and groups from the illegitimate use of research findings, but also to ensure its status as a legitimate and worthwhile undertaking. (May, 2001: 67)

May's statement is indicative of the significance he attributes to ethical guidelines, representing them as functioning concurrently for the good of the individual, society and the social science discipline. Whether it is feasible for statements of research ethics to incorporate all of these objectives is questionable, particularly in the increasingly complex social worlds that we inhabit. Acknowledgement of that complexity is evident in the reviews of ethical guidelines currently being undertaken by groups such as the BSA. We will now briefly review the current position of the key academic bodies pertinent to qualitative criminology. A range of codes are discussed linked to criminology, law, sociology and psychology reflecting the multi-disciplinary basis of the subject area. It will be noted that there are different standards of accountability and related sanctions across the disciplines reflecting the differences across paradigms. In particular the British Psychological Society (BPS) ethical statement published in 2000 amounts to a set of requirements, the breaching of which can lead to expulsion from the society, while the other groups pertinent to criminology offer a set of guidelines with less in the way of associated sanctions. The more stringent requirements made of psychological studies can be linked to a closer affinity with medical research. Fundamentally the common principles across all approaches are informed consent and that involvement with the research should involve no harmful effects for participants.

The BSA points to 'a set of obligations to which members should normally adhere as principles for guiding their conduct' (2002: 1). They argue for a position whereby should researchers choose to depart from ethical standards this should be a principled decision rather than one made out of ignorance. The association is explicit that they seek to inform rather than impose 'an external set of standards' (2002: 1).

The BSC adopted a written code of ethics in 1999, which was updated in 2003. Previously, as Baldwin (2000: 254) points out, 'resolution of everyday, but acute, ethical difficulties has been treated as a matter for the researcher's own conscience'. Again this code focuses on providing researchers with guidance rather than prescribed standards.

Some researchers working in the criminological and criminal justice fields have elected to turn to the written code provided by the Socio-Legal Studies Association (SLSA). This has existed since 1993, and at the time of writing is under review. Hoyle (2000: 401) in her work on domestic violence reports finding that guidance 'the most thorough and clearest of such statements'.

Having listed the key statements it is important to emphasize that attention to ethical issues is something that needs to be ongoing in the research process. There is a risk attached to having research plans vetted at the outset of projects that researchers may be lulled into thinking that they have a green light to proceed and are not required to maintain a critical eye to ongoing ethical issues. Those addressing ethical points, both as researchers and regulators, are increasingly acknowledging that best practice demands ongoing reflexivity and channels for providing the researcher with advice and support. Ethical issues can occur at different stages of the research process and will arise in relation to choice of topic; who is included; how the research is undertaken; and how the research data is handled and processed. Furthermore, the challenging scenarios that might be encountered can never be fully predicted in the planning stages of a research project. The researcher needs to be prepared for the unanticipated and can be helped in this by having an advisory committee to whom they can turn with any problems encountered. Similarly, codes of practice should only be seen as a starting point, with all of those that we have reviewed above emphasizing that the researcher will need to address ongoing issues. As the BSA identify their ethical statement cannot 'provide a set of recipes for resolving ethical choices or dilemmas' (BSA, 2002: 1). Liebling (2001: 481) similarly counsels that even where advance preparation has been undertaken 'dilemmas have to be resolved situationally and spontaneously'.

We will now turn to some of the core facets of an ethically-based approach, in part drawing on the work of those who have previously grappled with such problems:

Informed consent

Achieving informed consent is commonly promoted as a fundamental guiding principle for an ethically informed approach. This has been the case particularly among feminist researchers. Informed consent refers to research conducted in such a way that participants have complete understanding, at all times, of what the research is about and the implications for themselves in being involved. As Shaw (2003: 15) suggests 'the principle of consent includes an assumption of voluntary participation'. One of the difficulties in following such a wholly transparent approach is that certain participants may become defensive and unwilling to reveal sensitive facts or information. Such reticence can negatively impact on the validity of the findings that are achieved. It is for this reason that the researcher will sometimes have to balance competing questions of consent and validity. Jupp et al. (2000: 172) introduce the concept of 'trade-offs' between potentially competing principles emphasising that 'decision-making inevitably involves trade-offs, for example trading off the weaknesses of one course of action against the strengths of another'. Others have represented this as the need for researchers to develop an 'ethical compromise' (Fountain, 1993). Shaw (2003) also reflects on the challenges in applying ethical principles and the persistent requirement to balance competing priorities. House (1993: 168) asserts that 'the balancing of principles in concrete situations is the ultimate ethical act'.

As well as handling such trade-offs researchers will also need to ensure that information given and general communications are culturally sensitive. Informed consent requires complete understanding on the part of those participating in research. In some cases this will require translation of research materials and/or use of a language interpreter. On occasions materials will need to be made age appropriate, for example where children are participating in a research project. In Chapter 5 we offer some strategies for achieving informed consent when working with individuals held in custodial settings.

As Shaw (2003) discusses, there is an issue in being confident that one has achieved informed consent in ongoing qualitative research. For example, while the ethnographer, who is following an overt model, may achieve consent at the outset of their research, it might be suggested that to fulfil their ethical responsibilities they should return to the issue at regular intervals to check that consent is ongoing. The researcher might have understandable concerns regarding how such practices would impede their overall research task. In practice, they would hope as a participant observer not to have to highlight their researcher role, what Norris (1993: 131) refers to as making 'the research role invisible in the field'. Eisner (1991: 214) suggests that obtaining informed consent 'implies that the researcher knows before the event what the event will be and its possible effects. This is often not the case in qualitative research'. The qualitative researchers cannot rely on such an occurrence (Shaw, 2003).

Achieving universal informed consent among all potential research participants is also a particular challenge in communities, organizations or other group settings. Norris (1993) discusses the challenges of this in his ethnographic work shadowing police officers. He introduces the notion that researchers will produce 'serviceable' accounts of their work that may be adjusted depending on the intended audience for the account. For him 'such accounts are not untrue, but they are veiled. They construct the research role so as to make it understandable and acceptable to the researched' (1993: 129). Norris does, however, also acknowledge that he made the 'pragmatic' decision not to provide any explanation of his role to members of the public, thereby excluding them from the process of informed consent (see Chapter 10 for a discussion by Noaks on how her research role was constructed for competing audiences).

Despite this emphasis on the importance of informed consent there is a long standing tradition of covert research in the criminological field (Fielding, 1982; Holdaway, 1982). Such work can be viewed as a clear example of an approach that contradicts the principle of informed consent. We will now review the justifications that qualitative researchers have offered for following such an approach.

The ethics of covert research

Covert research is one of the most controversial issues in research ethics, and one which attracts substantive attention in ethical codes and guidelines. Feminist researchers, in particular, have argued for the importance of informed consent, something which is not achievable where the research is undertaken covertly. Despite this, some of those researchers who have used covert techniques have made a convincing case for their necessity. Holdaway (1992) who was responsible for some of the early work on the occupational culture of British policing provides a rigorous account of his decision to undertake a covert ethnography while working as a police officer. Fundamentally his justifications for adopting the approach are premised on the opportunity for unique access to an under researched and somewhat impenetrable group, and the contribution this would make to extending 'the body of knowledge' on policing (1992: 62). Having offered such justifications, Holdaway makes efforts to convey the stress and ethical challenges that he experienced in adopting such an approach. Such work cannot be said to overstep ethical guidelines because none of the associations cited above have offered emphatic opposition. The BSA (2002: 12) commends that 'as far as possible sociological research should be based on the freely given informed consent of those studied' but this position does not rule out the use of covert strategies in certain circumstances. Holdaway also points to the need for a continuum in our representations of research as either overt or covert. While research activity may be overt, researchers may choose to be covert about some of their objectives by providing what Norris (1993) terms 'serviceable accounts'. For Holdaway (1992: 62) such actions are 'as dishonest a strategy as covert research, if the latter is thought to be dishonest'.

Hoyle (2000: 401) in her work on the policing of domestic violence describes an approach whereby in home visits to victims of such violence (accompanied by a non-uniformed police officer) the victim was provided with an accurate account of the research objectives while the perpetrator was separately advised that 'the research was intended to examine public perceptions of the police handling of any disputes – not just domestic disputes'. Interviews with potential perpetrators were undertaken by the police officer in a separate room with the interviewee unaware that their partner was being asked about their violent behaviour. Hoyle acknowledges that such a 'ploy' facilitated her access to female victims enabling them to tell their stories but constituted an approach that was 'economical with the truth' (2000: 401). She recognizes that the routine presence of the police may also have put pressure on the women to talk to her and in seeking to balance that factor she was explicit with female interviewees regarding their right not to speak to her. As a case study Hoyle's work raises a number of ethical challenges and questions: for example, how comfortable would the woman feel in telling her story with the police present? how reassuring would it be to know that the violent partner was potentially within hearing distance in the next room? It also exemplifies the importance of a principled approach in choosing to set aside the concept of informed consent.

Privacy and confidentiality

When adopting an ethically based approach researchers will routinely follow a policy of non-disclosure of information shared and give research participants assurances about confidentiality. In a majority of cases this will be unproblematic. Pseudonyms will commonly be used to maintain privacy and confidentiality. The BSA (2002: 4) provide guidance on the safe storage of research data and sets down the responsibilities of researchers in that regard. Such requirements have been set down in the Data Protection Act, which is as applicable to those undertaking qualitative as quantitative research. However, social researchers working in the criminological field will encounter scenarios in which they have to face the dilemma of whether to breach confidentiality. Martin (2000: 229), drawing on her work in prison settings, argues that this should never be an action taken lightly. She represents this as a 'grey area' in which researcher discretion has to play a part. Her advice is that research projects should give advance thought to establishing the parameters of confidentiality and consider those situations when a breach of promises would be considered. King (2000: 307) argues that in his experience confidentiality can never be 'absolute'. In Chapter 5 we discuss how interviewees should be given a candid account of that information which the researcher may not be able to hold in confidence. This will empower the interviewee and enable them to make informed choices on what information they elect to share. In line with other experienced researchers we would support the need for a principled approach in deciding to transgress assurances regarding confidentiality. Despite this, researchers will sometimes receive information which they find personally distressing but which they choose not to disclose to official sources. We would concur with King (2000: 307) on the sensitivity of the reflexive account provided by Liebling (1992) in respect of her writings on suicide in prison. She sets out for the reader the ethical choices researchers will sometimes have to make when they handle sensitive material.

A commitment to respecting privacy is further problematized by the increasing complexity of what we understand by public and private space.

Wardhaugh (2000) in her work with street homeless people sets out the dangers of overemphasizing differentiations between that which is considered public and private. In a review of the ethics of conducting covert participation with such groups she points to the lack of 'clear separation between public and private domains: their whole daily round is carried out in public places, and they have no private space to which they may retreat, although they may contrive temporarily to define some places as semi-private' (2000: 326). Such complexity in definitions of privacy can also be linked to the intrusive capacity of the CCTV camera and the increasing extent to which our routine activities and movements are scrutinized. The importation of such cameras into the residential streets of our neighbourhoods reinforces the capacity for privacy to be breached, quite often without our knowledge. However, in the case of social research we should seek to respect privacy and acknowledge research participants' choices as to whether they allow us to share their personal space and choose to disclose their views, attitudes and feelings to us. In part, such questions are linked to decisions on the location for research, which Davies (2000: 88) links to 'practical, ethical and safety concerns'. As discussed in Chapter 5 on interviewing, attention to issues of privacy need particular attention for those in custodial settings who have limited control regarding their occupation of space. In community based work researchers will sometimes need to look to innovative solutions (Burman et al., 2001). Davies (2000: 89) describes using a local cafe in her interviews with female offenders as 'a compromise in terms of "home versus away"'. Smith (2003) in her research on taxi drivers' experiences of workplace violence often undertook interviews while sitting in their cabs.

As well as privacy issues linking to location, protection of personal identity can also be crucial. Sharpe (2000: 367) describes anonymity as a 'paramount' aspect of her qualitative research with prostitutes. She describes how the women had 'constructed elaborate stories, or had contingency plans organized, to explain their nightly absences ranging from a nightly baby sitting job to attending an evening class'. For them it was crucial that involvement with the research did not breach these accounts. Sharpe sought to guarantee this with the use of pseudonyms and the exclusion of any descriptive references that might have helped identify the women. Beck (2002) had to exclude the accounts given by black female police officers from her research. They constituted such a small minority in the police force that was researched it would have proved impossible to guarantee their anonymity.

Avoiding exploitation

Eisner (1991) suggests that it is virtually impossible for research not to be exploitative and from the point that the decision is made to undertake the work there is an element of using the experiences of others for one's own ends.

We do not like to think of ourselves as using others as a means to our professional ends, but if we embark upon a research study that we conceptualize, direct and write, we virtually assure that we will use others for our purposes. (1991: 225–6)

The danger of such a position is that it can serve to repress research activity. Instead qualitative researchers need to have an awareness of potential exploitation and deploy strategies to minimize such effects (see the case study in Chapter 10 for a detailed discussion of use of informants and how to respond to the acquisition of 'dangerous knowledge'). Payment to research participants can be one strategy to avoid potential exploitation – although this should not be oversimplified as buying off research subjects.

Offering payment to research participants has been used with relative frequency, although not always without controversy (Davies, 2000; Hobbs, 2001; Wardhaugh, 2000, and Chapter 9 of this book). Inducements can mean the use of methods other than monetary payment. For example, tobacco has a currency in the prison system. In the past Noaks has had experiences of interviewing prisoners when, although not a smoker, she would take in a packet of cigarettes for the prisoner to make use of during the interview. Martin (2000: 228) makes the point that prisoners will rarely agree to take part in research unless they can see that 'they will get something out of it for themselves', and refers to this process as the 'research bargain'. While many institutions have tightened up on the sharing of cigarettes with prisoners, either by social researchers or police officers seeking to achieve the writing off of crimes, Martin suggests that the skilled interviewer can still strike a bargain. She points out that in the mundane and boring world of the prison the prospect of talking with an unknown researcher can in itself be an inducement.

Ethical positioning

Ethical positioning refers to the status of the researcher in relation to their research participants. Pressures to move beyond the researcher role, whether into that of friend, advocate, colleague or collaborator, are a particular feature of qualitative work with its greater propensity for reciprocal relationship between researcher and researched. Maguire, in his work with street criminals highlights the 'risk of being swept along by the natural curiosity which every researcher possesses and crossing one of the ethical boundaries' (2000: 134). For Maguire, the ethical challenge related to an invitation from two known offenders to join them on a job. Such an experience made Maguire aware of the need for 'conscious setting of limits or "line drawing"'. For him the line was drawn in such a way as not to allow for his participation in the criminal act. He acknowledges that this has to be an individual moral decision for each researcher. Again this brings us back to the issue of interviewer discretion and an acknowledgement that neither methods texts or teaching can provide all of the answers as to how the researcher should behave. In practice others have gone further than Maguire and been prepared to play a part in criminal events (Ferrell and Hamm, 1998).

Issues regarding overstepping the researcher role are not restricted to experiences with offenders. Both Norris (1993) and Westmarland (2001a) describe the pressure to step out of the researcher role, potentially into that of whistleblower, in ethnographic work with police officers. Such decisions often have to be made instantaneously with little or no opportunity to consult ethical guidelines or project managers. In some cases such decision-making is linked to the concessions that have to be made to remain in the field and get the job done. In ongoing fieldwork this can also reflect the complexities of what Liebling and Stanko have referred to as 'feelings of ambivalence towards and allegiance with those we research' (2001: 422). Westmarland, drawing on the work of Brown (1996), also points to the potential shifts in researcher status as insider/outsider: 'an ethnographer may move along a continuum of insider/outsideredness, slipping backwards and forwards along it throughout the life of the study' (2001a: 527).

Qualitative researchers need to retain reflexivity in their relations with research participants. Smith and Wincup (2000: 343) describe the difficulty of avoiding being emotionally caught up with many of the traumatic experiences described to them by women in prison and bail hostels. They acknowledge that being the receptor of such information required 'emotional management' on their part. Liebling and Stanko (2001: 421) similarly refer to the 'emotional toll' that can be bound up with researching 'criminal harm'. Such challenges and the development of obligations and feelings of loyalty to research participants is a particular feature of extended fieldwork, including ethnographic projects (see Chapter 10 for an extended discussion of these effects in Noaks' work with a private security group). There may be pressure for academic researchers to take on the mantle of advocate and move away from the role of researcher. This will particularly apply in situations wherein researchers uncover maltreatment, injustices or potential miscarriages of justice. Again there are likely to be no easy answers and the researcher will be faced with balancing assurances regarding confidentiality and a desire to publicize inherent wrongs (see exercise 2 at the end of this chapter for an instance of this type of dilemma).

Concluding comments

The aim of this chapter has been to emphasize the need for reflexivity and ethical awareness on the part of researchers. We would concur with the Liebling and Stanko position that 'ethical predicaments cannot be avoided' (2001: 421). Such challenges are commonly encountered by the criminological researcher whose research will frequently bring them into contact with vulnerable groups. As we have evidenced, ethical decision-making is complex and there are rarely easy answers. Drawing on our own experiences and the increasingly reflexive accounts from some of our criminology colleagues we have sought to encourage researchers to follow their example in using a principled ethical approach.

Exercises

1 You are asked to undertake a piece of research evaluating the effectiveness of a local police force's operations in relation to maintaining the sex offender register. Part of the research will include interviews with individuals who are registered and residing in the community. Stage one: list the ethical issues that you would want to talk through with the project manager/supervisor before undertaking the interviews. Stage two: draw up a letter of introduction explaining the research to potential research participants.

2 As part of a project researching young people from minority ethnic backgrounds experiences' in Young Offender Institutions you observe a group of young white inmates racially abusing an 18-year-old Somali. The staff do not react and later tell you that it would be worse for the young man if they intervened as he would then be likely to be physically abused when they were not on hand. How do you respond as a researcher?

FURTHER READING

The following three recommendations provide invaluable reflexive accounts of the ethical challenges encountered when completing qualitative research projects.

*   *British Journal of Criminology* (2001), volume 41, issue 3 is a special edition on criminological research.
*   King, R. and Wincup, E. (eds) (2000) *Doing Research on Crime and Justice* is particularly recommended.
*   Norris, C. (1993) 'Some ethical consideration on field-work with the police'

Useful websites

British Society of Criminology   www.britsoccrim.org
British Sociological Association   www.britsoc.org.uk
The British Psychological Society   www.bps.org.uk
Socio-Legal Studies Association   www.kent.ac.uk/slsa
Social Research Association   www.the-sra.org.uk

Part 2

The Qualitative Research Process:
From Access to Analysis

4

Negotiating and Sustaining Access

Introduction

One of the key issues likely to confront researchers as soon as they begin to consider collecting data for their project is access, since all social research involves gaining access to data. Depending on the topic they select, qualitative researchers may need to negotiate access to documents (which may or may not be in the public domain), individuals, social groups or institutions. Access issues are not just problems which need to be solved at the beginning of a project but are also a continuing concern throughout the process of data collection. For these reasons, good researchers should be alert to potential problems at the outset and should 'adopt a reasoned, planned and modest strategy' (Blaxter et al., 1996: 143) to increase the likelihood of getting the access they need.

The purpose of this chapter is to sensitize researchers to the wide range of issues they need to consider when embarking on a research project. In order to do this the discussion draws heavily on our own experiences and those of other criminological researchers. The available literature is largely concerned with ethnographic research but we attempt within this chapter to identify considerations for all qualitative researchers, regardless of the approach they have selected. While access is in many ways a 'thoroughly practical issue' (Hammersley and Atkinson, 1995: 54), as we will explore in this chapter, researchers need to ensure that access negotiations follow appropriate ethical procedures. Hence this chapter should be read in conjunction with Chapter 3.

Getting in: negotiating physical access

Research settings vary considerably in the extent to which they are 'open' or 'closed' to public scrutiny. These differences, in turn, impact upon the nature and degree of negotiation necessary to secure access. To complicate matters further not all parts of the setting will be equally open. For example, as Baldwin (2000: 237) notes, 'conducting research within the criminal courts need involve no more than turning up with a notebook, finding a convenient vantage point, and watching whatever takes place'. This is undoubtedly true with the exception of the youth courts. However, the Lord Chancellor's Department (http://www.lcd.gov.uk/research/access.htm) *'strongly* advises consultation with members of the judiciary before you start' (italics in original). In our experience, courts sometimes object to researchers taking notes during court proceedings without prior permission. Should the researcher wish to look at court files or interview court staff, defendants, victims, witnesses, judges, magistrates or legal professionals they need to secure permission from the Lord Chancellor's Department. Even if this access is agreed this precludes researchers having access to particular groups and to particular settings. Researchers are actually prohibited by law from speaking to people who sit on juries, during or after the trial. Judges, lawyers and other court personnel have proved in the past to be unenthusiastic about participating in research (Baldwin, 2000; Morgan, 2000). In addition researchers often have access limited to the announcements of sentencing decisions on the 'front stage' rather than the decision-making process which takes place on the 'back stage', away from the open court.

For many researchers, whether they are investigating the workings of the criminal justice agencies or the activities of criminal groups, these settings are often relatively 'closed'. Hence negotiating access can be time-consuming and uncertain, not least because of the sensitivity of many criminological research projects. For researchers interested in the criminal justice process or seeking to secure access to offenders via a criminal justice agency, the political context can provide a further obstacle (see Chapter 2).

Enabling and constraining: the role of gatekeepers

In order to begin access negotiations key individuals, often known as 'gatekeepers', need to be identified. Gatekeepers can be defined as 'those individuals ... that have the power to grant or withhold access to people or situations for the purpose of research' (Burgess, 1984: 48). Knowing who has the power to open up or block off access, or who consider themselves and are considered by others to have this authority, is an important aspect of academic knowledge about the setting (Hammersley and Atkinson, 1995). Researchers need some insight into social relationships in a research setting before they can commence their study into these social relationships, but this may be based on commonsense rather than academic understanding. As Burgess (1984) emphasizes the 'getting in' process can reveal to the researcher the configuration of social relationships at a research site.

At this stage researchers need to present themselves and their projects to potential gatekeepers. This is a key research phase because the initial presentation will influence the ways in which potential research participants define the research. Useful advice is offered by Burgess (1984) in relation to accessing organizations, but it applies equally to research with individuals. He suggests that researchers should not offer a 'theoretical treatise or a research design' (1984: 50), but instead give a clear indication of those aspects of the setting which will be focused upon and the individuals that they would like to work closely with. The accounts given need to be plausible to those involved. In other words, researchers should be explicit about the implications of the research for the setting and those who work within it. In order to do this, researchers need to make an assessment of the demands their research requests will make on others so this can be conveyed to them. Such demands need to be realistic because potential research participants will be doing the researcher a favour if they agree to help, and some particularly useful advice is offered by Bell (1999) in this respect. She puts forward these words of warning:

> If at some time in the future, colleagues or other research workers ask for your co-operation with a project, would you be willing to give the same amount of time and effort as you are asking for yourself? If not, perhaps you are asking too much. (1999: 46)

However tempting it is to be economical with the truth in order to increase the chances of securing access, honesty is the best policy. Requests should be reasoned, planned and modest. As King (2000) notes in relation to prisons research, research always has costs for staff and prisoners. Research inevitably disrupts normal prison activities and will require greater or lesser input from staff. These inputs always have costs attached because every activity involving the research is at the expense of something else.

For the reasons outlined above, researchers often promise to give something back to gatekeepers. The researcher may freely offer this, either at the outset of the project or in the later stages. The gatekeepers may make requests for reciprocal help. They might be one of a number of conditions of access (see Chapter 10 for a discussion of the extent to which these conditions more or less constrain the researcher). Below is an extract from a letter received in response to a letter requesting access to a bail hostel:

> Dear Emma,
>
> I am writing to inform that that the 'Anyshire' Probation Service agrees to participate in your research project. This is on condition that the usual confidentiality of clients is ensured. We would also wish to receive copies of your research reports (including interim reports, journal articles and conference papers).

However, even if requests for assistance such as providing copies of reports are not a condition of access, researchers often feel a sense of duty to help, so the relationship established is one of mutual support. As researchers we have often promised the following to gatekeepers: copies of the final report or executive summary, running a workshop to disseminate the findings, presenting a paper at a conference, participating in policy development meetings. Whatever research bargains are negotiated they need to be something the researcher and the gatekeeper are willing and able to live with. Such agreements are sometimes included in contractual arrangements for funded research.

Researchers need to draw upon resources available to them to identify people who can help with access. Existing social networks can be used based on acquaintanceship, kinship and occupational membership (Hammersley and Atkinson, 1995). For example, a number of researchers have commented upon the key role that can be played by academic colleagues who can act as gatekeepers to the gatekeepers (Brookman, 1999; Smith, 1996). Below is an example of how gatekeepers can operate in a positive way, ensuring that the project gets off the ground. It is taken from Mary Eaton's research on women leaving prison which required her to gain access to 34 women who had previously served a custodial sentence:

> At this stage I was fortunate in receiving encouragement and help from Women in Prison, particularly from the director. She contacted a number of women on my behalf and asked if they would be willing to be interviewed. All agreed – I do not know whether this was as a result of the director's skill in choosing possible research subjects or her persuasive powers when explaining the project. (Eaton, 1993: 124)

Readers may want to reflect critically on the appropriateness of allowing gatekeepers to become so involved in the research project, and ask questions such as how far should the gatekeeper be responsible for selecting interviewees? Whatever the conclusions reached in this respect, the example does illustrate the centrality of gatekeepers to the research project. This is illustrated further below in the actions taken to negotiate access to women awaiting trial (Wincup, 1997).

1   Advice was sought from an experienced criminological researcher about suitable approaches to ensure access negotiations to bail hostels for women were successful because at the time there were only three hostels for women and access was required to two of them. This provided not only advice but also the name and contact details of a researcher working for the Association of Chief Officers of Probation (ACOP).
2   An initial letter and summary of the research was sent to the named person, followed up with a telephone call. It was suggested that having the approval of ACOP would help to facilitate access by adding credibility to the project. An invitation to include a summary of the research in the ACOP fortnightly bulletin was accepted. This led to one unsolicited offer of help. Unfortunately this offer could not be taken up because the hostel was some distance away from

the university and repeated trips and overnight stays were not possible given the small travel budget.

3 Letters and summaries of the research were sent to the Chief Probation Officers in the areas selected and were followed up by phone calls.

4 Invariably these letters were passed on to hostel managers, sometimes via the Assistant Chief Probation Officer with particular responsibility for hostels.

5 In the case of voluntary managed hostels the letters were then shared with the management committee. Typically hostels are managed by the probation board operating in the area and hence senior managers in the probation area can make decisions about access. Voluntary-managed hostels are run by management committees appointed by the charitable body who owns the hostel and hence access decisions needed to be made by this group.

See Wincup, 1997 for a more detailed discussion of the research design.

Fortunately all three areas agreed to participate and the whole process was relatively smooth running, even though it lasted for several months. Waiting to hear if the research could go ahead as planned was frustrating and stressful.

According to Hammersley and Atkinson (1995), one of the most famous gatekeepers is undoubtedly 'Doc' who sponsored, in a non-financial sense, Whyte's (1943, reprinted 1983) study of 'corner boys'. Doc agreed to offer Whyte the protection of friendship, and coached him in appropriate conduct and demeanour. Doc had no formal authority to grant or deny access but used his status within the group to open up the possibility of Whyte making contact with the young men he wanted to study. In informal settings gatekeepers act as people who can vouch for the researcher. They use their status and relationship with potential research participants to facilitate contact and trust between them and the researcher.

There are unquestionably plentiful examples in criminological research that illustrate the unwillingness of gatekeepers to help research, and how this can potentially threaten the viability of research studies. These examples rarely appear in the published literature and typically take the form of 'war stories' circulated at academic conferences or through other networks. One example here is King's (2000) study of the origins and operation of super-maximum security custody in the United States, which involved one of us (Emma Wincup) as a researcher from September 1996 to August 1997. Despite his experience of advising HM Prison Service on the feasibility of a supermax facility in England and Wales, which facilitated obtaining a letter of recommendation from the Director General for Prisons, he was twice refused access by the Federal Bureau for Prisons to their administrative maximum facility at Florence, Colorado. This was particularly puzzling because he had been previously granted access to a number of Federal penitentiaries, and no clear reason was given for the refusal to grant access. However, he was able to continue with his study by securing access to supermax facilities in other US states.

Between the extremes of gatekeepers excluding researchers or being willing to do everything possible to help are the typical responses faced by criminological researchers. They may be faced with a range of possibilities with gatekeepers being more or less willing to help, although often their ability to help may be compromised by other demands on their time. Gatekeepers cannot be disregarded once their initial approval has been obtained. They can continue to exercise influence over the research and hence the influence of gatekeepers goes beyond simply granting or denying access. As Denscombe (1998: 78) suggests, 'access, in the sense of permission from a gatekeeper, is necessarily renewable and renegotiable'. For these reasons he suggests gaining access should be perceived as a relationship rather than a one-off event.

Access negotiations in relation to specific projects are explored further in Chapters 9 and 10. Here we turn our attention to providing guidance on how to obtain access to criminal justice agencies, documents and criminal groups.

Access procedures and protocols: securing access to criminal justice agencies

Access procedures vary considerably between criminal justice agencies but there is some common ground. For access to be granted, the research project needs to be at least acceptable to the agency, and preferably perceived as beneficial to them. Some institutions and organizations may insist that researchers complete an application form as part of their formal procedures for requesting permission, while others are happy for researchers to send a letter and short research proposal. It is also possible that some institutions and organizations may additionally request that the research has been approved by an ethics committee (see Chapter 3).

As Liebling (1992) notes, in relation to her study of suicide and self-harm, formal access procedures can have hidden advantages. Working in prisons with the fewest operational problems cleared the way for the research. This was particularly important as the research was conducted at one of the most turbulent times in the recent history of prisons. She also suggests that repeated contacts with Home Office researchers and policy-makers facilitated intense scrutiny of the research design and provided expert advice and comment throughout the negotiation process. Her views may not be shared by all. Other researchers may view such guidance as intrusive and be alarmed at HM Prison Service steering her away from young offender institutions which accommodate remand prisoners, and as a consequence those prisoners most likely to commit suicide or self-harm. Researchers need to be aware that strings may be attached if access is agreed and they need to consider the implications of these. However, as Liebling points out, while this resulted 'in a possible bias towards the smooth end of the young offender spectrum' (1992: 123), it allowed her to question why suicide and self-harm are widespread even amongst sentenced young offenders in relatively smooth-running institutions? For Liebling, the bottom line was that not agreeing with the gatekeepers would necessitate abandoning the study. Her experience is encapsulated in the quotation below:

> Negotiating access is a balancing act. Gains and losses now and later ... must be traded off against one another in whatever manner is judged to be most appropriate, given the purposes of the research and the circumstances in which it is to be carried out. (Hammersley and Atkinson, 1995: 74)

For Liebling, the gatekeeper was HM Prison Service. Researchers need to identify influential gatekeepers at a national or local level, and this is dependent on the scope of their study. In general terms, only large-scale studies need to secure permission from a national gatekeeper. Further information is provided in Table 4.1.

TABLE 4.1   *Gatekeepers in criminal justice settings in England and Wales*

Organization	Examples of national gatekeepers	Examples of local gatekeepers
Police force	Association of Chief Police Officers	Chief Constable
Court	Lord Chancellor's Department	Magistrates' court committee; Crown court manager
Prison	HM Prison Service	Governor
Probation area	Association of Chief Officers of Probation	Chief Probation Officer in a probation area
Youth offending team	Youth Justice Board	Youth offending team manager
Victim Support	Chief Executive, National Association of Victim Support Schemes	Co-ordinator for a Victim Support Branch

Getting in: accessing documents

The use of documentary sources is attractive to many researchers because of their accessibility. Increasingly vast amounts of information are available to the public without requesting permission. Access may be immediate and free, particularly as documents are often available on the Internet. While documentary research may appear to pose fewer access problems than the use of other qualitative research methods, researchers need to remind themselves that not all forms of documents are freely available. Denscombe (1998: 166) distinguishes between three types of documents: 'public domain', 'restricted access' and 'secret'. Below are some examples of the types of documents which may be of interest to criminological researchers interested in qualitative research:

1   *Public domain*: newspapers, annual reports produced by criminal justice agencies, websites.

2   *Restricted access*: files belonging to criminal justice agencies, prisoner letters and diaries, audio and video recordings of police interviews.
3   *Secret*: minutes of government meetings, e-mails produced by companies illegally trading.

As Denscombe notes the first two types are those most commonly used by academic researchers. The latter are typically used for fraud detection and under-cover work and investigative journalism (see Rawlinson, 2000 for a discussion of the blurred boundaries between investigative journalism and academic research). To access such documents requires insider knowledge, participation and decep-tion. No access negotiations are needed to access those documents in the public domain. In a conclusion to a chapter analysing the politics of criminological research, Morgan (2000) reminds readers that it is possible to conduct research without having access problems to overcome. He suggests that 'the great fortune of the British criminologist is that he or she inhabits a domain in which there is more than enough data available for secondary analysis' (2000: 85).

Below is an example of a criminological research project which required negotiating access to police murder files, restricted access documents.

Police murder files are a type of documentary source rarely used by researchers (Brookman, 1999) but were used by Brookman to obtain data for her study of patterns and scenarios of masculine homicide and violence across England and Wales. The data gathered supplemented the qualitative data obtained from in-depth interviews and quantitative data acquired from the 'Homicide Index', a large statistical database managed by the Home Office. Brookman explores the 'complex, dynamic and ongoing process'(1999: 48) in which she had to engage in order to secure access to the files she needed. As she remarks, the process required numerous forms of correspondence and contact, both formal and infor-mal, with police officers of differing ranks in three police forces. This resulted in differing negotiations processes in the three force areas with differing outcomes. The most important variations included the length of time taken to locate (or more appropriately 'unearth') the relevant documents, the extent to which access was granted to the complete files and the extent to which potentially significant documents were missing. Two valuable lessons for researchers can be gleaned from Brookman's account: firstly, it is ill-advised to assume the documents, even highly sensitive and confidential ones, may be neatly filed away, and secondly, negotiating access to sensitive documents is highly dependent upon 'who you know'.

Getting in: accessing criminal groups

Negotiating access to criminal groups in their natural setting is fraught with difficulties, leading some researchers to focus their efforts on securing access to offenders via criminal justice agencies or to adopt covert techniques (explored later in this chapter). On this point, regardless of whether an overt or covert stance is adopted, researchers need to identify the group of interest and find some way of establishing a relationship with them. For Polsky (1971) this necessitates asking around to secure an introduction to a criminal or finding out where one or more can be met. This is easier for some researchers than others because of their networks. Most of the introduction to Winlow's (2001) book on violent men is dedicated to offering a reflexive account of the research process, and within this account the impact of his personal biography on the nature and quality of the research is discussed at length. While critics might suggest it is at best self-indulgent and at worst irrelevant, Winlow argues that it was vital to successful commencement and completion of the study. His previous detailed knowledge of working-class North Eastern England 'subculture', his continued contacts with it and his working-class accent are described by Winlow as 'tools' which helped him to negotiate access and conduct the research. In this way, he suggests that he was able to conduct a study that few educated, middle-class and middle-aged British researchers could because they would have so little in common with their research participants. The book is dedicated to his parents and he suggests that without their guidance he would have been the subject of the book rather than the author!

Social access

Physical access is a prerequisite for social access but does not guarantee it. Social access describes the process of 'getting along' through establishing a research role, building up rapport with participants and securing their trust. Sparks (1989: 119, cited in Liebling, 1992) argues that the researcher entering a prison for the first time appears naïve, green, uncomfortable and out of place. This could equally be applied to research in all criminal justice settings and to research with criminal groups. Particularly for ethnographic research, access needs to be sought to new people, places and events as further research questions begin to emerge. This happens as the data are analysed and the research design evolves. To become accepted researchers need to be willing to fit into the timetables of institutional life. This applies also to research with criminal groups because researchers will soon become familiar, and need to fit in with, their routine activities. They also have to become acquainted with, and be seen to accept, the culture of the group they are investigating as the following case study illustrates vividly.

Sharpe's (1998) study of prostitution utilized first-hand lengthy observation and the methodological issues raised are explored in a chapter published in 2000. Her research had three central concerns: to analyse why women enter the world of prostitution, to examine the importance of prostitution in the individual's life and to observe how prostitution was policed. Inevitably these research concerns would require the police to have a major input in some form. The issue for Sharpe was that she had not only negotiated access to a police force in order to research their activities, but also to seek their co-operation to secure access to women working as prostitutes. Other agencies such as the Probation Service were not able to offer direct help. Motivated by 'practical expediency' rather than demonstrating 'political or ideological allegiance' (1998: 18), conducting research on and with the police required her to manage diverse relationships in the field between potentially conflicting groups. It was difficult for her to assess the extent to which the study was compromised by her relationship with the police, although she does conclude that the 'research was completed largely *in spite of* the police, not because of them' (1998: 21; emphasis in original). She also suggests that while the world of the prostitutes is perceived as a hard world to enter, the same might be said about the police due to the collection of behaviours and attitudes typically described by police researchers as 'cop culture' (see Reiner, 2000b for a more detailed discussion). As a female researcher the masculinity of police culture came as a considerable shock. Female researchers conducting studies within other criminal justice agencies are also likely to encounter some form of masculine culture.

The research took place in an established red light district known as 'the patch'. This comprised three streets within an isolated non-residential area of a city (which remained anonymous in the published account) where the police tolerate prostitutes soliciting for business as part of a policing strategy for containing and controlling prostitution. In the course of one year, 29 patrols were accompanied, resulting in 120 hours of observation across all days of the week. These plain-clothed officers were part of a Divisional Enquiry Team, known to the prostitutes as 'the vice'. This is a misnomer because the remit of their work also included a wide range of other sexual offences, locating missing persons and drug offences. Interviews were also conducted with both prostitutes (40 in total and 95% of those working regularly in the area) and police officers (12 in total), taking an unstructured form with the former group and a semi-structured form with the latter.

Sharpe's honest account of the research process highlights some of the likely problems that researchers might encounter. These are detailed below:

- Access negotiations are often time-consuming and may lead to the project developing in a different way than originally anticipated.
- Access may have to be negotiated with different layers of the organizational hierarchy divided by authority and power. Members of each layer may not share the same interests.
- Researchers may not be trusted (at least not initially) and their trust may be continually tested.
- Potential participants may have good reasons for not wanting to take part in the study, especially if they are involved in criminal activities.

Research roles

There is a large amount of literature on research roles in relation to qualitative, particularly ethnographic, research. Space precludes a detailed discussion of this and instead we aim to highlight the most pertinent themes. A recurring theme in published accounts of the research process is that establishing a research role takes time, and researchers may need to adopt different roles throughout the research process (Hammersley and Atkinson, 1995). For these reasons, researchers need to engage in 'impression management', which may take different forms with different groups, in order for their research role to be accepted. For example, Adams (2000) explores how she engaged in 'dressing up' and 'dressing down' depending on whether she was interviewing suspects, solicitors or police officers. This is discussed further in Chapter 5. Impression management is only possible to a certain extent because aspects of a researcher's biography such as age, sex and ethnic origin influence the researcher's role. This has been particularly highlighted by feminist scholars (see Gelsthorpe, 1990; Rawlinson, 2000; Smith and Wincup, 2000).

Our own experiences have led us to the conclusion that the research role is not always fully understood and may be treated with suspicion. Hence alternative roles are assigned to researchers to make sense of their presence in the research setting. These are detailed in Table 4.2.

TABLE 4.2   *Examples of ascribed roles in criminological research*

Researcher(s)	Research topic	Ascribed roles
Carter (1994)	Occupational socialization of prison officers	'Plant' from the Home Office; Member of Group 4 security engaged in a feasibility study for privatization
Noaks and Christopher (1990)	Assaults on police officers	Female CID officer
Sharpe (2000)	Prostitution and policing	Social worker; journalist, official from the Home Office
Wincup (1997)	Bail hostel provision for women awaiting trial	Hostel worker; social worker; 'cop'

Alternatively researchers may adopt 'cover' roles. Table 4.3 includes some examples of such roles and their usage in criminological research. These researchers were not conducting covert research but felt the need to create an acceptable social role in order to be in the setting in the first place. In both cases the role adopted was limited but helped to overcome the awkwardness inherent in conducting research.

TABLE 4.3   *Examples of 'cover' roles in criminological research*

Researcher(s)	Research topic	Cover roles
McKeganey and Barnard (1996)	Prostitutes and their clients	Quasi-service provider engaging in harm reduction work e.g. giving out condoms
Wardhaugh (2000)	Criminalization, victimization and homelessness	Volunteer in a day centre

There is an important distinction to be made between researchers assuming 'cover' roles and conducting covert research. The latter issue is discussed in the section which follows.

Conducting research without access

Covert research

Sometimes it may be judged that the relevant gatekeepers will almost certainly block entry altogether. If the research is to go ahead then one solution is to resort to covert research. This involves the researcher adopting a plausible role so they can blend into the background. There are a number of examples of criminological research which have been conducted in this vein including Holdaway's (1983) study of the British Police, Ditton's (1977) analysis of 'fiddling' in a bakery, and Hobbs et al.'s (2003) research on door supervisors or 'bouncers' as they are more traditionally known. The difficulty faced by researchers is deciding whether to request access. Sometimes permission to conduct research can be given when it is not expected. One example of this is Fielding's (1982) study of the National Front, an extreme right-wing political organization in the UK with explicitly racist views. These views are frequently condemned and therefore negotiating access to this group seemed unlikely.

It might be argued that all research is more or less covert. As Hammersley and Atkinson (1995: 265) argue, 'even when operating in an overt manner, ethnographers rarely tell *all* the people they are studying *everything* about the research' (emphasis in original). While researchers do not work in a covert manner it is fair to say that some studies involve what could be euphemistically described as being economical with the truth and perhaps more accurately described as deception. This issue is considered in Chapter 3. Burgess (1984) makes similar arguments and remarks that the decision to do covert research is often posed as an alternative to overt research. However he suggests that it is not as straightforward and simple as this. To support his argument he outlines a number of points summarized below:

1   In some instances where access is openly negotiated not all individuals will know about a piece of research. For example, if a researcher has negotiated access to a local prison, which accommodates unconvicted, unsentenced and short-sentence prisoners, the daily turnover of prisoners will make it difficult to ensure all prisoners are aware of the research.

2   Even if all individuals are aware of the research they are likely to hold differing interpretations about what is being done. For example, a study of equal opportunities and policing may be interpreted by male officers as a study of sexism and by white officers as a study of racism.

3   Some researchers may establish open access with some groups while closing off details of the research to other groups. For example, an observational study of shoplifting might involve negotiating access through store managers but details may not be given to all staff, and certainly not to customers within the store.

The ethical dilemmas raised by covert research mean that it is rarely used by researchers. However there are some recent examples such as Winlow's (2000) study entitled *Badfellas: Crime, Tradition and New Masculinities*. His choice of covert observation to explore the everyday world of violent men is a contentious one, but it is a tried and tested one by researchers studying similar groups (see for example Calvey's, 2000 study of 'bouncers'). This raises numerous ethical issues (see Chapter 3). Polsky famously urged researchers to steer clear of covert approaches:

> In doing field research on criminals you damned well better *not* pretend to be 'one of them', because they will test this claim and one of two things will happen: either you will ... get sucked into 'participant' observation of the sort you would rather not undertake, or you will be exposed, with still greater negative consequences. (1971: 122, emphasis in original)

Pretending to be 'one of them' is precisely what the covert researcher is expected to do. For Winlow this involved engaging in a type of masculine bravado with which he was not entirely comfortable but also skirting the boundaries of criminality on a number of occasions. His research therefore involved the risk of being arrested and violent attacks from drunken young people. Deciding to conduct covert research does not solve access problems instantly because researchers have to tread carefully to ensure their deception, and hence their true identity as a researcher, is not unveiled.

As Burgess (1984: 48) notes, covert research bypasses the negotiation of access with a gatekeeper but the trade-off is that limitations are placed on the research. One of the difficulties of assuming a covert role is that the researcher is unable to make field notes as incidents take place. Instead field notes have to be written up after leaving the setting. Winlow used the strategy of jotting down key words and phrases immediately after leaving the field and then used these as *aide-memoires* to develop detailed field notes the next day. This can be time-consuming, and the ethnographer is reliant on reconstructing events based on what they can recollect some time after they took place. For covert research this is the only option but even if research is conducted overtly, taking field notes can still be problematic. It can be both intrusive and impractical to take notes in front of participants. Despite claims made about ethnographers making frequent trips to the toilet to catch up on note taking, this is probably apocryphal.

Alternative strategies

Researchers need to be sufficiently adaptable to ensure the research continues, even if it is not in the form that they originally envisaged because access negotiations do not work out as intended. Many researchers do not end up studying precisely what they intended at the outset. In part this is because access negotiations can be unpredictable although there may be many other explanations.

Qualitative research techniques are particularly suited to studies which are exploratory. For these reasons, researchers should not stick rigidly to the initial research design but allow the research to evolve in a controlled rather than an ad hoc way.

Blaxter et al. (1996) offer six strategies to consider if access is denied. These are listed below with some criminological examples:

1 *Approach other individuals*: This is frequently done in criminological studies involving interviews. For example, if one prisoner refuses to be interviewed then researchers simply approach others.

2 *Approach other institutions*: For instance, Punch's (1979) inability to gain access to police forces in Britain led him to eventually study the Dutch Police instead. This is an extreme example but it is not uncommon for an individual police force to say no, so the researcher has to approach others.

3 *Approach another individual in the same institution*: For example, if a researcher is interested in probation practice with sex offenders and the officer responsible for delivering programmes with this client group refuses to participate, then it may be possible to access this group by contacting other officers such as probation hostel manager. This is unlikely to be possible if the Chief Probation Officer has declined access.

4 *Try again later*: This is rarely an option for researchers because of time constraints, but waiting until a resistant chief constable has moved on or a HM Inspectorate of Constabulary visit has been completed can be fruitful. Securing access is, of course, never inevitable.

5 *Change your research strategy*: This might involve using different methods, modified research questions or studying alternative groups and organizations. For example, McEvoy (2001) informally explored the possibility of conducting interviews in Northern Ireland prisons for his study of paramilitary imprisonment. He was told frankly that this was 'not a mission' (2001: 371) and a formal approach via a letter was ignored. His solution was to secure access to prisoners after they were released or were on Christmas or summer leave programmes. The attendance of prison officers on university courses allowed him to identify prison officers willing to participate.

6 *Focus your study on the research process*: This is rarely an option for researchers but students required to write a short dissertation could select this option, drawing on their own experiences and those of other researchers. The latter may be elicited by means of qualitative interviews with criminologists or by a virtual focus group using an electronic mailing list (see http://www.jiscmail.ac.uk for details of suitable lists).

Saying goodbye: leaving the field

Snow (1980) commented that the process of leaving the field was a neglected problem in qualitative research. A claim such as this is now no longer valid, however, it is fair to say that the researcher's departure from a particular setting has yet to receive the same systematic treatment as their entrance and presence. Much has been published since then on the process of leaving a diversity of research settings (see for example Shaffir et al., 1980 and Shaffir and Stebbins, 1991), although it is still difficult to find accounts by criminologists. Common themes within the published accounts are that the process of leaving involves reflecting on when to leave, managing the relationships formed and deciding whether to return. A further theme is that the researcher's departure, if misunderstood or viewed unfavourably by research participants, may strongly affect the efforts of future researchers in the same or similar settings. As King (2000) argues, the reputation of all researchers can depend upon the legacy left behind by any one individual. For these reasons he recommends avoiding making promises that cannot be kept, taking time to discuss and explain the research throughout, being alert to rumours so they can be quashed as quickly as possible and tying up loose ends before leaving the field.

Wolf's (1991) discussion of leaving an 'outlaw' society is one of the few criminological accounts available on leaving the field. The group studied was a motorcycle club whose members were often involved in minor crimes and sometimes engaged in major organized crime. This group, one of approximately 900 in existence in the United States and Canada at the time of the research, was perceived as a deviant subculture. Wolf's account begins by acknowledging the relationships between the different progressive stages in his fieldwork career from entering the field, maintaining field relations, leaving the field through to writing up. All are interdependent and as he notes the difficulties he faced in leaving the field were because his initial access negotiations had gone *too* well, leading to the ironic situation that for a time he felt unable to leave and write up the study. The very purpose of the time he had spent with the group appeared to be under threat. He was experiencing over-rapport and appeared to be 'going native', abandoning the analytic role for full participation, thus rendering him incapable of making any kind of detached analysis.

Wolf's study was unusual in that it moved from being a covert to an overt participant observation study. This was largely the consequence of one member of the club inviting him to conduct research at a time when Wolf was struggling to broach the subject of how to reveal the genuine nature of his interest in the group; as he notes this was 'an incredible stroke of luck' (Wolf, 1991: 218). As he moved from group member to ethnographer, his role as biker became contrived and he became excluded from the group. In his words, he 'faded away' (1991: 222). While he had initially planned to maintain ties of friendship this was not realized. The special world of the outlaw bikers necessitated intense comradeship and nothing less than this would suffice.

There is an important distinction to be made between getting out and getting away. Leaving the field physically can be relatively easy but getting away emotionally can prove more challenging, leading some researchers to describe the process as a 'psychological problem' (Shaffir, 1991: 210). As King (2000: 308) suggests, 'some researchers find it hard to leave the field, mostly because in the course of the research one inevitably makes rewarding relationships'. Some ethnographers (for example Shaffir, 1991) have suggested that research participants often expect researchers to continue on a permanent basis with the personal commitments they have established during the course of the research. However, when researchers physically leave the field they often find themselves consumed with analysis and writing, hence interest in their research participants diminishes, which can lead to feelings of betrayal and disloyalty. Neither of us are familiar with this scenario, or at least we are not aware that any of our research participants having experienced such emotions. Instead, as one of us has explored elsewhere (Smith and Wincup, 2000), a more common experience is that researchers encounter problems in 'letting go'. The analysis process serves as a constant reminder of who researchers have met, the stories they have told and the emotions they displayed when telling their stories.

Taylor (1991) suggests that there are three questions that researchers need to pose as they approach the final stages of the data collection process. The first concerns how and when to conclude a study by stopping collecting data and beginning the serious work of intensive analysis and writing. The second question is how to manage the personal relationships formed with research participants? Taylor suggests that this is a personal decision, and it depends upon how the researchers sees the people and the nature of the relationship developed with them. Finally, researchers need to consider the social, political and ethical implications of the research. These issues are discussed elsewhere in this book in Chapters 2 and 3.

There is no straightforward answer to the first question. While researchers often set themselves goals to be achieved (or they are set for them by funders or academic supervisors) such as a certain number of interviews or fixed period of observation, the most straightforward answer to the question is that a study is complete when the researcher has gained an understanding of the setting or aspect of social life that they set out to examine. Nonetheless, this response is unsatisfactory because there is a sense in which studies of the social world are invariably incomplete and imperfect. Researchers need to strive for a 'good enough' understanding otherwise they run the risk of never completing the study. For these reasons, Taylor (1991) suggests that a more appropriate question to ask is 'when does fieldwork yield diminishing returns?'. Using a jigsaw puzzle as a metaphor, he suggests that the study nears completion when it becomes apparent how the pieces of the puzzle will come together and it becomes obvious what picture the whole puzzle portrays. At this stage, missing pieces can be identified but the search for these missing pieces also generates pieces that the researcher is already aware of. What was once strange has become familiar and field notes and interview transcripts become repetitive. Leaving the metaphor aside, staying a while longer helps to confirm hunches and to find better examples of themes identified in the research. At this stage the data collection can become tedious. All experienced researchers can relate to the sense of research fatigue, which includes becoming bored by the data collection process, and physically and emotionally drained. The peculiarities of criminological research, which often expose researchers to situations of danger and distress and uncomfortable settings, can lead to this sense of fatigue taking hold at an early stage. Regular breaks can help to sustain the researcher to ensure that sufficient data are collected, but as King (2000) proposes, research projects pursue a natural trajectory; hard work at the outset to win support followed by a core period of productive collaboration, but this fades towards the end of the study.

The reality is that researchers, whether they are postgraduate students or working on funded research projects, have to work with the constraints and pressures that flow from employers and/or funders. Deadlines for the submission of theses or reports are set and researchers sometimes have to stop collecting data before they have collected all the pieces of the jigsaw. It is tempting to stay in the field longer than needed. Wax (1971: 104) in a text on fieldwork subtitled 'warnings and advice' confesses to being plagued by an impulse to stay longer than necessary and an irresistible urge to gather more data. The opportunity to conduct an additional interview or to observe a further court case is often seized, even if it is likely to produce data that are repetitious. Qualitative researchers sometimes work under the misapprehension that this adds weight to their conclusions in the same way that a large sample size does for quantitative research. This is, in some respects, ironic because it results in the qualitative researcher gathering more data than they can handle. Back (2002) warns of the dangers of becoming a 'fieldwork junkie' suffering from the 'one more interview syndrome' in an article focusing on doctoral research.

> Remember it is not the quantity but the quality of what you write about that matters. One of the frightening things about doing a PhD is that at the end of the day it's only possible to include a fraction of the empirical material you have recorded. So don't stay in the research phase longer than necessary. (paragraph 3.16)

Back's words of wisdom are also applicable to all forms of qualitative research.

Snow (1980: 101-2) suggests that one of the 'litmus tests' for indicators of what he terms 'informational sufficiency' is heightened confidence about their knowledge of their area of study. For novice researchers, and indeed for many experienced ones, feelings of self-doubt can lead to delaying the decision to leave the field. Moreover, if researchers are honest, part of the temptation to stay in the field is because it delays the difficult process of analysing fully the data collected which is necessary to build up an understanding of the social world.

Related to the decision to stop collecting data is the decision whether to return to the field? King (2000) advises prison researchers to leave one loose end hanging, explicitly or implicitly, to provide an opportunity for going back if need be. However, again the most appropriate response is this should only be done if it will enhance the level of understanding, and often limited time and resources will preclude this. Researchers may also return to discuss their analysis of the research data with their research participants. This is explored further in Chapter 8.

Concluding comments

Negotiating access is a continuous and frequently demanding process. Access is rarely negotiated on a single occasion but negotiated and renegotiated during different phases of the research process. As King (2000: 297) argues 'initial access is only the first hurdle. In fact negotiating and renegotiating access takes place on almost a daily basis once the research is underway'. Negotiating access, data collection and analysis are not distinct phases of the research process but significantly overlap (Hammersley and Atkinson, 1995). To this list we can also add the process of disengaging from the field.

Researchers need to be aware that access cannot be taken for granted and it is risky to assume it will be OK. Permission to carry out an investigation must always be sought at an early stage. One of the roles researchers must adopt is one of salesperson, trying to convince those who are in a position to help of the importance of their research. Equally the researcher must adopt a diplomat role, engaging in explicit discussions or more subtle processes, to facilitate access to the data needed. Access negotiations often do not run smoothly but the good news is that some form of research is usually possible if researchers are willing to be flexible and think imaginatively about other possibilities, 'Ultimately, therefore, research comes down to focusing on what is practically accessible. Research is the art of the feasible' (Blaxter et al., 1996: 145).

Exercises

1 Request an application form for undertaking research in prisons from the Prison Service. Select one of the following projects and try to complete the form: the nature and extent of self-harm in young offender institutions; illegal drug use in female prisons; staff attitudes to prisoner education. Alternatively look at the Lord Chancellor's Department website (http://www.lcd.gov.uk/research/info.htm), develop a research idea related to the administration of justice within the criminal courts and prepare a letter to the Research Secretariat which provides sufficient information to request access.

2 Select one of the following topics: experiences of victimization amongst homeless people; school-aged children's attitudes to drugs; stress and policing. Outline how you would secure access to enable you to carry out your research. Can you identify any potential problems with regard to access?

FURTHER READING

There are few texts devoted solely to negotiating and sustaining access, and most of those available focus on ethnographic research. However, the following are particularly recommended:

- Hammersley, M. and Atkinson, P. (1995) *Ethnography: Principles in Practice*, especially Chapter 3 on access and Chapter 4 on field relations.
- Lee, R. (1993) *Doing Research on Sensitive Topics*, particularly Chapter 7 on the access process in research on sensitive topics and Chapter 8 on covert research.
- Shaffir, W. and Stebbins, R. (eds) (1991) *Experiencing Fieldwork: An Insider View of Qualitative Research*. This book is divided into four sections: getting in, learning the ropes, maintaining relations and leaving and keeping in touch.

Discussions about access negotiations in relation to criminological research are typically covered in edited collections which bring together reflexive accounts of the research process. Useful discussions can be found in the following:

- R. King and E. Wincup (eds) (2000) *Doing Research on Crime and Justice*, particularly the chapters in part four.
- V. Jupp, P. Davies and P. Francis (2000) (eds) *Doing Criminological Research*, particularly the chapters by Davies, Martin and Hughes.
- D. Hobbs and T. May (1993) *Interpreting the Field: Accounts of Ethnography*, particularly the chapters by Armstrong, Norris and Fountain.

In addition, PhD theses are a useful source of information on access negotiations. These can be found in university libraries.

5

Interviews

Introduction

This chapter will review the range of possible interview techniques employed in criminological research. The approaches discussed will range from more structured methods through to unstructured in-depth techniques. Attention will be given to biographical approaches, focus groups and other forms of group interview. The chapter will include a discussion of the advantages and disadvantages of various interview techniques and will pay particular attention to the requirement in many criminological research studies to interview vulnerable individuals regarding sensitive topics.

The skilled interviewer

As others have acknowledged (Arksey and Knight, 1999) the media provides a plethora of role models for the skilled interviewer. If we analyse such skill it typically consists of an ability to establish an instant rapport thereby facilitating disclosure from the interviewee. Revelations and insights will often be couched in a conversational style which can lead us to take for granted the skills of the interviewer. Tony Parker, whose in-depth interviews with offenders have subsequently been represented as *Criminal Conversations* (Soothill, 1999), provides an important role model for interviewers.

This chapter will seek to analyse the required interview skills for a successful social researcher working in the criminological field. Problematizing the interview and deconstructing what works for the interviewer and interviewee owes much to feminist researchers (Finch, 1986; Oakley, 1981) who have done much to challenge the early dominance of scientific paradigms and their contribution will be reviewed. This chapter will also set out the required stages in effective interviewing, including planning, preparation and attention to detail in conducting an interview.

Selection of method

Before moving on to consider the style of interview that should be adopted, researchers need to begin by thinking about the appropriateness of interviewing for their research task. The interview strategy will need to be weighed against other possible methods, including documentary analysis and self-completion questionnaires. In some cases interviewing will be used alongside other methods as part of a triangulation process (Arksey and Knight, 1999 and see Chapter 10 for an example of a multi-method approach).

Theorizing the interview

As suggested above, feminist theory has been particularly influential in the evolution of qualitative methods. In acknowledgement of that we devote a section below to tracing how feminist approaches impacted on qualitative interviewing. However, as discussed in Chapter 2, the increased use of qualitative methods precedes the re-emergence of feminism in the second half of the twentieth century. The adoption of such methods is linked to a desire for research to address 'constructions of reality':

> qualitative research is concerned with constructions of reality – its own constructions and in particular those constructions it meets in the field or in the people it studies. (Flick, 1998: 11)

This approach has particular implications for interviewing strategy because it encourages interviewer discretion and reflexivity. It also allows for a different form of input from the person being interviewed. One of the unique features of qualitative methods is that it seeks to start from where people are at and actively looks for the means to enable them to share their experiences. Interviewing is one of the strategies by which this is achieved but with a resistance to the closed instrument, such as the questionnaire, which stifles and allows no opportunity for interviewee flexibility. Probing the interviewee perspective is at the core of qualitative research with such activity typically represented as a distraction in the quantitative approach.

The emergence of qualitative methods owes much to the symbolic interactionist tradition which sought to identify social actors' ascribed meanings and understandings. While the approach was influential in the promotion of ethnography as a method (see Chapters 1 and 6) it was also significant for the style of interviewing that was used. Downes and Rock (2003: 179) argue that symbolic interactionism required 'a particularly patient, cautious and attentive methodology to chart such a delicate and complicated process as social life'. The more unstructured qualitative interview techniques were recognized as a vital tool in achieving such understandings. As we shall go on to discuss the challenge to positivist approaches was continued by feminist researchers.

The contribution of feminism

Feminist researchers were responsible for mounting a major challenge to the scientific paradigm that dominated early social science research. As the feminist movement began to re-emerge in the 1960s those scholars involved with empirical research sought to question accepted wisdom on the research task. Feminists looked to go beyond the objectification of the subject as represented in positivist approaches thereby opening the way for greater use of qualitative methods (Oakley, 1981). Feminist researchers were explicit in acknowledging the hierarchical power relations that were embedded in the traditional dichotomy between researcher and researched. They highlighted the potentially exploitative character of such methods. In contrast, feminists sought to conduct egalitarian research through striving toward partnership in the researcher/researched relationship. This was typically premised on reciprocal relations, which might be mutually self-revealing, rather than disclosure only being forthcoming from the interviewee. Rather than favouring separation and distance in research relations feminists favoured a fusing of roles and a greater acknowledgement on the part of the researcher of their active contribution. Oakley (1981) questioned the validity of so called objective scientific approaches and called for more reflexivity from the researcher on how they impacted on the process. However, while feminists are questioning of the notion of objectivity this does not equate with rejecting the need for rigorous scholarship. As Gelsthorpe (1992: 214) notes, 'a focus on experience in method does not mean a rejection of the need to be critical, rigorous and accurate'.

Developing the work of early feminists more recent scholars have also warned against the dangers of seeing a feminist position as being free from the potential for exploitation. Subsequent work has also problematized the feasibility of achieving an equal partnership in the research task. This has included a questioning of issues such as interviewer disclosure as a means of dismantling the hierarchical relationship between researcher and researched. With some scepticism regarding the appropriateness of such disclosure on the part of the interviewer, Owen (1995: 255) acknowledges that 'regarding the research in its entirety, from conception to production, the researcher will have a measure of control that the research participants will not (and indeed may not want to) have'.

In terms of the interview, the influence of feminism has seen a preference for the less structured and more open approach which allows the interviewee greater scope in making an input. This is not to naïvely suggest that feminists are rejecting of quantitative methods. Some important work has been done on how feminist ideologies can be brought to bare on quantitative approaches. Kelly et al. (1991) emphasize that quantitative methods can be important in identifying the scope of social issues and when sensitively applied may be more revealing and less traumatic for some subjects. For those, however, who use qualitative methods the more open unstructured approach is favoured as providing more opportunity to incorporate the interviewee perspective. An interview based on closed questions overwhelmingly serves the interests of the interviewer. The qualitative approach gives more scope for the interviewee to set their own agenda and typically provide a more in-depth response to questions posed. In that context, in a subsequent section we deal with how the interview can be constructed with an alertness to the needs of the interviewee.

Closed and open questions

In a neighbourhood study of fear of crime, residents were asked in a door step interview about their image of crime in their community. This was achieved by asking an open ended question: what kinds of crime are committed around here? The framing of the question allowed them to volunteer responses without prompting from the interviewer. They were then read a list of questions and asked if this category of crime was a problem in their area. The list consisted of burglary, vandalism, car theft, assault, robbery, sex crimes, drug use, teenage nuisance and rowdiness. The subsequent analysis was able to distinguish those crimes that were volunteered and those that were probed. Vandalism was the most commonly cited crime, 60% volunteered and 29% probed. Burglary ranked second with 56% volunteered and 26% probed. Certain crimes were mainly mentioned once the probing question was used. This applied to drug use, 2% volunteered and 14% probed and robbery, 3% volunteered and 14% probed. These crimes could not be said to be in the forefront of residents minds as contributing to the crime problem in their area (Noaks, 1988).

A typology of interview strategies

The term interview is a generic one which incorporates a range of research techniques. The continuum ranges from delivery of the quantitative research instrument, typically a structured questionnaire, through to the semi-structured or in-depth case study (May, 2001). Interviews can be undertaken on a one-to-one basis or follow a group format. Focus groups provide one example of the latter approach with the interview role merging with that of facilitator (Bloor et al., 2001). May (2001: 125) proposes that the main distinction between the group interview and the focus group is the explicit encouragement in the latter format for the participants to talk to each other.

The interview strategy adopted will be influenced by a number of factors including characteristics of the research population, the sensitivity of the topic, the location of the interview and timescales. Interviews undertaken in the criminological field will often involve working with vulnerable groups. Research undertaken with victims of crime provides an example of the need for the interviewer to be sensitive to the emotional impact of the experience on the interviewee. Beck's (1999) work exemplifies the emotional effects, both positive and negative, of asking victims of indecent exposure to re-visit the experience. With an alertness to such issues we include a discussion below of how the interview can be conducted in a manner that is sensitive to the needs of the interviewee while at the same time meeting the research requirements.

Criminological research can sometimes involve direct work with children and young people, either as victims of crime or assailants or both. There is an emerging body of work that sets down best practice for direct work with such groups (Arksey and Knight, 1999; Butler and Williamson, 1994; Christensen and James, 1999; Lewis and Lindsay, 1999). Qualitative researchers have also developed some innovative methods to facilitate engagement with children and young people. Wilby (forthcoming) has used pictorial methods with American and British children as young as seven in a comparative study on representations of the police.

The location of an interview can also be a significant factor. In criminological research location can be something outside of the control of the interviewer. This is commonly the case when access has been gained to interviewing subjects in criminal justice institutions. Both Noaks and Wincup were involved in interviewing remand prisoners about their experiences in a local prison (Brookman et al., 2001). While a room was set aside on the remand wing for interviewing, some prison officers insisted on leaving the door of the room open and entering at uninvited moments. Their rationale for such actions was the security of the researchers (all female). However, the risk of being overheard can be inhibiting for some respondents and may impact on the material they are prepared to share. The rigour with which the daily routine of the prison is managed can also impact upon the interview experience with interviews precipitously curtailed to fit with other deadlines, for example meal times, family or solicitor visits and workshop requirements.

The location of the interview can also be something that the interviewer needs to think about in relation to their own safety and peace of mind. While institution based interviews can be problematic, those undertaken in the community can pose other difficulties. Hudson (2003) conducted interviews with convicted sex offenders in both custodial and community settings regarding their experiences of therapeutic programmes. She paid particular attention to protecting her anonymity in not divulging her full name to interviewees and instructing staff in her institution not to do so. Noaks (Noaks and Christopher, 1990) interviewed a group of individuals who had allegedly assaulted a police officer offering them the opportunity to give their version of events. While some of the interviews were prison based the majority were undertaken in the interviewees own home. As a female interviewer, mostly interviewing alone, some basic precautions were followed in leaving details of planned whereabouts at the office base. It is also important in such scenarios for the interviewer to emphasize their neutral stance and their lack of affiliation to a pre-conceived viewpoint. In this case a carefully thought out letter was sent emphasizing that the interview was an opportunity to give the alleged assailant a voice. Knowing that such measures have been taken allows the interviewer to be more relaxed and at ease during the interview.

The skill base

The skills required of the interviewer will vary with the type of research undertaken. Table 5.1 provides a typology of the key skills pertinent to particular interview techniques. In the more structured interview the focus needs to be on the neutrality of the interviewer. This style of approach is more common in large-scale studies when there are commonly a team of interviewers working with a large sample of respondents. Such an approach requires that the interviewers are trained to enhance standardization of approach. Such a strategy offers no opportunity for improvization or prompting on the part of the interviewer. We include a discussion below of telephone interviewing as a device for data collection, where it has been argued that the potential to supervise interviewers allows for enhanced standardization.

The semi-structured interview offers more opportunity to probe, typically with the use of follow-up questions. The interviewer will be equipped with an interview schedule but there is more flexibility in the order in which the questions are asked. There will commonly be a standardized section in relation to demographic data delivered at either the beginning or end of the interview. The semi-structured interview offers more opportunity for dialogue and exchange between the interviewer and interviewee. An important feature of this approach is that the interviewer has an understanding of the context of the project to facilitate alertness to significant themes.

In contrast, the unstructured and open-ended approach is typically used in life history, biographical and oral history work. In such work the interviewer has a

TABLE 5.1   *Typology of interview strategies*

Type of interview	Required skills
Structured interview	Neutrality; no prompting; no improvisation; training recommended for the interview task.
Semi-structured interview	Some probing; rapport with interviewee; a need to understand the context of the project to aid in identification of significant themes.
Unstructured interview	Flexibility; rapport with interviewee vital; social skills important.
Focus group	Facilitation skills; flexibility; an ability to stand back from controlling the discussion and allow group dynamics to emerge.

broad aim in mind but allows the interviewee the freedom to talk and ascribe meanings. This approach requires flexibility from the interviewer but allows for the discovery of meanings. Qualitative researchers would typically see this as contributing to the richness of the data achieved. Establishing a rapport in the interview is vital in this approach, particularly as it can be the case that interviews are conducted over several sessions. Active listening is at the core of such an approach and in practice the more unstructured the interview the more significant the interviewer's communication skills, including attention to non-verbal cues.

Cockcroft (1999) adopted an oral history approach in his work with former Metropolitan police officers. The research sought to explore their experiences of how the police culture had shifted over time. The sample consisted of 26 officers who had joined the force between 1930 and 1960. In taking oral histories from such individuals he sought to go beyond the official accounts represented in force documentation. It was also hoped that as former officers they would be more prepared to be open and revealing in their accounts. Semi-structured interviews were undertaken in a face-to-face setting with snowballing used as a means of gathering the sample. Cockcroft achieved detailed and revealing accounts:

> You knew full well ... you had to stretch the evidence a bit. To get a conviction you could rely a hundred percent on whatever you said would be backed up by your fellow officer. It didn't matter who it was. You sort of had a ... you could rely on one another but the thing was you never, ever got an innocent man down. If you knew that person was guilty you did anything you could to make sure that he was convicted ... but you never, ever stretched it a bit to get an innocent man in the dock.

> I think anyone who's a decent person and has worked in the CID ... especially at that time ... can't look back without regretting a lot of the stuff they've done ... a lot of it was wrong but we were young and we thought what we were doing was right. (1999: 133)

He also identified some of the problems attached to the oral history approach, including unreliability of memory and the influence of hindsight. For example, when individuals are being asked to give retrospective accounts of events which occurred some time ago, there is a risk that with the passage of time one gets a different account of events to that which would have been provided in a contemporary interview.

Goodey (2000) has also highlighted the potential value of the biographical method for qualitative studies in criminology and criminal justice. She acknowledges that historically the method has been relatively under used by criminologists, even though Clifford Shaw, one of the founders of the Chicago School, incorporated accounts written by boys on parole into his 1920s study of juvenile delinquency (Shaw, 1930). Subsequently she traces a measure of scepticism regarding the value of an individualized focus to criminological research. Despite this, she makes a convincing case for the manner in which life story accounts of criminal acts, particularly the focus on critical events, can be informative regarding 'the direction individual lives take with respect to crime and victimization' (Goodey, 2000: 474). Carlen's (1985) book entitled *Criminal Women* and Campbell's (1984) *The Girls in the Gang* both provide important examples of the biographical approach being employed by criminologists. Carlen's piece incorporates detailed accounts of four women with crime and their related experiences with the criminal justice process. Campbell's work also reflects on the female experience focusing on young women members of New York gangs in the early 1980s. Both books represent pioneering pieces of work with their exclusive focus on women's criminal experiences.

Particular skills are also important in conducting group interviews and focus groups which we will now turn to.

Group interviews and focus groups

Up to this point we have primarily concentrated on the one-to-one interview. It is, however, possible for interviews to be undertaken in a group context. Group interviews have been used in a range of criminological studies. For example, Cohen and Taylor (1972) made early use of the method to gather evidence on prisoners' experience of long-term custody. In recent times the most commonly used group interview strategy is the focus group which allows for communication between the group participants. Such forms of data collection do not necessarily involve face-to-face work and the focus group can be undertaken in the virtual arena (Bloor et al., 2001). What distinguishes the focus group from the group interview is that the former is particularly concerned with the social dynamics which occur between group members.

Focus groups typically have between six and 12 participants, although the virtual medium lends itself to larger groupings. The interviewer, often referred to as a facilitator, will set out the agenda for the session and the prescribed time limits (typically lasting between 60–90 minutes). However, in this approach as well as following the researcher's agenda there is a social dynamic of respondents reacting to each others input. The interviewer will need to be alert to the interactions and sometimes manage those, for example, by drawing in silent group members. Conducting such interviews can be complex and demanding and the presence of a second interviewer to support the main facilitator is an advantage.

Focus groups can be used at different stages of the research process. They may be used at the outset of a project to gather contextual material, as a core data gathering tool or as a means of disseminating findings. Commonly focus groups are used as part of a multi-method approach. The innovative recent development is the extension of the focus group to an on-line environment. Outside of the virtual focus group, Bloor et al. (2001) are pessimistic about the future use of the approach as a stand-alone method. While acknowledging the convenience of the method they also highlight the disadvantages:

> When it comes to documenting behaviour, focus groups are less suitable than individual interviews: there is an understandable tendency for atypical behaviours to be unreported or under-reported in group settings. (2001: 8)

However, they are much more optimistic about the focus group as an adjunct to 'other methods' (2001: 8).

Loader et al. (1998) used focus groups with various groupings of citizens (for example, the young, older people and upwardly mobile 'twenty-somethings') in constructing an 'ethnography of anxiety' in a suburban English community. Their rationale for undertaking focus groups consisting of separate categories of people was that complex inter-relationships existed between the individual citizen, their assessment of crime-related risk and their connection with their locality. Acknowledging residents' potentially diverse relationships to place, the focus group provided the opportunity to explore the extent to which fear of crime reflected personal biography and affiliations with the community.

> The intensity and type of identification individuals make with 'fear of crime discourse' (Hollway and Jefferson, 1998) arises not only from their direct or indirect experiences of victimization. It also intersects with their place within prevailing social hierarchies and their resulting relationship to a particular geographical community: how much time one spends there, the kind of emotive and financial investments one has in it, the 'thickness' of one's social networks, whether or not one has children, how long ago one arrived, and the extent that one feels able – should the need arise – to up and leave. (Loader et al., 1998: 395)

Careful attention to how the focus groups were constructed allowed this diversity of experience to be drawn out.

Williams (Williams and Robson, 2003) used the virtual focus group strategy to explore deviant activities in on-line chat rooms. Using this method he was able to explore experiences of victimization on-line and attitudes to the sanctions that should be used against those who were culpable. Use of the virtual approach has the advantage of allowing the researchers to extend both the size and duration of the focus group.

Having addressed the different forms that interviewing can take we now move on to consider one of the unique features of the qualitative approach in terms of acknowledging responsibilities to the interviewee.

Responsibilities to Interviewees

Responsibility to the interviewee needs to be addressed at the various stages of the research process. This includes the initial approach; during the interview; and in subsequent handling of information acquired.

The initial approach

It is important in agreeing to participate in an interview that an individual fully understands what the research project is about and why they are being asked to be part of it. Such expectations are set out in the various ethical codes discussed in Chapter 3. The objective is to achieve informed consent. However, this can be problematic when interviewing individuals in institutional settings where much of the decision-making may be taken out of their control. Typically in such cases the first stage of access will have been negotiated with the organization (for example, the prison or probation area) rather than the individual. This should not prevent a revisiting of the issue with the individual at the outset of the interview when time should be devoted to checking out understandings. As an example of misunderstandings, Toor (2001) found in her interviews with young Asian women in custody that no-one had explained to them the purpose of her visit. In the initial checking out process one woman revealed that she thought Toor was her parole officer and that the interview was to deal with her possible early release. Initial time given to checking out understandings allows for any such misconceptions to be addressed. In some cases a leaflet might be provided giving brief but accessible details on the objectives of the research. In ideal circumstances such material should be made available to prospective interviewees ahead of the interview taking place. Both Brookman (2000) and Hudson (2003) employed this approach when interviewing convicted prisoners in custody.

In this initial phase the ground rules of the interview and possible uses for the information acquired need to be established. It is important that researchers make explicit to what uses the data will not be put, as well as how it will be used. A recurring issue in criminological and criminal justice research is the question of protecting the identity of the individual and/or organizational setting. Where an assurance of confidentiality is provided it is essential that this is complied with. However, when in the field the researcher may receive certain information which they do not feel able to hold in confidence. This can apply to statements from interviewees regarding potential self-harm and abuse and details regarding offending. What is needed is a strategy for when the assurance regarding confidentiality might be breached. While it is difficult for researchers to predict all of the ethical dilemmas that they may encounter, some forethought needs to be given to how such challenges will be handled. Social researchers, unlike members of the medical profession, do not take a Hippocratic oath and will sometimes need to balance the interests of the individual and that of their research.

During the interview

Qualitative interviewing is typically premised on the interviewer achieving an effective rapport with the interviewee. It is important that the interviewer acknowledge and maintain an awareness that they will frequently be dealing with personal sensitive issues that can generate emotional effects for the individual being interviewed. Even in the most cursory brief interview such feelings can be aroused and part of the interviewer's responsibility is to take account of such reactions. Both the construction of the interview schedule and how it is conducted are important in fulfilling such responsibilities. While the semi-structured interview has flexibility in how topics are ordered, the interviewer should seek to ensure that sensitive issues are embedded in the interview procedure and begin by asking about less emotive issues. One strategy is to begin with collecting basic demographic data and include other neutral topics at the beginning of the interview. Attention also needs to be given to concluding an interview. Where interviewees have found the experience emotionally taxing they need to be given the opportunity to reach an equilibrium before the interview is brought to an end. It is important therefore to also finish with a more neutral topic, although as suggested above, the timing of this can be challenging in institutional settings where there is a risk that interviews can be curtailed precipitously. In research conducted on fear of crime, Noaks (1988) began by asking about interviewees attitudes to their community and neighbourhood networks before moving onto their fear of crime and victimization experiences. The interviews ended with questions about their attitudes to policing and demographic data, including a final question on what pets they had. The semi-structured interviews were thus designed to embed the more sensitive issues of their experiences of victimization and fears and anxieties in relation to crime in the heart of the interview.

Fundamentally the interviewer needs to have an ongoing alertness to how the interviewee is responding emotionally and to have constructed the interview to allow space and time for emotional recovery. On some occasions this will mean taking time out from the interview and where appropriate the switching off of a tape recorder. We discuss below a strategy whereby the interviewee can be empowered in this process. However, while acknowledging that an interview can generate an emotional reaction it is not feasible or appropriate for the interviewer to take on the role of counsellor or therapist. Where the person being interviewed is disclosing confidential information for the first time or finds it rare to have someone prepared to listen to their account, they can seek to gain ongoing emotional support from the interviewer. The challenge of being drawn into the role of counsellor has been encountered by many qualitative researchers working with sensitive topics. While it is inappropriate for the interviewer to extend their input in such a way, they can be alert to such possibilities and have available means of putting the interviewee in touch with support networks. One strategy is to have lists of relevant contact points available that can be shared with the interviewee if appropriate.

After the interview

Responsibilities to the interviewee extend beyond the completion of the interview. Assurances regarding confidentiality are important, including taking care in the handling of data to ensure that breaches do not occur. Qualitative data is as subject as quantitative data to the requirements of the Data Protection Act 1998, and it is the responsibility of the interviewer to ensure that data (for example, field notes, interview schedules, audio tapes) are adequately protected.

Contemporary feminist scholars have also suggested that responsibilities to the interviewee extends to their inclusion in the research dissemination process (Beck, 1999; Maynard and Purvis, 1994). Rather than seeing the interview as a one-way process with the interviewee providing information and the interviewer receiving, they seek to build the person interviewed back into the dissemination loop. One of the strategies adopted to meet this end is providing those interviewed with a written report of the analysis and inviting comment. Maynard and Purvis (1994) see this approach as an ethical imperative and a means of checking the validity of the researcher's analysis. Beck (1999: 107) who followed this approach with victims of indecent exposure, reports the gain described by interviewees in being able 'to see the whole picture as they had previously seen their own experience as unique'. This style of follow-up is sometimes proffered to those participating in focus groups (Bloor et al., 2001).

Attention to the best interests of those interviewed has routinely been seen as part of good research practice. However, such issues are increasingly being monitored at an institutional level. For example, universities and research organizations are increasingly alert to potential legal action where questions asked might be said to have a traumatic effect on those interviewed. As discussed in Chapter 3, those conducting interviews are increasingly likely to have the ethics of their approach scrutinized by a committee or advisory group in order to pre-empt such eventualities.

Tools for gathering information

It is important that the qualitative researcher think carefully about the tools that they will use to gather information. Some qualitative researchers will choose to commit to memory rather than intrude on the research relationship by taking notes. The disadvantage of this approach is that some detail will be lost and recall cannot be complete. However, it may be the case that at certain points in the interview the note taking may be suspended. This can sometimes be influenced by the sensitivity of the material that is being shared. Noaks conducted research in the early 1990s in a series of police CID departments. In an interview with a senior officer, where notes were being taken, he began to talk about his experiences of police interrogation practices prior to the Police and Criminal Evidence Act 1984 and made a specific request that she stop writing things down. That was a clear example where to continue to take notes would have cut across the rapport that had been established.

Where written notes are taken it is important to minimize the detrimental effects of being engaged in writing things down. For example, taking a full written account during the interview will hinder the researcher in maintaining eye contact and being able to observe non-verbal cues. Where notes are taken these should be an *aide-memoire*, typically of key words and phrases, to be written up in full as soon as possible after the interview. The disadvantages of having the interviewer engaged with note taking is one of the reasons for the increasing use of audio recorders as a means of gathering information. With increasingly small and compact recorders available this can be an unobtrusive tool for the researcher. Criminological researchers should however be aware that there has been some resistance to the use of recording equipment in penal establishments and those undertaking such research commonly have to rely on note taking. Where a recorder is employed it is important that the ground rules on usage are established. In the first stage of the interview there needs to be confirmation that the interviewee is comfortable with a recording being made. This is part of gaining informed consent and should include advising how the interview materials will be used. Where pseudonyms are to be used this needs to be established. It is also good practice to reiterate such agreements at the end of the interview.

As well as checking out that the interviewee is comfortable with use of the tape the option of discontinuing recording needs to be made explicit. As a means of redressing the inherent power imbalance between interviewer and interviewee the machine can be placed in such a position that the person being interviewed can control the on/off button. An initial statement needs to be made by the interviewer that turning the machine off is an option, thereby going some way to redress the typically passive role of the interviewee. Linked to this, all interviewers should make it clear that the interviewee has the right to refuse to answer questions. Interviewees typically ascribe considerable power and status to an interviewer (however inexperienced and nervous you may sometimes feel) and can lose sight of their right to refuse to answer your questions.

On a practical level, while the audio tape has become an invaluable tool to the social researcher, care needs to be taken that the machine is functioning effectively. Back-up batteries should be available and a good supply of tapes carried. Where audio recorders are used in focus groups the second facilitator can be charged with ensuring that the machine works appropriately.

Other options for data collection are telephone interviews and internet based interviews, either group or individual. Historically, telephone interviews were particularly used in the gathering of large-scale survey data and this usage applied to early research on-line. However, more recently both approaches have begun to be used as qualitative research instruments (Williams and Robson, 2003). Some of the delay in adopting such methods for qualitative work was linked to concerns regarding the difficulties in establishing rapport. Proponents of the methods now argue that there can be a positive advantage in having a lack of visual contact when asking about sensitive issues. They argue that 'respondents who may be concerned about being judged by the interviewer feel less exposed, and thus more able to answer honestly' (National Opinion Poll, 2000). The relative cost effectiveness of such methods has also been highlighted as a distinct advantage.

Finally, we are left with the tools for capturing visual images. As with Wilby's work (forthcoming) discussed above, this can be as simple as pen and paper used for artwork. As highlighted by Silverman (2001: 193) qualitative criminologists, in line with other followers of this tradition, have made limited use of video recording as an interview tool.

Concluding comments

This chapter has emphasized the range of interviewing techniques that are available to social researchers. We have identified the key features of qualitative interviewing in relation to criminology and criminal justice research and the unique issues that pertain to interviewing in custodial settings. As indicated above, much of the work is with vulnerable groups and researchers need to be aware of the implications of that for their research design. Research undertaken in relation to law and order issues can sometimes mean that interviewees are disclosing potentially illegal matters or other forms of sensitive material and it is crucial that researchers have a strategy to deal with such events. While it is difficult to predict all of the challenging issues that may arise during an interview the researcher should have given some advance thought to how they will cope with certain scenarios. As with other forms of qualitative research it is also important that the researcher retains a reflexive approach in how the interview is conducted and their own responses to information that is forthcoming.

Exercise

Draw up an interview schedule for the scenarios set out below. In each case you can assume you have received the necessary permissions with regard to official access. However, time constraints on the project are such that you will not have the opportunity to undertake repeat interviews and will only be in a position to see the individual on a single occasion. Your schedule should have a particular focus on how you would order the items to be included. Also think about the tool that you would use for data collection and compare and contrast the advantages of your chosen method with at least one other strategy.

- **Scenario 1:** to interview a 13-year-old boy from Wrexham two weeks after his admission to a Secure Training Centre in Kent. *Objective of the interview:* to explore his experiences of custody.
- **Scenario 2:** to interview a 35-year-old Asian woman convicted of manslaughter of her 42-year-old husband and eight months into a four year prison sentence. *Objective of the interview:* to explore her experiences of custody as an ethnic minority prisoner.
- **Scenario 3:** to interview a 19-year-old male remanded in custody, charged with grievous bodily harm on a police officer and pleading not guilty. *Objective of the interview:* to explore any obstacles experienced in his access to justice.
- **Scenario 4:** to interview a 52-year-old male who has served 12 years in prison for rape and is about to be discharged to his home community. *Objective of the interview:* to explore his experiences of resettlement.

FURTHER READING

Both of the following are important texts which provide an overview of issues with interviewing.

- Arksey, H. and Knight, P. (1999) *Interviewing for Social Scientists.*
- Kvale, S. (1996) *InterViews: An Introduction to Qualitative Research Interviewing.*

The following books are significant examples of the output from interviews in the criminological field:

- Bennett, T. and Wright, R. (1984) *Burglars on Burglary.*
- Carlen, P. (1985) *Criminal Women.*
- Hobbs, D. (1988) *Doing the Business.*
- Reiner, R. (1991) *Chief Constables.*

- Worrall, A. (1990) *Offending Women.*
- Spradley, J. (1979) *The Ethnographic Interview* is a classic text in relation to ethnographic interviewing.
- Bloor, M., Frankland, J., Thomas, M. and Robson, K. (2001) *Focus Groups in Social Research* provide an important contribution in relation to focus groups.

6

Ethnographic Approaches to Researching Crime and Deviance

Introduction

Within criminology the ethnographic tradition is long established. Indeed some researchers have gone so far as suggesting that ethnography has been especially reliant on studies of deviance (Adler and Adler, 1995; Lofland, 1987; Manning, 1987), leading to studies of youth subcultures, gangs, prostitution, professional and organized crime and illicit drug use (see Hobbs, 2001 for an overview). This is a contentious view but it can be argued that some of the most important contributions to the sociology of crime and deviance have developed out of ethnographic work. Coupled with the use of ethnographic approaches to explore the workings of the criminal justice system, ethnography has proved its value as a way of conducting criminological research. Broadly speaking ethnography involves a researcher participating, overtly or covertly, in people's daily lives for an extended period of time and collecting whatever data are available to throw light on the issues that are the focus of the research (Hammersley and Atkinson, 1995). This leads to the creation of 'long-term and multi-stranded research relationships that provide the detailed contextualisation characteristic of good ethnographic research' (Davies, 2002: 419). The extended tradition of adopting ethnographic techniques within criminological research studies implies the appropriateness of this approach to researching issues of crime and criminal justice.

The basic shape of the chapter is as follows. It begins with an attempt to define ethnography and to dispel some of the myths which surround this approach to social science research. This is followed by a chronological account of the rise and, some might argue, fall of ethnography in criminology, and in so doing it considers the relationship between ethnography and a variety of theoretical perspectives. Case studies are used to illustrate some of the practical, ethical and methodological issues connected with ethnographic research on criminological topics. These reflect our personal preferences and readers are directed to alternative examples in the section on suggestions for further reading.

What is ethnography?

A close examination of the methodological literature reveals a lack of clarity about what ethnography actually is. In part this reflects the difficulty of defining many concepts in the social science. For instance, within criminology this is illustrated by the lack of consensus surrounding its basic subject matter; 'crime'. Ethnography is no exception and Hammersley and Atkinson (1995: 2) suggest that the boundaries around ethnography are 'necessarily unclear'. Nonetheless the obscurity surrounding ethnography can also be attributed to the tendency for ethnography to be misunderstood and to be oversimplified. A numbers of myths surround ethnography and these will be dispelled below:

1   *Ethnography is synonymous with participant observation.* While ethnography is typically associated with participant observation it can involve the use of different research methods, either on their own or together. Pearson (1993: ix) suggests that for some ethnographers the 'participant observer' method 'is the key-stone of the claim to authenticity'. He also argues that for other ethnographers this claim derives from conducting in-depth interviews. Frequently ethnographic work involves mixing methods and contemporary ethnography tends to be multi-method research combining participant observation, in-depth interviews and documentary analysis. By utilizing different approaches ethnographers are not naïvely suggesting that this will increase the validity of their data or that data gathered from different sources can be used to produce a single unitary picture of the 'truth'. Instead it helps to uncover multiple versions of reality. For instance, an ethnography of drug use within prison has the potential to reveal the conflicting perspectives of prisons, prison officers and the prison service about the nature and extent of drug problems within a prison.

2   *Ethnography is 'telling it like it is':* Naturalistic realism is built into ethnographic methodology. Naturalism is a methodological approach which proposes that as far as possible the social world should be studied in its 'natural state', undisturbed by the researcher. Thus ethnographers need to adopt an appreciative stance and to describe cultures though obtaining direct access to 'objective' knowledge about them. This latter principle is also true of realism, a methodological position which

also advocates that there is an external world independent of people's perceptions
of it. The naturalist realist notion that researchers can 'tell it how it is' and can
write ethnographic accounts which present social reality in an unproblematic
way has come under attack as postmodern critiques have been developed (see for
example, Denzin, 1997). The inherently political nature of the research process (as
discussed in Chapter 2) and the construction of ethnographic texts has been
brought to the fore (Atkinson, 1990; 1992). 'Telling it like it is' implies presenting
an account of the social world from the perspective of those being researched;
telling the story as they would tell it (based on the unlikely assumption that all
would tell the same story). This is an overly simplistic view because if an ethnographer was able to do this he or she would have 'gone native', in other words
become so immersed in the culture they were studying that they had left their
academic culture behind. Ethnographers are required to be in two places at the
same time as they assume the role of storyteller and scientist (Fetterman, 1989)
in order to bridge the gap between the research participants and research audiences. Ethnography has been described as the 'art and science of describing a
group or culture' (Fetterman, 1989: 11) but these ethnographic descriptions are
'partial, selective, even autobiographical in that they are tied to the particular
ethnographer and the contingencies under which the data were collected'
(Brewer, 2000: 24–5). This debate is explored in more detail in Brewer (2000,
Chapter 1) and Hammersley and Atkinson (1995, Chapter 1). A highly accessible
but brief summary is given in Denscombe (1998, Chapter 5).

3   *Ethnography is simple to do*: As Hammersley and Atkinson (1995) note, it is often
assumed that ethnography is unproblematic, and requires little preparation and
no special expertise. Novice researchers are sometimes misled that they can head
off armed with pen and paper to find a suitable group to study. Ethnography's
resemblance to the routine ways in which people make sense of the world in
everyday life through watching what happens, listening to what is said and asking questions helps to fuel this myth. To conduct ethnographic research properly, requires some degree of training and preparation. As Delamont et al. (2001)
argue, the former is sometimes rejected and ethnographic techniques are perceived as an innate quality rather than a masterable skill. Similarly the need for
preparation is refuted because the course of ethnography cannot be predetermined. While this is true would-be ethnographers can be instructed to expect
the unexpected, to develop a research design; to reflect on how they might gain
access to the setting and manage field relations within it, to consider strategies
for recording data and to learn about techniques for analysing it, and finally to
select the most appropriate way of writing the final account.

4   *Ethnographic research lacks rigour*: As LeCompte (2002) notes, since ethnographic
research lacks experimental controls and fails to generate the reliable and
replicable results widely perceived as the only hallmarks of legitimacy, critics
may suggest ethnographic research is not rigorous. For these reasons, she suggests that ethnographers need to be active lobbyists of their work to convince
suspicious academic audiences and policy-makers.

There is considerable confusion surrounding whether ethnography can be appropriately described as a research method or whether it might be more accurately described as a methodology. The former describes a data collection technique and the latter a theoretical and philosophical framework. This debate is explored in detail elsewhere (see for example, Brewer, 2000, Chapter 2). Suffice to say here that it is helpful to see ethnography as a research strategy rather than a method which is linked especially with two data collection techniques: participant observation and in-depth interviews. While ethnography was traditionally associated with one methodological stance, known as naturalism or naïve realism, the postmodern critique has destroyed this linkage by allowing the development of different methodologies with the common aim to distinguish ethnography from lay accounts of social life (see Brewer, 2000).

It should be evident at this stage in the chapter that developing a universally accepted definition of ethnography is an impossible task. Nonetheless, a working definition is offered below.

> Ethnography is the study of groups of people in their natural setting, typically involving the researcher being present for extended periods of time in order to collect data systematically about their daily activities and the meanings they attach to them.

The origins of ethnography

Brewer (2000) argues that the roots of ethnography are ancient, noting that travellers and outsiders of different kinds have for centuries lived among strangers and recorded their way of life. Similarly, in a brief historical sketch of ethnography, Wax (1971: 21) suggests that 'descriptive reporting of the customs, inclinations accomplishment and accomplishments of foreign people is almost as old as writing itself'. In common with attempts to identify the birthday and parentage of criminology as a discipline (Coleman and Norris, 2000), it is difficult to be precise about the origins of ethnography. Not least this is because, as we have already noted, it resembles the routine ways in which people make sense of the world in everyday life. However, the turn of the twentieth century is usually perceived as the point at which ethnography emerged as a specialist skill.

Ethnography, as described above, has its origins in anthropology. The work of Malinowski is significant because as well as claiming to be the first British social anthropologist to pitch his tent in a village and observe and record what was actually going on, he was also the first professional anthropologist to give his readers a relatively detailed account of the experience of conducting fieldwork (see Wax, 1971 for a discussion of his influence). Traditionally anthropologists like Malinowski attempted to immerse themselves in the particular culture of the society under study in order to develop 'thick description' (Geertz, 1973); in other words rich and detailed description of the accomplishment of everyday life. Typically this involved studying pre-industrial cultures radically different from those of Western (mainly British) anthropologists. This work has been described as the product of an undesirable colonial legacy of exploitation and domination and contemporary anthropologists have explored issues closer to home (see for example, Hall's, 2000 study of youth homelessness).

The Chicago School and its legacy

The development of ethnographic fieldwork in criminology is inextricably linked to the development of the Chicago School. As Deegan (2001) describes, the Chicago School was particularly influential in sociology between 1892 and 1942. A powerful and prolific subgroup of these sociologists created the Chicago School of Ethnography. They produced analyses of the everyday life, communities and symbolic interactions characteristic of specific groups, particularly in the period from 1917 to 1942. Many of them were doctoral students supervised by Robert Park and Ernest Burgess. In a lecture to undergraduate students at the University of Chicago in the 1920s, Robert Park urged his students to conduct their own fieldwork by advocating 'Gentleman go get the seat of your pants dirty in real research'. The gendered language should be noted here, and feminists have been influential in unearthing women's involvement in the Chicago School (see for example, Delamont, 2003). Park hoped to inspire students (and he succeeded in doing so) to study deviant groups within their natural setting and to make connections between their lifestyles and the social turbulence of Chicago at that time. Park had studied psychology and philosophy but it was his background as a journalist which encouraged him, and others, to go out on the streets to collect information by whatever means they could. Park's own work is testimony to the view that ethnographic studies can consist of multiple research methods, including those leading to the generation of quantitative data.

As detailed in Chapter 1, the Chicago School made important theoretical and methodological contributions and launched a tradition of conducting ethnographic research on aspects of crime and deviance. The second Chicago School (Fine, 1995), developed in the post-World War Two period, continued to be dominated by ethnographies of deviance. Undoubtedly the most well-known of these is Becker's study of marijuana users (Becker, 1963). His ethnographic work explored the social processing involved in becoming deviant by examining the process by which a particular behaviour is labelled deviant and the impact this labelling process has on the individual who has been labelled deviant. In this way he highlighted the socially constructed nature of crime and deviance. Hobbs (2001) goes as far as to suggest that Becker's work has assumed iconic status with successive generations of scholars. In a chapter describing the social organization of British criminology, Rock (1994) reports on a survey of criminologists (106 in total), Becker's *Outsiders*, described by Rock as an 'interactionist manifesto' (1994: 141), was named most frequently as the publication which had had the greatest influence on them.

Brewer (2000: 13) suggests that by focusing on deviant subcultures, the Chicago School helped to create a common-sense view that ethnography 'offers mere description of things foreign, exotic and peculiar'. This is ironic given that conducting ethnographic fieldwork with these deviant groups can be a prosaic business. Even in the supposedly action-packed lives of youth gangs or drug users, there is a measure of repetition. The same is true of ethnographic research within criminal justice agencies. The criticism Brewer describes probably relates more to the type of theoretical work with which ethnography has been associated rather than being a direct criticism of ethnography itself. In the post-war period ethnography was the main tool used to develop a sociology of the underdog and to develop the labelling perspective, typified in the work of Becker. This was crudely characterized as the sociology of 'nuts, sluts and perverts' (Liazos, 1972) by critics who went on to develop more radical approaches for explaining crime and deviance.

A new twist: the Deviancy School and ethnography in the UK

The ethnographic tradition came alive in the UK in the mid-1960s when the hegemony of positivist criminology was threatened (Bottoms, 2000). Positivism has at its heart a belief that criminality is a characteristic of individuals. Hence the challenge for criminology is to identify the causes of crime by emulating the methods used by natural scientists. Ethnography has different emphases; rejecting the idea that social phenomena can be studied in the same way as natural phenomena, stressing the importance of deep involvement in the everyday lives of research participants and offering a commitment to understanding the meanings human beings attribute to their actions.

The National Deviancy Conference of 1968, with the benefit of hindsight, marks a watershed in British criminology. Dissatisfaction with positivism coupled with a lack of faith in interactionism created the intellectual space for alternative theoretical frameworks to develop. Sumner (1994) notes that the National Deviancy Conference had no collective position, hardly surprising because it consisted of interactionists, anarchists, phenomenologists and Marxists, and it made few theoretical advances other than developing deviancy amplification theory. This involved consideration of the role of the mass media in highlighting and developing further what it perceived to be 'deviant' threats to social order. The New Deviancy theorists adopted a more politicized approach than earlier sociologists of deviance. For example, the work of Stuart Hall and his colleagues analysed conflict between 'deviant' groups or subcultures and disapproving establishment forces including the media and the State (see for example Hall et al., 1978).

Ethnography was championed in rhetoric but the reality was that few papers based on ethnographic research were presented at subsequent colloquia (Hobbs, 2001). Stan Cohen's (1973) study of Mods and Rockers is one of the most well-known examples of ethnographic research by an author involved in the National Deviancy Conference. Cohen's study involved a number of methods including participant observation, interviews and documentary analysis of media reports. He examined the battles between two opposing working-class youth subcultures on public holidays in British seaside towns in the mid-1960s. His research led to the development of the concept of 'moral panic' to describe the media and political over-reaction to the perceived threat these groups (cast as 'folk devils') posed to societal values.

Feminist criminologies and ethnography

The second wave of feminism, which began in the late 1960s, introduced a new dimension to criminological debates. It began by developing a critique of the different explanations of crime and noted that women who offend are typically neglected or misrepresented. Feminist critiques of criminology almost always explore the shortcomings of ethnographies conducted by men on men (see for example Millman, 1975). Ethnographies of crime and deviance have been inclined to marginalize female offenders; and as feminist criminologists have argued, such ethnographies tend to be conducted by men on men (Hobbs, 2001 for an overview).

The notion of an exclusive feminist method has been challenged by researchers working inside and outside the feminist tradition. There is no blueprint to follow but feminist researchers do not simply use pre-existing research techniques, rather they adapt them to mesh with their gender-conscious theoretical position. Gelsthorpe (1990) suggests four common themes in feminist research: choosing topics which are relevant or sympathetic to women and to the women's movement; a preference but not an exclusive focus on qualitative research; a reflexive approach and a concern to record the subjective experiences of doing research. The debate has moved on from an uncritical acceptance that a methodological approach can be adopted which is fully congruent with feminist concerns, to a stance which argues for the need to consider the potentials and dilemmas of methods used in feminist research.

The relationship between feminism and ethnography has been explored by a number of feminist researchers (Clough, 1992; Olesen, 1994; Reinharz, 1992; Stacey, 1988; Wolf, 1992). Of particular concern is Judith Stacey's (1988) claim that feminist ethnography is fundamentally contradictory. She suggests that feminist scholars have identified ethnographic methods as ideally suited to feminist research because of their contextual, experiential approach to knowledge, emphasizing empathy and human concern, and because they facilitate equal and reciprocal relationships between the researcher and research participants. However, Stacey argues that paradoxically such methods subject research participants to greater risk of exploitation, betrayal and abandonment than positivist research. Her concerns lie with the research process and its product. Fieldwork, she points out, inevitably represents an intrusion because it intervenes with a system of relationships that the researcher can leave more freely. Moreover, there are difficult compromises to be made between respect for participants and producing authentic accounts when research participants are promised control over the final product. Despite this she believes the potential benefits of a 'partially' feminist ethnography seem worth the serious moral costs involved.

This view is not shared by all (see Skeggs, 2001 for an overview of the debate). Indeed, many feminist researchers have drawn our attention to the dilemmas of feminist ethnography, yet at the same time do not regard feminist ethnography as a contradiction in terms. For example, while acknowledging the potential of feminist ethnography to make women's lives visible, Reinharz (1992: 65) notes that 'feminist ethnography is burdened with many controversies and dilemmas'. She labels these the problem of trust, the closeness/distance dilemma and the dilemma of complete participant/complete observer. The problem of trust refers to the realization that rapport and trust are not immediately established on the basis of shared sisterhood. Instead this needs to be worked at. A further dilemma is that the development of closeness to further understanding may be seen as 'going native' or 'over-rapport'. This is problematic in two ways in which it might be seen to compromise the very academic understanding that feminist ethnographers set out to achieve, but it can also be seen as exploitative in the sense that superficial friendships are created for the purpose of data collection. Total immersion in the social world in which they are studying through complete participation in it is viewed positively by some feminist researchers as a means of integrating their selves into their work and eliminating the distinction between subject and object (Roseneil, 1993; Stanley and Wise, 1993).

These dilemmas cannot be easily resolved and they shatter any images of ethnography as simple to do. What the critiques elude to, a point that Hammersley and Atkinson (1995) make explicitly, is the need for reflexivity. Within the ethnographic tradition calls for reflexivity have been made strongly. One particular area of focus has been on the ways in which gender has been experienced in the field.

Reinharz (1992) suggests that feminist ethnographers typically make double contributions when they conduct their research. They contribute to our understanding of feminist ethnography as a research strategy and they contribute to our understanding of the subject matter they choose to study. Every feminist ethnographic project generates its own new set of concerns, in addition to touching on existing ones. Despite the controversies within feminist ethnography, ethnographic research has enormous potential to make visible the lives of women in general, and the lives of women in contact with the criminal justice system as victims, offenders or professionals in particular. Later in this chapter we will explore further examples of feminist work.

The decline of ethnography?

In the conclusion (subtitled 'whither ethnography?') to his text on ethnography, Brewer (2000) suggests that the future of ethnography is uncertain. In addition to facing the challenge of the postmodern critique, ethnography has had to defend itself from the march of globalization. People are now often described as living in a 'global village' in which people live their lives on a larger scale. They are exposed almost immediately to events happening elsewhere in the world as they watch or read global media products and travel more extensively. Moreover, the growth of cultural homogeneity and recognition that people's lives are shaped by events outside the control of the nation state and its economy is a major threat to ethnography. Ethnography thrives upon researching difference through attempting 'to bridge between the experiences of actors and audiences' (Pearson, 1993: xviii).

Ethnographers assume that they are researching a social group with clear boundaries and distinct social meanings. As LeCompte (2002) notes, ethnography has traditionally been thought of as the investigation of the culture of small, relatively homogeneous, naturally or artificially bounded groups. Brewer (2000) recognizes that globalization potentially robs ethnography of the specificity of the local, yet notes that global processes are always mediated locally. Ethnography can elucidate these processes. For example, an ethnographic study of victimization in Islamic communities in Britain could be used to demonstrate how events on September 11 2001 impacted on ethnic relations in British communities, as well as considering the nature and extent of victimization and the meanings attached to such acts.

As a means of conducting criminological research, ethnography faces further challenges. As Maguire (2000: 121) notes 'criminologists nowadays spend surprisingly little of their time talking to "criminals"'. Similarly, Parker (1996: 282) points out that British criminology has 'largely retreated from qualitative, ethnographic community-based studies of subculture and deviant lifestyles'. It would be wrong to give the impression that criminologists do not spend any time talking to offenders. They do, but in many respects they do not resemble the ethnographic studies of previous decades. Criminologists often tend to access offenders through criminal justice agencies, particularly through police forces, prisons and young offender institutions, probation areas or youth offending teams. These constitute artificial settings and institutional timetables and resources influence the type of research methods which can be utilized. Characteristically this is a formal interview. More often than not, these interviews are likely to focus not on their offending behaviour but on their experiences of being arrested, remanded in custody, undertaking a community punishment order or other aspects of the criminal justice process.

It is not difficult to imagine why criminologists have been reluctant to commit themselves to conducting ethnographic work. It presents a range of practical, ethical and personal safety dilemmas and these are explored in the following two sections through discussion of two ethnographies. In order to complete an ethnographic study researchers need to be highly skilled and to be sufficiently convinced of the appropriateness of their approach to defend it when faced with criticism that it is unscientific. Most of all they need to be passionate about their research topic so they enjoy all stages of their work and can produce a well-crafted ethnographic account in spite of the problems they are likely to encounter along the way. In addition a willingness to talk openly, and at length, about the process of conducting research is also one of the characteristics of a first-rate ethnographer. Both the authors we discuss have done this either in their published research monographs and/or through separate confessional tales.

Contemporary ethnographies of crime and criminals

As Hobbs (2001: 207–8) argues, 'ethnographies of deviance, both authorship and subject, are dominated by men'. In this section, and in the one that follows, we have deliberately included ethnographies conducted by female researchers, which have involved the study of females as offenders and criminal justice professionals. We have also deliberately chosen ethnographers who have been prepared to offer honest accounts of the research process either in their published research monograph or in separate publications.

Case study 1: Avril Taylor (1993) Women drug users: an ethnography of a female injecting community. Oxford: Clarendon Press

Taylor's (1993) research monograph purports to be the first full ethnographic account of the lifestyle of female (illicit) drug users. The author presents an empirical account of the lives and experiences of a group of intravenous drug users in Glasgow, told from the perspective of the women themselves. The data were gathered through 15 months participant observation of over 50 women and through in-depth interviews with 26 women carried out at the end of the fieldwork period. The findings of the study challenge the predominant view of female drug users found in popular discourse as passive, socially inadequate women who were chaotic, out of control of their own lives, and incompetent unfit mothers.

In her introductory chapter Taylor describes the theoretical influences on her work. These include insights gained from 'general social theory' (Bottoms, 2000: 36) as well as theoretical concepts derived from the analysis of data gathered from previous qualitative studies. Weber's theory of 'social action' and his *verstehen* sociology of interpretative understanding (Weber, 1949); symbolic interactionism as advanced by Mead (1934) and Blumer (1969) and feminism are examples of the former, while the concept of 'career' is an example of the latter. As Taylor discusses, previous studies of male drug users had challenged the stereotypical view of drug users as pathological individuals and demonstrate that drug users are rational agents, making decisions based on the contingencies of both their drug using careers and their position within the overall social structure. These theoretical perspectives and concepts represent more than an eclectic mix of influences and help to construct a theoretical framework to guide the research process.

The theoretical framework selected inevitably affected the type of ethnographic account presented. As Taylor outlines in the introduction 'much of the text is devoted to allowing the women to speak for themselves, describing their lifestyles in their own words' (1993: 7). In their own words involves the use of words or expressions which are peculiarly Glaswegian or Scottish. A glossary is provided for readers because it was felt that to translate their 'eloquent and insightful comments' into 'standard English' would have meant losing the 'tone, intensity and sincerity of what the women had to say' (1993: 29). Hence extensive quotations are used from the women's accounts to elucidate the main aspects of their lifestyles: starting off (becoming a drug user), scoring (procuring drugs) and grafting (financing drug use), their social networks, their relationships with their children and coming off (ending their drug using careers).

During the fieldwork period Taylor was exposed to a number of risks. She suggests that they took three forms: legal, health and personal, and all needed to be managed in the field. Health risks included the risk of contracting HIV or Hepatitis B. While it is fairly difficult to become infected with the HIV virus it is still possible unless contact is avoided. Hepatitis B is common among intravenous drug users and highly infectious, especially in unhygienic conditions. In discussing the further risks she was confronted with, Taylor explores the difficulty faced by all criminologists, but particularly ethnographers, of being aware of illegal activities. The latest British Society of Criminology Code of Ethics (2003) suggests that researchers work within current legislation, should not breach 'the duty of confidentiality' nor pass on any identifiable data to third parties without participants' consent. This is an ongoing debate that we cannot do justice to here (see Feenan, 2002 for a recent discussion of these issues) but we can point some ways in which ethnographers can avoid being accessories to crimes. It may be appropriate, as Taylor did, to warn the local police in advance of the research but please note that this does not guarantee immunity. In addition, ethnographers should give thought in advance to consider where they want to 'draw the line' (Polsky, 1971); in other words to think about what they are willing (and perhaps most importantly not willing) to be told about so this can be clearly communicated to research participants. This means that the researcher avoids promises of total confidentiality. Since ethnographic work takes place over a period of time, participants may need to be continually reminded of this. Taylor also considers the range of personal risks that she felt that she and her family were potentially exposed to, and notes that this is a neglected issue in the research literature. In order to protect her family, she never gave out her address and she changed her phone number to an ex-directory one so she could control who had access to it and her address (giving out a mobile number is now a possibility if it is necessary). She also tried to ensure that only essential people knew of her research plans to avoid her children being stigmatized due to her contact with people with HIV and AIDS.

Contemporary ethnographies of criminal justice agencies and institutions

The use of ethnographic approaches to study organizations owes a great deal to the work of Goffman. His symbolic interactionist work on 'total institutions' such as prisons and asylums paved the way for ethnographic research on a range of criminal justice agencies. Studies of policing have been the most popular (see Reiner, 2000a for an overview of police research) and two examples of these are presented here.

Case study 2: Louise Westmarland (2001b) Gender and policing: sex, power and police culture, Cullompton. Cullompton: Willan Publishing

This study examined gender and operational policing in North-East England, enabling Westmarland to construct an ethnographic account of 'the real world of street policing and gender issues which are a central part of this' (back cover). To this end a case study approach was adopted of two contrasting police forces: a rural 'county' force and a large, urban, metropolitan one. Approximately six months were spent in each police force over a three year period. Data gathered from participant observation were supplemented by interviews and focus groups with police officers and statistical analysis of policing data. Overall over 400 hours of observation took place, mostly of weekend night and evening shifts, and including being on patrol, in the patrol car and the police van.

The ethnographic account constructed explores four areas of policework: dealing with women and children as victims and offenders, policing of sexual offences, uniformed patrol work and specialisms such as work with firearms. In developing her account Westmarland (2001b) drew upon sociological work on the gendered body and masculinities to consider 'the ways in which categories such as "masculinity" and "femininity" are defined within police occupational culture' (Westmarland, 2000: 27). Much has already been written about 'cop culture' and the challenges it presents for researchers (see Reiner, 2000b). As Westmarland (2001b) observes, to collect valid ethnographic data on policing, permission is needed at an organizational level, but access needs to be renegotiated on a day-to-day level. This is a challenge for any researcher but the following helpful strategies can be gleaned from her experiences.

- King (2000: 298) writing about prisons research suggests 'you have to do your time'. This is what Westmarland did and it reaped rewards in demonstrating to the police officers her commitment and perseverance. It demonstrated her continued interest in them and their work and as they got used to her being around it became easier to study them.
- Complain about shift work, lack of sleep, boredom and poor working conditions in order to demonstrate solidarity with your research participants but never suggest academic life is a better alternative or claim and special treatment as a woman unless you want to commit 'ethnographic suicide' (Westmarland, 2000: 30)!
- Be prepared to pass informal initiation or 'bottle' tests to test your emotional and physical strength. These include encounters with violence and sudden death (Westmarland, 2000: 30).

Writing in a volume about risks and ethics in social research (Lee-Treweek and Linkogle, 2000a), Westmarland (2000) proposes that attempts to exclude the possibility of risk from the research are counter-productive to the ethnographic endeavour. This is not to suggest that measures such as adhering to safety procedures should not be taken to manage such risks but to advance the view that risky experiences can give us greater insight into the world of our research participants. While researchers should attempt to maintain their role as 'informed stranger' (Westmarland, 2001b: 11) and avoid 'going native' by experiencing danger in this way, it is possible to demonstrate that the researcher is 'one of them' and this helps to build up trust and rapport.

The need to demonstrate solidarity with your research participants is a dilemma which Westmarland returns to on a number of occasions in her published accounts of the research process. Sometimes it is against the researcher's better judgement and the ethical response might be to 'blow the whistle'. One example of this is witnessing police brutality and subsequently reporting it. Researchers typically do nothing and in so doing collude with the behaviour through inaction. Doing something would result in their access being ended because solidarity is expected and forms part of the occupational culture of the police (see Westmarland, 2001a for a more detailed discussion). Ethnographers lack instruction manuals, which in any case are likely to be of little use, and instead have to decide what best to do based on their own moral and ethical beliefs.

Concluding comments

We began this chapter be dispelling some of the myths surrounding ethnography. Through exploring the varying ways in which criminologists have employed ethnographic approaches we have elucidated some of the key characteristics of ethnography, and these are listed below:

1 Ethnography involves studying people in their natural setting and revealing the complexity of their social world, their experiences and their subjective attitudes.
2 Ethnography is flexible and can be used to study a wide variety of social groups and settings using a range of theoretical frameworks.
3 Ethnography contributes to the development of theoretical knowledge. It offers much more than amassing detailed information about aspects of social life. An ethnography which only did this would be indistinguishable from the docusoaps which have come to dominate our TV schedules.
4 Conducting ethnography is a 'messy business' (Pearson, 1993: vii). This is reflected in the confessional tales of ethnographers which stand in stark contrast to the sanitized accounts in 'research methods' texts.

We hope that we have also demonstrated that while ethnographic research appears deceptively simple it is challenging yet rewarding. This is vividly described by Sharpe below in a chapter reflecting on researching prostitution,

> The research was not a dull experience. It ranged from being extremely interesting, hilariously funny and enjoyable to being conversely tense, frustrating and totally exhausting. Providing you are not of a nervous disposition and do not mind getting freezing cold, mercilessly teased, tried out and 'tested', sworn at, laughed at, generally abused and half frightened to death, it is a research strategy that makes library based research seem a trifle dull in comparison. (1998: 12)

It is tempting to end this chapter with 'criminologists don't do ethnographies like they used to' but this would do a disservice to the contemporary ethnographies we have discussed above. Ethnographies are now rare but are often carried out meticulously. Social scientists warn against constructing rosy views of the past by comparing the present to a mythical golden age. To suggest that contemporary ethnographies compare unfavourably with classic ones glosses over the lack of methodological sophistication of some of the classic ethnographic studies of deviant life. This aside, it is easy to arrive at Maguire's (2000: 126) conclusion that this methodology had 'a hugely liberating effect on criminology', allowing researchers to get close enough to offenders to understand their social worlds.

While the number of researchers who continue to conduct ethnographic work is small, they have generated some important criminological work. Perhaps one of the most worrying trends is that ethnography has become an approach adopted by researchers studying for a PhD and this approach is abandoned through personal choice or more likely necessity once they embark on an academic career. Many of the published studies discussed in this chapter have been developed from doctoral studies. Hobbs (2001) also makes this observation suggesting that his review of ethnographies of deviance indicates that the ethnographer's craft is practiced for the most part by younger academics, just launching a career. We end with concurring with Maguire's (2000: 122) view:

> There is a strong case for 'righting the balance' in current patterns of criminological work, by encouraging – and allocating more funding to – research with offenders.

Exercises

1   Go to http://www.qualidata.essex.ac.uk, the Qualidata website. Qualidata is a UK service for the acquisition, dissemination and re-use of qualitative social science research data. One of the datasets is from Stan Cohen's study entitled 'Folk Devils and Moral Panics' and includes in-depth and unstructured interview transcripts, participant observation field notes and press clippings. It is possible to request access to this data but your task here is to consider the advantages and disadvantages of making use of ethnographic data collected by other researchers.
2   Select a criminological topic which you feel is suitable for study using an ethnographic approach and imagine you are attempting to secure funding for this work. How would you justify the use of this approach?
3   Try to anticipate your critics and consider what feedback you might receive.

FURTHER READING

There are a number of excellent general methodological texts on ethnography. Two classic texts are:

- Hammersley, M. and Atkinson, P. (1995) *Ethnography: Principles in Practice.*
- Burgess, R. (1984) *In the Field.*

A more recent addition to the literature is:

- Brewer, J. (2000) *Ethnography.* This text contains a number of examples from criminological research, including the author's own fieldwork on the Royal Ulster Constabulary.

The most comprehensive text is:

- Atkinson, P. et al. (eds) (2001) *Handbook of Ethnography.* The chapter by Dick Hobbs on ethnography and the study of deviance is particularly recommended.

For a text focusing specifically on crime, deviance and field research, readers should look at:

- *Ethnography at the Edge* edited by Ferrell, J. and Hamm, M. (1998).

In addition to the ethnographies discussed in this chapter any of the following are good introductions to the challenges and complexities of conducting ethnographic research on criminological issues. We have deliberately selected some of the most recent ethnographies to give a flavour of the realities of conducting ethnographic research today. However, classic ethnographic texts are still worth reading.

- Armstrong, G. (1998) *Football Hooliganism: Knowing the Score.*
- Foster, J. (1990) *Villains: Crime and Community in the Inner City.*
- Hobbs, D. (1995) *Professional Criminals in Modern Britain.*
- McKeganey, N. and Barnard, M. (1996) *Sex Work on the Streets: Prostitutes and Their Clients.*
- Rock, P. (1993) *The Social World of an English Crown Court: Witness and Professionals in the Crown Court Centre at Wood Green.*

The following journals are also recommended to familiarize experienced and novice ethnographers with recent debates surrounding ethnography.

- *Qualitative Research* published by Sage.
- *Journal of Contemporary Ethnography* published by Sage.

7

Using Documentary Evidence in Qualitative Research

Introduction

This chapter will explore the value of the written word and other forms of documentary evidence to the qualitative researcher. It will review the broad range of possible documents and sources to which the criminological researcher might turn, including crime data and media representations of crime and deviance. We will discuss the various functions of documentary evidence as a useful starting point for research, particularly in organizational settings, as a means of authenticating other research findings, as providing a unique historical perspective, and as a tool in analysing representations of the self. The chapter will also highlight some of the risks related to an over reliance on documentary sources and acknowledges their status as socially constructed products.

Potentially there are a broad range of documentary sources that qualitative researchers can use. In the criminological field these have been as diverse as official statistics, reports and archival material, through to an analysis by Brown and Heidensohn (2000) of the representation of women police officers in humour and cartoons. Such material can serve as a stand alone focus of research activity or as an adjunct to other work. Students undertaking qualitative research for their dissertation are likely to find documentary evidence to be a valuable resource, particularly where access to criminal justice organizations or actors is problematic.

As well as its potential as a stand alone method, documentary evidence also has an important part to play in triangulation of methods. Drakeford (1999: 7) graphically describes how his research on criminalization of the 1930s *Greenshirt Movement for Social Credit* involved a piecing together of interviews and archive material collected by members of the movement. He acknowledges the diversity of the archive material, which included formal public documents such as pamphlets and publications (some in book form), what he refers to as 'ephemera' including notices of public meetings and tickets to events, materials produced by the movement but not intended for public consumption including minutes of meetings and confidential materials including letters and diaries. This rich tapestry of documentary evidence enabled Drakeford to produce a detailed and informed account of the activities of the movement and criminal justice responses to them. In using such materials we should not lose sight of the concept of informed consent. Drakeford provides an endearing and reflexive account of gaining consent from very elderly past members of the movement to make use of the materials in his research. Scott (1990) highlights the distinction between public and private documentation and proposes the categorization of closed, restricted, open-archival and open-published. As might be expected different access issues will arise in relation to the distinct categories.

For our purposes Drakeford's work also exemplifies the various forms that documentary evidence can take. Plummer (2001) emphasizes this point with his most recent publication discussing the resource potential of letters, photographs and diaries (including video diaries). May (2001: 175) also points to the manner in which documentary material can be a resource for those involved in ethnographic research as a point of comparison 'between the observer's interpretation of events and those recorded in documents relating to those events'.

Documents as a resource and a focus of research

Researchers who deploy documentary sources (Brookman, 1999; Zedner, 1991) have typically distinguished between the use of such information as a means of finding out about specific issues and their use as means of exploring those who produce such materials. Brookman (1999: 52) summarizes this distinction between documentary sources as 'a resource *for* social research or as a topic *of* social research' (emphasis in original).

Documentary sources as a resource for social research

We discuss below the value of organizational documents in providing an insight into professional cultures. However, such documents should also be valued as an informational resource regarding the organization. Typically impenetrable groups such as police forces, which may be particularly challenging for students to access, are required to provide annual reports which provide a plethora of detailed information on the structure of the organization and their activities. All police researchers will find such documentation of value as a starting point for their research or, in some cases, as a stand alone resource. In the latter case annual reports are a useful resource for comparing the structure and performance of different police forces. Although qualitative researchers will need to approach such data from a stance of critical interpretation.

Another important source of information on criminal justice organizations are the reports provided by external regulators and inspection bodies. Again such reports are commonly in the public domain, providing important insights into the activities of typically closed institutions, for example prisons and young offender institutions. The reports forthcoming from Her Majesty's Inspectorate of Prisons and the Prisons Ombudsman have provided important information on the treatment of prisoners, in some cases acting as a significant catalyst for change. Topics addressed have included issues of self-harm and suicide in prison and the treatment of female prisoners and lifers (HM Chief Inspector of Prisons, 1997).

For those involved with community based research the requirement under the Crime and Disorder Act 1998 that localities publish a crime audit can be a valuable resource. Such publications carry a statutory requirement that they must be based on a collaborative approach, directly involving key players and agencies in the community. In that sense the documentation will throw light on who the community identifies to be key players in relation to crime and disorder matters, levels of resident participation, official accounts of community priorities and local levels of crime and disorder. Noaks (2000) made use of the local crime audit in her research on a community based private policing group. The audit made no mention of a possible contribution to crime prevention or control from the private police and/or a possible diversion of reported crime from the public to the private police. This is despite the fact that the private group had operated in the area for five years and were reported by residents to be a key factor in falling crime rates. These findings went some way to supporting the private group's view that their contribution to crime prevention was ignored and that they failed to feature as a key local player.

Documentary sources as a topic of social research

Documentary evidence can be particularly functional for social researchers in facilitating access to organizational cultures and related representations of them. Official reports will typically be available to researchers (increasingly on the Internet) and provide an important perspective on how the organization or group chooses to manage its public representation. May (2001: 176) refers to such representations as 'particular readings of social events'. For example, annual reports produced by police forces can reveal a great deal about the force's relative priorities on crime control, special initiatives, trends in staffing; representations of ethnic minority officers, numbers of special constables, and regional crime patterns. Such annual reports are produced in-house, a fact which makes them particularly revealing on organizational agendas and priorities. It is interesting, for example, to compare changes in the structure of such reports over time. We note that recent reports are much more likely than those of 20 years ago to comment on citizens' anxieties and fears regarding crime. Such commentary was absent from earlier reports, a change that can be linked with criminology's increasing focus on fear of crime (Hale, 1996). In the face of a substantial increase in recorded crime in that period, and more recently a particular focus on rising violent crime, the impact on local citizens' fear of crime has commonly become a performance indicator for policing. In other words while the police may be less able to represent themselves as controlling crime they can seek to show themselves as positively influencing an individual's construction of their local crime problem. While researchers need to be alert to the social construction of such reports, acknowledging their subjective rather than objective status, this in itself can make them valuable as illustrative of organizational cultures.

As well as annual reports other output produced by organizations can provide a significant insight into shifts in organizational culture and climate. For example, attention to pre-sentence reports (formerly known as social enquiry reports) produced for the courts by the probation service gives a valuable insight into the radical changes that the service has experienced in the last decade. The change in name of such reports is significant in itself. Currently such reports are typically written to a required formula set down in National Standards (Home Office, 2000). Among other things, the standards require the probation officer to undertake and report a risk assessment, both for the individual and the community in general. Overall, the content and style of the reports lacks the discretion and individualism that was evident in the social enquiry report. This can be linked to the recent reconfiguration of the probation role as outside of the social work world that it previously occupied. Historically there was some ambivalence for probation officers in balancing their duties to the court and to their individual clients. The privileging of their responsibilities to the court was made explicit with the removal of probation officers from social work training and a shift in discourse to replace clients with offenders. Probation officers are no longer part of the social work profession, a change that can be directly linked to the movement to strengthen community penalties and represent them as a genuine alternative to custody (Cavadino and Dignan, 2002). An analysis of reports for the court will reflect these changes in a reduction of the attention (typically as a form of mitigation) given to the social circumstances of offenders and a more narrow focus on the impact of their offending behaviour. As well as giving an insight into shifts in organizational culture such reports have also been used by criminological researchers as a vehicle for researching specific issues, for example discrimination (Gelsthorpe, 1993).

Historical research

Documentary evidence has also been a particularly important source of information for historical research. Those who favour such approaches have argued that historical work has a contemporary significance in providing an important baseline for the measurement of both continuity and change with regard to criminal justice matters, while others have argued that the precursors to our current criminal justice processes are worthy of study for their own sake. Beck (2002: 36), in addressing the position of police women in early twentieth-century Britain, argues that 'an historical perspective provides useful insights into current problems and also guards against research being atemporal'. Jones (1996: xiii), writing about crime and policing in nineteenth- and twentieth-century South Wales, acknowledges how contemporary debates can be 'circumscribed by the absence of a historical dimension', requiring such an approach to give insights into 'the historical roots of today's fears, myths and prejudices'. His detailed and meticulous accounts rely heavily on archival material, typically pieced together from a variety of sources. Other historical accounts of policing have been able to combine archival documentary evidence with interviews with surviving police personnel. Cockcroft (1999: 131) in his study of the Metropolitan Police in the period 1930–60 combined the use of historical texts with an oral history approach, involving interviews with former police officers who served in that period. For him the historical texts provided 'orthodox' or conventional accounts' and he relied on the oral histories to provide the officers' own perspective and interpretation of events. Cockcroft's distinction is an important one. It brings us back to an important theme in documentary research that the social construction of the materials should never be lost sight of.

May (2001) cites the work of Pearson (1983) as providing an important historical piece that addresses continuities over time in citizens emotional responses to crime and the fear of crime that can be generated. Pearson took an historical approach in exploring moral panics related to 'hooliganism', a phenomenon which was represented as a product of declining moral standards in 1970s Britain. Using documentary evidence dating from the Victorian period Pearson countered claims establishing the mythology of golden-ageism 'with identical fears being expressed in each period considered' (May, 2001: 177).

Other historical work has elected to focus on events that received relatively limited research attention at the point that they were occurring. Feminist scholars have particularly noted the lack of attention to women and other minority groups in historical work. They have sought to rectify this position adopting an approach which is described by Beck (2002: 37) as applying 'insights of modern feminist criminology in order to explore their historical subjects'. Arguments regarding the marginalization of women and the invisibility of gender issues have proved to be applicable both to offenders (Carlen, 1985) and those working in the criminal justice process (Beck, 2002; Heidensohn, 2000). Such marginalization has demanded careful and detailed attention to documentary evidence to draw out and identify the unique experiences of such groups.

Ballinger (2000) provides an important example of such an approach in her study of the 12 women executed in England and Wales between 1900–55. Her analysis of court records and related media accounts of both the trials and executions are particularly revealing with regard to social responses to the women and their offending. Ballinger identifies how the discourses regarding the women and their crimes gives insights into representations of women and issues such as motherhood, sexuality, race and power. In her detailed case study of Styllou Christofi, a Greek–Cypriot woman convicted and executed in 1954 for the murder of her German daughter-in-law, she raises issues of a failure to identify mental illness and racial issues. Drawing on the documentary evidence Ballinger (2000: 161) recounts how the prosecuting council referred to Christofi as a 'stupid woman of the peasant type'. Readers are advised that she spoke very little English and the trial was conducted with the deployment of an interpreter. Despite being diagnosed as 'mentally deranged' by the Principal Medical Officer at Holloway, the defendant refused to plead insanity. As a consequence her medical report only became public knowledge a few days before the execution. Ballinger describes how a small group of Labour MPs failed in their efforts to prevent the execution in the light of the medical evidence. Ballinger highlights how the case attracted little public concern, quoting a subsequent *News of the World* conclusion that 'Nobody raised a fuss when Mrs Christofi was hanged in 1954. But then who was Mrs Christofi? A dark skinned foreigner' (Ballinger, 2000: 163).

Ballinger's (2000: 165) own conclusion is that 'Christofi found herself located at the receiving end of both judicial and cultural misogyny'. She also points to the 'ultimate irony of a criminal justice system which throughout history has attempted to categorize relatively "normal" women as "mad", while the mental state of criminal women who may have qualified for this category is ignored'.

Turning to women working in the criminal justice process, Beck (2002: 37) addresses how both Radford (1989) and Heidensohn (2000) point to equivalences in the experiences of early pioneer police women and those struggling against potentially sexist practices and forms of exclusion toward the end of the twentieth century. In reaching such a conclusion they draw on historical accounts, often provided directly by early British police women. Such accounts included personal biographies, diaries and work logs which provided a fascinating insight into some of the coherence between the experiences of early and contemporary female police officers in Britain.

Court and police records

Ballinger's research demonstrates the ways in which court records can be pivotal in providing information on criminal justice issues. Such information has commonly been at the core of large-scale quantitative studies in criminology (Hood, 1992) but also has a place in the work of the qualitative researcher. Prosecution files and the transcripts of trials by their particularly detailed character can be an important source of information and evidence. Wilczynski (1995) deployed such materials in her study of filicide (child-killing by parents or parent substitutes) in England and Wales in the mid-1980s. Her study involved attention to 65 files from the Director of Public Prosecutions (DPP) in 1983 and 1984 (immediately prior to the establishment of the Crown Prosecution Service in 1985). Wilczynski (1995: 167) notes that previous work in this area had particularly focused on psychiatric elements in the cases, while her study concentrated upon 'the motivation for the crime, the common background features of the cases, and the criminal justice response to offenders'. She was also particularly concerned with exploring any gendered responses to the offenders, with women in a majority in her sample. Drawing upon DPP files she is able to report.

> most of the killings ... were not instrumental or premeditated–they were usually sudden and impulsive. (1995: 168)

> Numerous social stresses are a very prominent feature of filicidal parents' histories, such as financial and housing problems, youthful parenthood, marital conflict, lack of preparation for parenthood and children who are difficult to care for. (1995: 172)

> Women are less likely than men to be prosecuted, or convicted of murder, and more likely to be granted bail and to receive psychiatric treatment before trial. (1995: 174)

Having identified the distinctive treatment experienced by women and men in relation to this offence, Wilczynski's case study approach allowed her to report that such differences were sometimes attributable to differences in prior convictions but also reflected a contrasting social response to the committal of filicide by women. Equivalent offending on the part of men is represented as more understandable and something for which prosecution through the usual routes for any other violent crime is appropriate. In contrast, such crime on the part of a woman is abhorrent and far less understandable. As such it is much more likely to attract a psychiatric label. In Wilczynski's words:

> When a woman kills her own child, she offends not only against the criminal law, but against the sanctity of stereotypical femininity: it is therefore assumed that she must have been 'mad'. (1995: 178)

Brookman (1999) also reports on the value of documentary evidence to her qualitative study of male on male violence, including homicide, in England and

Wales. While acknowledging the value of the Homicide Index as a source, predominantly of quantitative evidence, she turns to police murder files as a 'documentary source rarely used by researchers' (1999: 46). The Homicide Index is a national database which was able to provide her with contextual information on trends in homicide, but it was to three police forces' murder files that she turned for qualitative analysis of the nature of the acts. Ninety-five covering reports from police murder files were scrutinized with such reports able to provide details of the:

> events surrounding the homicide and ... details of offenders, victims, circumstances leading up to the homicide and previous histories of the victim and offender. (1999: 47)

Brookman is anxious to point out that this approach is not without its pitfalls, not least due to the challenge of gaining access to such materials. In one of the three forces information needed to be accessed on the computerized HOLMES system (Home Office Large Major Enquiries System) requiring her to rely heavily on individual police officers for each episode of access and culminating in more restricted data. In practice the transfer of data from hard copy to the computer system had resulted in more condensed accounts with some of the detail lost. This illustrates the need for the qualitative researcher to be alert to the social construction of the product and the purpose for which it was originally produced. In the case of such cover reports they are particularly intended to provide the Crown Prosecution Service with a detailed summary of what can be vast files and dossiers generated by a murder inquiry. However, with the acknowledgement of their original purpose, cover reports potentially provide the researcher with a unique perspective on the dynamics of a violent event and the actions of the key players, alongside an insight into the attitudes and values of those producing the reports. Brookman (1999: 55) reports how the latter became evident to her as the research progressed, leading her to describe the reports as 'not neutral documents'.

Media sources

Media representations of crime and deviance provide a unique documentary source for qualitative research. Criminology has an established history of using the media as a research tool to access public understandings of crime (Ditton and Duffy, 1983; Wykes, 2001). In part this is attributable to the fact that the majority of the public still derive their image of crime from mass media accounts. As with the distinction previously made, the media can provide a source of data with its interpretive accounts of criminal acts, investigations, arrests, trials, appeals and crime-related issues in general or can be the object of study in its own right regarding its representation of crime. In the latter case much of the debate has focused on the potentially 'criminogenic consequences of the mass media' (Reiner, 1997: 189), something which Reiner identifies as a 'perpetual refrain'. In particular this refrain concerned itself with the extent to which the disproportionate focus on violent crime, typically written about in sensational and dramatic language, acted as provocation to the commission of further crimes.

An important theme in research on the media is the social construction of the product. The early work of radical criminologists in the 1960s and 1970s highlighted the lack of neutrality in media reporting and the, sometimes insidious, influence of powerful factions (Cohen and Young, 1973; Hall, 1979). This early work generated a whole school of media studies. Feminist scholars took up this approach with both Naylor (1995) and Wykes (1995) focusing on the representation of violent women in the British press. Their analysis of press discourse leads them separately to conclude that:

> Men in these accounts are accounted for as breaking the law rather than as breaking any taboos of masculinity. In contrast, women are depicted as having broken taboos of gender behaviour three times more often than men. (Wykes, 1995: 69)

> Gender is treated as central when a woman is violent. Deviance from (or at times conformity to) gender roles for women is itself seen as causing the violence, and provides the base from which the story is presented. (Naylor, 1995: 93)

Despite Reiner's (1997: 192) assertion that '"content analysis" so called has been colonized by this positivist and quantitative approach', both manage to achieve an analysis of value to the qualitative researcher (see Chapter 8 for a discussion problematizing analysis of content). In discussing documentary sources this chapter is primarily concerned with magazine and newspaper accounts, while acknowledging a small body of work concerned with representation of crime in fiction (Reiner, 1997). Self-evidently mass media output can incorporate TV, radio and film which others have discussed (Reiner, 1997; Wykes, 2001) but which we will not focus on here. Work on documentary sources has typically identified the disproportionate amount of newspaper print devoted to coverage of violent crime. Williams and Dickinson (1993: 40) report that in one month of 1989 64.5% of newspaper reporting on crime was concerned with violent offences, at a time when the British Crime Survey reported that only 6% of offences reported by respondents were violent. While acknowledging that the survey data may reflect some under reporting by victims, it remains the case that coverage of offences of violence are disproportionate. Reiner (1997: 200), citing the work of Williams and Dickinson (1993), goes on to report that:

> The percentage of studies dealing with crimes involving personal violence, and the salience they were given (as measured by where they appeared in the layout and the extent of pictures accompanying them) increased considerably the more down market the newspaper studied ... While on the one hand, the *Independent*, the *Guardian* and *The*

Times devoted 3–4% of their news space to crimes of personal violence, this was over 19% in the *Sun* and the *Star*.

Reiner also points to ways in which the media provide a skewed picture of crime and disorder. Firstly, he points to a disproportionate focus on police success, often directly linked to a disproportionate focus on violent offences for which police clear-up rates are higher. Secondly, he provides evidence of a disproportionate focus on high status and older offenders in the national press, although he problematizes this and suggests that the profile might be a more accurate reflection than that provided by crime statistics. Thirdly, he points to contradictory evidence on whether the media disproportionately focus on offenders from ethnic minority groups. Fourthly, he confirms the arguments advanced by that of Naylor (1995) and Wykes (1995) regarding disproportionate attention to women offenders. Finally, Reiner notes a disproportionate focus on the victimization and 'risks faced by higher status, white adults of becoming victims of crime' (1997: 210).

Qualitative analysis has also been extended to crime fiction, both in book form and the magazine style true crime stories genre (Reiner, 1997). Brown and Heidensohn (2000) also provide an analysis of the representation of police women carried in policing journals up to the 1970s. Beck (2002: 39) points to the 'blatant caricaturization' that such images convey and reflects their conclusion that 'such depictions of women officers are a distillation of negative views'.

Political and personal accounts

As suggested above, criminology and its related studies are typically embedded in political processes (see Chapter 2). Qualitative researchers seeking to follow trends or shifts in policy will commonly find it of value to look to original material and sources to throw light on such shifts. Such political material can include Hansard (official reports of UK parliamentary proceedings), political speeches and manifestos and the proceedings of select committees. Such sources can prove an important starting point for excavation of the political ideologies that underpin the evolution of law and order policies and legislation. Such sources have proved vital to Jones and Newburn's (2002) efforts to trace the major influences on criminal justice policy in England and Wales at the turn of the last century. Their focus was comparative with a particular interest in identifying the sources for the emergence of zero tolerance policies and the rise of privatization in the criminal justice processes of late twentieth-century England and Wales. In the latter case, while acknowledging the ongoing presence of private services throughout the late nineteenth and twentieth centuries, their starting point is the marked upsurge in the deployment of such services in the 1990s. Private prisons expanded markedly both in number and role (for example, they began for the first time to take sentenced prisoners) and private security personnel increasingly outstripped public police in their presence on our streets. In seeking to trace the political thinking that facilitated such changes the researchers looked to political speeches and statements and the output of government think-tanks, select committees and working parties. In particular they were interested in how far politicians and senior civil servants had become 'policy tourists', particularly looking to the United States as the model for developments in the UK. This piece of research is a good example of work where the documentary evidence provides an effective starting point for the study, to be followed up by interviews and the opportunity for interpretation with key players. In this case Jones and Newburn (2002) undertook such interviews with key politicians, civil servants, senior police officers, prison personnel and pressure groups on both sides of the Atlantic.

Hudson (2000) adopted a similar triangulated approach in her work on sentencing patterns with young burglars. Her starting point was the crime figures which revealed that between 1980 and 1996 the use of imprisonment with burglars initially fell by 10%, only to rise by 20% between 1992 and 1996. Having established such trends Hudson sought to 'explain these changes in the context of new penal strategies', which are themselves 'consequent upon the twists and turns in the politics of law and order' (2000: 187). In constructing her analysis she looked to a variety of sources including contemporary Home Office publications and output, 'insider accounts' from civil servants and researchers, accounts by academic criminologists and wider social theory ('which explain general movements and trends, for which crime and punishment might provide examples but are not the whole subject matter' (2000: 187)). Crime statistics may be one source of data used by criminologists looking to documentary sources, although researchers should be alert to the social construction of such figures and the partiality of the perspective that they provide (see Maguire, 2002). Those following a qualitative approach can use such figures as a reference point but should seek to supplement them with evidence from other sources. This data might be gathered using a range of qualitative strategies.

Finally, we would make a plea for the qualitative researcher not to ignore the personal accounts of interaction with the criminal justice process that are available to us. Over time, such accounts have been forthcoming both from offenders (Carlen, 1985; Peckham, 1985) and personnel working within the criminal justice process. In the latter case this has included former police officers, lawyers, judges, executioners and the former director of the prison service (Lewis, 1997). Evidently by their very nature such biographical accounts are subjective and provide the author's version of events. However, once their status has been acknowledged they provide a rich vein of personal accounts and experiences, which have sometimes proved inspirational to subsequent work.

Approaches to using documentary evidence

Having reviewed the variety of forms that documentary evidence can take it is important to comment on the approach that researchers should adopt in making use of such materials in their research. The divergence of possible sources should not deflect researchers from adopting a coherent and consistent strategy on how they approach documentary sources. In the following section we will highlight some of the key principles that researchers need to follow to conduct high quality documentary research.

In that regard it is important that qualitative researchers who deploy documentary sources stay true to the principles of reflexivity and methodological rigour. Reflexivity should underpin the choices that are made by researchers in selection of documentary sources. As discussed above, the potential range of documentary sources in the criminal justice field is vast and researchers need to be alert to the ways in which their personal biography influences selection.

May (2001) argues that Scott's (1990) typology for assessing the quality of the evidence available from documentary sources is particularly helpful. This consists of four criteria: 'authenticity, credibility, representativeness and meaning'.

- *Authenticity* refers to the researcher's reflexive judgement that the documents that are unearthed are attributable to the organization or individual to whom they are ascribed. In making such judgements the researcher will need to be alert to the source, structure and format of any documentary materials.
- *Credibility* refers to content of the materials and the researcher's assessment on the 'extent to which the evidence is undistorted and sincere, free from error and evasion' (Scott, 1990: 7). In this regard May (2001: 197) makes the point that while the Internet has increased accessibility to documentary sources it is vital that researchers retain 'critical reflexivity' regarding the representation of self that those investing in Internet based materials are seeking to achieve.
- *Representativeness* refers to the extent to which the materials can be said to be 'typical' of other connected materials. However, as May (2001: 190) points out 'typicality' will not always be of concern to the qualitative researcher and the atypical documentary source should not be overlooked.
- Finally, Scott's typology is concerned with *meaning*, something which he further subdivides into intended, received and content meaning (May 2001: 193). For May (2001: 190) this final criteria is concerned with 'the clarity and comprehensibility of a document to the analyst'.

In addressing all of these criteria the analyst will need to draw on their knowledge of the social context in which documentary materials are compiled. Having achieved documentation that meets the above criteria the methodologically rigorous approach also needs to be extended to the analysis of documents.

Working with documentary sources is not without its methodological challenges and researchers will sometimes need to think innovatively to overcome possible difficulties. Jones (1996) found that his historical research on policing in South Wales had to contend with shifting police force boundaries which problematized the comparative dimension to his work. Wilczynski (1995) drew upon a sample of 65 case files from the Director of Public Prosecutions records for her study of filicide in England and Wales. The records applied to 1983 and 1984 and involved many hours of meticulous research at the London based records office. There were issues of time and cost for a postgraduate student based in Cambridge and student researchers will commonly need to take such factors into account in deciding the scope of their study. Wilczynski (1995: 167), however, points out that the challenges would have been even greater if she had drawn her sample from a year later when the establishment of the Crown Prosecution Service meant that homicides were prosecuted regionally and a centralized national sample would have been far more difficult to obtain. Brookman (1999) also pointed to the challenge of accessing some of her intended sources and those undertaking documentary research should be alert to adopting a realistic approach both in terms of the actual materials they seek to use and the volume of data analysed.

Silverman (2001) also emphasizes the importance of limiting data to that which is manageable. He also highlights the need for clarity of analytic approach that is theoretically derived and explicitness of analytic strategy that demonstrates the connections between coded elements. In this regard he contrasts the coding of qualitative and quantitative data calling for the former approach to 'show how the (theoretically defined) elements we have identified are assembled or mutually laminated' (2001: 42). In other words, he encourages qualitative researchers to make explicit the particular theoretical approach that informs their work.

The studies we have included in this review demonstrate such features with Ballinger, for example, setting out her commitment to Foucauldian feminism which for her:

> rejects the notion of a pre-given subject and hence by implication, cannot accept a unitary category of 'Woman'. Instead it concerns itself with analysing how subjects come into being via discourses – the 'discursive construction of the subject' ... prostitutes, bad mothers or women alcoholics therefore do not exist in an a priori state, waiting for institutions to act upon them ... [but] are being continually constituted and ... also constitute themselves through language/discourse. (2000: 54)

It is intended that sharing these experiences of conducting documentary research will encourage others to see the valuable evidence that can be uncovered. Despite some of the potential challenges that have been reviewed it is to be hoped that all researchers will be encouraged to recognize the value of documentary sources and the insightful material that they can provide.

Concluding comments

It is hard to think of qualitative research activity that does not place some reliance on the use of documentary evidence. This may be as minimal as scrutinizing diaries or work logs in institutional settings through to what is sometimes referred to as library based research which relies totally on documentary and archival material. Despite such regular usage, deployment of documentary sources is rarely scrutinized as a method (May, 2001). In countering this lack of critical attention we would hope this chapter encourages researchers to be reflexive about their use of such materials. Acknowledgement of the potential diversity of materials used should also foster a rigour of analysis and an appreciation of the enhanced understandings that can derive from using documentary sources. In collating such knowledge researchers should, however, hold on to the distinction put forward at the beginning of the chapter that documentary evidence can be used both as focus of research as well as a research tool. It is also worth reiterating and re-emphasizing the social construction of all potential documentary sources, and the difficulties, in practice, of separating their construction from the evidence that we can take from them.

Exercises

1 (a) Read a report produced by either your local police force or Her Majesty's Inspectorate of Prisons, (b) draw up a list of six key research themes which you might write about after you have read the report and (c) list other sources of information that you might follow up to extend your knowledge on the topic.

2 Follow the newspaper accounts of a trial in two newspapers. This might either be a recent event or an historical account. You can either choose to access hard copy or via the Internet. Compare and contrast the style of reporting with particular attention to any differences in style, use of visual images and use of language in tabloid and broadsheet newspapers. Be alert to any gender or racial issues in the accounts.

3 Draw up a list of questions that you want to ask about crime in your local area. Trace the most recent audit for your locality. Analyse the key players and the main priorities as identified in the document. Identify any omissions from the accounts and reflect on the capacity of the document to answer your original questions. How would you account for any shortfall?

FURTHER READING

May, T. (2001) *Social Research: Issues, Methods and Process, Buckingham Open University Press* is highly recommended. Chapter 8 entitled 'Documentary research: excavations and evidence' provides a useful overview of some of the issues discussed in this chapter. More detailed overviews can be found in the following texts.

- Plummer, K. (2001) *Documents of Life 2.*
- Prior, L. (2003) *Using Documents in Social Research.*

The following accounts provide important personal accounts of what it means to conduct documentary research.

- Brookman, F. (1999) 'Accessing and analysing police murder files'.
- Naylor, B. (1995) 'Women's crime and media coverage'.
- Wilczynski, A. (1995) 'Child-killing by parents: social, legal and gender issues'.
- Wykes, M. (1995) 'Passion, marriage and murder'.

8

Analysing Qualitative Data

Introduction

This chapter addresses approaches to managing, analysing and presenting the main types of qualitative data collected by criminological researchers. In particular we will provide a review of the grounded theory approach, consider alternative approaches such as discourse and conversational analysis, and emphasize that the process of analysis needs to be ongoing and is not a distinct stage completed at the end of a project. Computer packages designed to aid analysis will also be discussed. We will provide data to give illustrative examples of the process of analysis.

Analysis is variously represented by methodologists as daunting, complex and difficult to achieve through to Coffey and Atkinson's more tantalizing perspective that it is potentially 'artful and playful' (1996: 10). Tesch (1990) rejects representing it as a prescribed rule-bound activity. For her the variety of possible data sources and analytic strategies precludes adopting a standardized approach that can be used in all circumstances. This is not our intention and we acknowledge that qualitative research requires imaginative and reflective input from the researcher. Our overall aim is to go some way to demystifying analysis, particularly for the novice researcher. In setting out what we see to be helpful pointers and practical advice we draw on our own research experiences and those of our students and colleagues.

While flexibility and an openness of approach is a vital feature of analysis of qualitative data the adoption of such methods must not entail an abandonment of rigour on the part of the analyst. By their very nature qualitative methods can generate a vast amount of rich and detailed data. The challenge for the researcher is to make sense of that data and provide an illuminating analysis. This chapter seeks to facilitate that task for the social researcher and set out some of the commonalities and fundamental ground rules that, in our experience, aid the analytic process.

Establishing the research questions

It is important that attention to analysis is a feature of the early planning stages of a research project. It is essential that researchers think ahead regarding how they envisage analysing the data that their research will generate. All research begins with the identification of a research question. In the criminological field this can be as diverse as considering the experiences of offenders, victims or those employed in the criminal justice system. Whichever group or groups are the focus of study the project must begin with identifying the particular facets of their experience that the research will address. In this initial planning stage researchers should think ahead to the areas of thematic interest that they envisage addressing. This early planning should be flexible. Researchers need to remain open to emerging themes but in our experience early planning facilitates achieving subsequent analytic focus.

As suggested above, one of the most important rules is that the researcher should never see the completion of the data collection stage as the point at which they begin to think about and plan for analysis. Advance attention to analytic requirements will influence choice of research sites and subjects and the questions that are asked of them. As far as possible researchers need to give advance thought at the outset of projects to the key themes that they wish to address and to have designed their project accordingly. Early reflection on the research questions will influence project design including the approaches that will be adopted in managing and analysing the emerging data. For the qualitative researcher this will not be a static and inflexible process and best practice will incorporate a willingness to adapt and adjust accordingly.

The grounded approach

Some qualitative researchers favour a pure grounded approach whereby analytic themes emerge from the data collected. Following such an approach the emphasis is on the researcher avoiding going into the field with preconceived ideas and a thematic focus but allowing such themes to emerge from the field-work, this constitutes a grounded theory approach as advocated by Glaser and Strauss (1967). Such an approach bridges the gap between theoretically uni-formed empirical research and empirically uniformed theory by grounding theory in data. It is based on the premise that theory at various levels of gen-erality is indispensable for deeper knowledge of social phenomena but theory ought to be developed in close relationship with data. The principle is that detailed analysis of the data helps to produce an emergent theory to guide data collection focused on making comparisons. In due course theoretical satura-tion is reached where additional analysis no longer contributes to discovering anything new about a category. The results are then written up with 'thick description' (Geertz, 1973) with the presentation of specific incidents from field notes and interviews organized around analytic themes and discussion of an empirically-grounded theory. This inductive method is particularly useful for those undertaking ethnographic research, who are typically seeking to analyse the natural setting. In the case of those conducting interviews, however unstructured, there is likely to have been more advanced planning in relation to identifying, addressing and analysing key themes.

For all qualitative researchers the main points of thematic interest and related analysis will be developed and evolve as the data are collected. While there might be said to be something of a continuum in the extent to which quali-tative researchers follow a grounded approach, advocates of grounded theory are marked out by the openness of their approach and a lack of rigidity in the planning stages of their research. Such openness is intended to be receptive to the themes that emerge from the fieldwork and may not have been anticipated by the researcher. Silverman (2001: ix) gives an illuminating account of how it was 'nagging doubts about the credibility of my research ... the need to go beyond my data in various unforeseen ways so as to obtain the sort of answers I wanted', that led him away from following a quantitative approach to a qual-itative one. Others, particularly feminist scholars, have favoured the method as a means of giving a voice to those participating in the research. Many scholars have rejected the imposition of a rigid agenda by the researcher and turned to qualitative methods as a counter to that. Beck's (2002) work on equal oppor-tunities in policing is a good example of triangulation where her focus group with policewomen and her interviews with female and male officers are intended to complement the quantitative survey undertaken with a large sam-ple of officers from the force studied.

However grounded the method, the data that are generated will need to be subjected to an analytical strategy. Research needs to be about telling both the how and the why. But despite this, as Coffey and Atkinson (1996: 2) describe, it is not uncommon for the qualitative researcher who has gathered a vast amount of data to be without any clear plan in how they might use that data to construct explanations and develop theoretical concepts. Bottoms (2000: 15) points to how addressing the relationship between theory and research can be daunting for all scholars. Our aim is for this chapter to provide help and support to potentially floundering individuals, while at the same time encouraging ongoing attention to the appropriateness of their analytic strategy on the part of those with more clearly established plans.

The hidden skill

We might ask why researchers commonly visit issues of analysis as an afterthought in the research process and something which they only seek to address once the data are collected (Coffey and Atkinson, 1996). Some of this is likely to be attributable to the relative lack of attention in many methods books to issues pertaining to analytic strategy. In addition, while accounts of qualitative research typically provide details regarding access and the subsequent findings that emerged in the field, relatively little attention is given to setting out, and being explicit about, the analytic procedures that were deployed. Silverman (2001: 229) also reports a similar lack of transparency regarding strategies adopted to ensure the reliability and validity of data generated by qualitative methods. As suggested above, while giving research participants a voice is a vital component in some researcher's repertoire of skills, such outputs cannot stand alone as valid qualitative accounts. While telling their story is important, authentic research requires analytic attention to key themes and concepts. Attention to such themes can never be addressed at too early a stage in the research process. In that regard it is important that the qualitative researcher retain reflexivity regarding how their key themes are selected. Such selection and choice of themes may reflect personal biography. The influence of such biography cannot be excluded in relation to choice of research site, relations in the field and the subsequent thematic focus and analysis.

Matching data and analytic strategies

A broad variety of analytic strategies are available to criminological researchers and it will be impossible to review all of them in this chapter. In the light of the variety of data sources that criminologists have available to them it is unsurprising that an array of analytic tools have been developed. Such data can include narrative and textual accounts. Narrative accounts are provided by the multiplicity of social actors that make up the criminal justice process, which include victims, witnesses, offenders and criminal justice professionals. Textual accounts can take the form of court transcripts, police files, charge sheets, witness statements, custody records and others. The range of potential tools to analyse such sources continues to expand, particularly with the advent of an increasing number of computer assisted packages (Fielding and Lee, 1998).

In recent years computer packages such as NUD*IST and Ethnograph have been developed to aid the analytical process. As Fielding and Lee (1998) point out, computer software packages have shifted from their traditional role as a tool for statistical analysis to a resource for the analysis of qualitative data and suggest that 'CAQDAS (Computer Assisted Qualitative Data Analysis Software) has ceased to be a novelty and has become a palpable presence' (1998: 1).

While only a minority of contemporary qualitative researchers could envisage not making use of a computer in the organization and management of their data there is a principled decision to be made in whether one elects to use an analytic software package. A major consideration will be the time required for data organization where software packages are deployed. As Wincup (1997: 69) reflects in relation to a small-scale project, 'Personally, I felt that a danger attached to dedicated software packages is that too much time can be spent sorting and retrieving data at the expense of writing'.

The scale of projects is a key consideration here with smaller projects in our experience not warranting use of a package. It is recommended that students familiarize themselves with what software packages have to contribute.

Triangulation

Qualitative researchers commonly favour a combination of analytic strategies. While Coffey and Atkinson acknowledge the value of such triangulation they press for avoidance of an over simplified understanding of the process. They suggest:

> We can use different analytic strategies in order to explore different facets of our data, explore different kinds of order in them, and construct different versions of the social world. That kind of variety does not imply that one can simply take the results from different analyses and stick them together like children's building blocks in order to create a single edifice. (1996: 14)

In other words while different methods can provide varying perspectives on our data, researchers need to think carefully about the linkages and interconnections between such output and make principled decisions on why they elect particular combinations of analytic strategy (Coffey and Atkinson, 1996). Once choices have been made it is important that the researcher continues to reflect critically on the appropriateness of the analytic strategy for the task in hand. Following what Coffey and Atkinson (1996: 6) refer to as a 'cyclical process' such reflexivity at the analytic stage will commonly identify a need for further data collection and analysis.

Devising strategies for data collection and management

As we are representing appropriate analysis of data as a journey rather than a single event we will now take the reader through the research process highlighting the analytic issues that need to be considered.

Considerations regarding analysis need to inform decisions relating to how the data are collected and any instruments (for example semi-structured interview schedules) that are deployed. Such decision-making will include whether to record or rely on handwritten accounts of research encounters. Given our commitment to providing practical advice it is important that we provide a brief discussion regarding the possible tools that can be used for data collection and storage. For some commentators organization of data forms an integral part of the analytic procedure, with others representing it as something of a preamble to the intellectual scholarship required for the development of theoretical understandings:

> For some authors, analysis refers primarily to the tasks of coding, indexing, sorting, retrieving, or otherwise manipulating data ... From such a perspective, the task of analysis can be conceived primarily in terms of data handling. Whether it is done by hand or by computer software, data analysis at this level is relatively independent of speculation and interpretation ... For others in the field, analysis refers primarily to the imaginative work of interpretation, and the more procedural, categorizing tasks are relegated to the preliminary work of ordering and sorting the data. (Coffey and Atkinson, 1996: 6)

Whichever position one adopts effective organization of data should enhance the researcher's capacity for data retrieval and manipulation, and the subsequent capacity to develop theoretical explanations.

Effective data handling needs to begin with careful attention to how the data will be collected. Increasingly researchers make use of CDs, audio tapes and digital tape recorders. Modern recording equipment is particularly compact and easy to transport, although we would recommend the routine carrying of back-up batteries and careful checking that the tape (or equivalent) and machine are working effectively before the interview. It is important not to lose time at the beginning of an interview having to check the tape and there can be few worse scenarios for the social researcher than to have achieved access for a particularly valuable interview only to be let down by non-functioning audio equipment. Recording equipment is typically used in recording focus groups. In our experience the smooth running of such groups is helped by having two facilitators, one of whom takes responsibility for monitoring that the tape is working as required, leaving the other to focus on facilitation of the discussion. Focus groups also require some attention to sound levels and background noise. Our recent experiences of conducting such groups with children as young as four pointed to the need to have an initial check that the equipment was picking up the children's voices.

Another option for recording data is the use of video equipment. The same rules need to apply regarding participant consent with particular attention to questions of confidentiality. Effective means are also available for the recording of telephone interviews although we would want to stress the importance of informing the interviewee that a recording is being made and gaining their consent. During a telephone interview it will not be evident to the respondent that a recording is being made and it is therefore particularly important that the researcher is explicit that they intend to record the interview. The respondent's wishes should be checked carefully. One of us (Noaks) recently conducted a telephone interview with a middle manager in the social care field. While they gave their consent to the interview being recorded and transcribed the sensitivity of the information led them to request that, even with assurances regarding confidentiality, the tape and transcript be destroyed after the research had been completed.

While the use of recording equipment is increasingly common, scenarios are encountered in criminological research where their use is not allowed or they are not deemed appropriate. In our experience their use is rarely allowed during prison-based interviews and the researcher will commonly have to rely on the more traditional method of note taking. Devoting attention to writing down what is said can detract from achieving a rapport with the interviewee and the researcher's observation of non-verbal cues. Our advice is that key elements are noted during the interview and a full account written up immediately after the interview is completed. There may also be research situations in which the researcher chooses not to use an audio tape. For example, tape recording of interviews has particular meaning for the police and those who have been arrested, linked to the Police and Criminal Evidence Act (1984) requirement that interviews with suspects are audio taped, transcribed and form part of the subsequent dossier of evidence. In that respect we have tended to avoid the use of such tapes in our own police interviews believing that it may suppress their willingness to provide honest accounts. Other respondents should also be provided with a clear and accurate account of how the recordings will be used, whether in relation to transcription of recordings or written accounts of interviews with the requirements of the Data Protection Act (see Chapter 3 for a fuller discussion of this issue).

Content analysis

Where documentary evidence is used as either a stand alone method, or an adjunct to other strategies, decisions will also need to be made on the analytic approach to be adopted. Content analysis is an approach commonly used in the analysis of documentary materials. While content analysis can involve a quantitative approach such as counting the number of times a particular word is used, a qualitative approach to content analysis involves exploring the documentary materials for cultural meanings and insights that the text can provide. May (2001: 191) defines the qualitative form of content analysis by drawing on the work of Ericson et al. (1991) highlighting their emphasis on 'the fluidity of the text and content in the interpretive understanding of culture'.

Wykes uses a content analysis approach in her book *News, Crime and Culture* (2001: 1) and describes crime news as 'the site of our national conscience and

TABLE 8.1   *Wykes' typology of intimate murders*

Name of murderer	Details of the murder
Sara Thornton	Convicted of murdering her husband. Initially served a life sentence but was released on her second appeal (1997) on grounds of diminished responsibility.
Joseph McGrail	Killed his female co-habitee and was given a two year suspended prison sentence. Also said to have been 'offered twelve months' psychiatric supervision to help overcome his feelings of remorse'.
John Tanner	Convicted of murdering his girlfriend and sentenced to life imprisonment.
Linda Calvey	Convicted of murdering her male partner for which she received a life sentence.
John Perry	Convicted of murdering his wife and sentenced to life imprisonment.
Pamela Sainsbury	Convicted of manslaughter of her husband on grounds of diminished responsibility.

moral codes'. She uses content analysis of output from the news media to trace representations of black communities in inner city Britain, youth in Britain, homelessness and interpersonal violence. In the latter case she provides a detailed review of intimate murders with an analysis of the newspaper cover-age of six cases involving as perpetrators the following: Sara Thornton, Joseph McGrail, John Tanner, John Perry, Linda Calvey and Pam Sainsbury (2001: 149). Table 8.1 provides a detailed synopsis of the circumstances of each case.

Wykes' research question was whether the journalistic accounts demon-strated that 'the press was acting ideologically in reproducing traditional gen-der power relations in accounts of intimate killing and to assess the implications of any such process' (2001: 149). Her detailed analysis led her to conclude that questions of gender were rendered invisible in the reporting of crime by male perpetrators while such questions were the focus of accounts regarding women. She concludes that:

> The sales pitch was that women were to blame for both their own and men's violence because they were deviating from conservative femininity. The articles analysed consis-tently linked both female violence and male violence to non-traditional femininity. The net effect was to promote marriage, monogamy, maternity and moderation as safe, nor-mal and responsible for women. In contrast, feminists, femmes fatale, foreigners and feck-less women drive men to badness and themselves to madness. (Wykes, 2001: 161)

In adopting such a strategy it is important that the approach is rigorous and methodical, often with attention to the frequency and regularity with which particular forms of content feature. May (2001: 191) points to value of com-puter assisted packages in this regard and also the accessibility of retrieval of newspaper accounts via the internet as a data source. Students undertaking research for dissertations will find the Internet to be a particularly valuable route for accessing data (see exercise 2 at the end of this chapter). However, as discussed in Chapter 7, the distinguishing feature of the qualitative form of content analysis is striving to go beyond mapping the profile of the document to achieve an interpretive understanding of meaning and impact.

Transcription

Having collected the data the next stage in the process is the issue of transcription. When recordings of interviews are made they will need to be transcribed. Researchers need to be aware that this is a costly procedure both in time and, where professional support is acquired, money. A one hour taped interview can take anything between six and ten hours to transcribe. This can be balanced against the fact that researchers transcribing their own work will have the opportunity to enhance their familiarity with the piece and to become steeped in the nuances of the interview. The transcription process offers the opportunity for reflection on the data and attention to emerging themes and should be seen as an integral part of the analytic process. Such opportunities for familiarization need to be balanced against the speed and efficiency of a professional typist for those research projects where funds exist for transcription. In such cases proof reading of data can facilitate reflection and an analytic focus. Whichever strategy is adopted, the time spent on familiarizing oneself with the data is invaluable, with one of the distinguishing attributes of qualitative analysis being the need for close reading and re-reading of data.

Where handwritten field notes or word-processed interview transcripts are used the same principles apply in relation to the importance of familiarization with the data. Such familiarity is essential for the analyst's subsequent decisions regarding coding of the data. As suggested elsewhere (see Chapter 5 on interviewing) handwritten notes should be attended to as soon as possible after the interview or period of fieldwork. Immediately revisiting them will allow for more graphic recall of those details which the researcher might not have been able to capture during the interview. As suggested above, the use of key words can facilitate this procedure allowing the researcher to focus on maintaining rapport with their interviewee. Adopting this approach will mean that familiarity with handwritten field notes is more likely to be an ongoing process. In contrast audio tapes may be stored up and more time allowed to lapse between the collection of the data and the full transcription, not losing sight of the time that will need to be devoted to such transcription.

Students, particularly those producing shorter (for example 10–12,000 word) dissertations, will need to think about the scope of their project and in some cases transcribe and analyse the most relevant part of an interview rather than the full piece. As others have acknowledged (Arksey and Knight, 1999: 141) transcripts vary in the level of detail that they include. There are issues, for example, about the extent to which the transcript should include grunts, groans, chuckles, 'um's, 'ah's and pauses. Such elements in the delivery of speech can be highly telling and their inclusion will communicate more to the reader about the attitude and state of mind of the interviewee. While resources may not run to extending this type of transcription to the full data set such an in-depth approach might be deployed with the more significant segments of an interview. Again it is important that the researcher consider carefully the reasons for their style of transcription and be explicit about their rationale for the format adopted.

The theoretical perspective that is adopted is significant here with some approaches, particularly ethnomethodology, requiring the highly detailed level of transcription described above. Examples of the application of an ethno-methodological approach to criminological studies include Bittner's (1967) classic study of the police role in peace keeping in an American urban setting and Watson (1990) on the elicitation of confessions in murder investigations. Hester and Eglin (1992: 134) explore both studies in some detail, for example they describe how:

> Watson's data consists of two videocassette recordings of police interrogations of murder suspects, Lewis Strawson and Stuart Riley, in a large North American city. Strawson is accused of having killed and dismembered a young woman and Riley is suspected of three murders. Both of them confess and Watson seeks to examine aspects of the 'methods' through which these outcomes are achieved interactionally.

Coding of data

Once the data collection process is underway the next task in the analytic procedure is coding. Coding entails bringing a measure of organization to the data and identifying conceptual categories. At this point the researcher will work with the data to produce categories in line with areas of thematic interest. Such activity is achieved by reviewing the data and attaching what have variously been referred to as tags, labels or memos. Such activity should not merely be seen as a mechanical process but as an opportunity for further reflection and thought on the part of the researcher regarding the messages that are emerging from the data. This is one of the ways in which qualitative analysis differs significantly from that deployed with quantitative data. In the case of quantitative data, the focus will be exclusively on quantification rather than ascribed meanings. While the qualitative researcher will be interested in the regularity with which particular events, emotions or feelings are reported (May, 2001: 164 points to the importance of the 'probability' of phenomena to the qualitative researcher in mapping their typicality) they will want to extend their analysis beyond this to consider meanings and understandings. Such analysis should begin early in the data collection phase allowing the opportunity to check out emerging findings as the collection of data proceeds. This reinforces our earlier point that delaying analysis until all the data are collected precludes the opportunity to explore and check out new and emergent research questions. This approach also facilitates the researcher keeping an open mind and flexibility in relation to their analytic focus.

Grounded theory

As described earlier in this chapter Glaser and Strauss (1967) represented grounded theory as an approach requiring from the researcher an alertness and reflexivity to the messages that emerge from the data. So while the researcher is recommended to give early thought to analysis, and in doing so to have reflected on the analytic codes they expect to deploy, they should also remain open to the categories that emerge from the data and which they had not anticipated discovering.

Coding forms an important part of the data analysis process. The stages of coding are delimited by Strauss (1987). Open coding opens up the enquiry, asks questions of the data and searches for answers. This initial and unrestricted coding leads on to axial coding whereby each category is analysed intensely and linkages between categories are explored in search of a core category. Finally, selective coding can take place around the core category guided by the coding paradigm. We set out below a reflective account from Wincup on the decision to adopt such an approach:

> Looking in detail at the texts written on the process of data analysis, my main concern was that some of them were too prescriptive (Miles and Huberman, 1994; Spradley, 1980) and I was wary about imposing a structure on my data that was not appropriate. The stages of open, axial and selective coding overcome this problem by allowing the researcher to use the data to think with. This was a two stage process: looking first at my data as a whole to highlight important themes which would form the basis of chapters and secondly, to focus on these themes in turn at look at them in a more detailed way. (1997: 69)

In similar vein Coffey and Atkinson's (1996: 32) approach is to distinguish a 'start list' of codes that pre-date the researcher's reading of the data and derive from reading of the literature and preliminary research questions and the 'bottom up' more grounded approach whereby codes are allowed to evolve from the content of the data.

Approaches to coding

The physical task of coding can either be undertaken manually or electronically. For those who favour working in hard copy the coloured marker pen is an ingenious invention. Such colour coding can also be applied to work on screen and the cut and paste facility in word processing packages used to support organization of the data.

The amount of data collected will influence the number of conceptual categories that the researcher will be working with. As the example below shows researchers can work to different levels of analytic complexity in the extent to which they seek to categorize and sub-categorize a segment of data. Those addressing large and intricate data sets will find packages such as NUD*IST particularly useful. Some segments of text will be particularly rich in data and as such are likely to produce several overlapping codes.

Such packages should be seen as tools to facilitate the researcher's analytic processes rather than a substitute for them. Coffey and Atkinson (1996: 12) caution against the danger of such packages stifling researcher's own analytic skills. They emphasize that such packages typically provide useful 'forms of coding of data' but that such procedures are not 'synonymous' with analysis.

Computer packages as an analytic resource

Several computer packages exist designed to facilitate the coding procedure. May (2001: 140) describes how packages such as NUD*IST and Ethnograph can be used to search for participants key words and to identify their frequency and the context in which they are used in the data. He counsels against allowing such computer packages to detract from the researcher's own familiarity with the data. What is not recommended is a situation where the data is carefully stored on the computer but not embedded in the thinking of the researcher. Dey (1993: 61) suggests 'the computer may be able to handle an enormous amount of data; but the analyst may not'.

As we suggested above, some qualitative researchers remain cautious about the time that needs to be invested in using CAQDAS while others reach an alternative view, 'The ability to interrogate data and revise conceptualizations through searching and retrieving categorized data promises to introduce a new flexibility and rigour into qualitative analysis' (Dey: 1993: 59).

Whatever approach is adopted the important factor to hold on to is that coding in itself does not constitute analysis. Pivotal to analysis are the linkages and theoretical connections that the researcher makes between the analytic categories. As Coffey and Atkinson (1996: 27) propose 'the important analytic work lies in establishing and thinking about such linkages, not in the mundane process of coding'. So while coding of qualitative data must allow for reflection and thoughtfulness, it is an incremental stage in the interpretative process facilitating the final goal of considering the relationships between the conceptual categories.

In this regard May (2001) points analysts to the Loflands' (Lofland and Lofland, 1984: 71) use of 'units' as an analytic tool. Units are described as 'a tool to use in scrutinising your data' and are said to 'emerge as the scale of organization increases' (May, 2001: 166). Their deployment is incremental with the use of linked units systematizing the approach to the data. Their use helps the analyst not to become overwhelmed by what can be large amounts of data. Linking of data can also be achieved electronically with the use of 'hypertext' (or 'hypermedia' link). These various approaches to identifying related meanings in the data is a vital stage in beginning interpretation.

We are persuaded by Coffey and Atkinson's argument that coding should be seen initially as a reductive process which facilitates manipulation of the data as a preamble to 'going beyond the data, thinking creatively with the data, asking the data questions, and generating theories and frameworks' (Coffey and Atkinson, 1996: 30). We provide an example below to show how a data extract can be coded and categorized and then deployed as part of the bigger task of interpretation. We would encourage novice researchers to practice coding their own data or to make use of the exercises provided at the end of this chapter.

The data presented were collected during a study of residential work with offenders (Wincup, 2002) and are extracts from two interviews with two female members of staff working in two different bail hostels for women.

Emma Wincup	What are your thoughts on mixed hostels?	
Residential worker 1	I guess I'm not opposed to them but I would say there has to be hostels for women only. I think one of the things we offer the women is that they come here and they've been given a breathing space. They know that this hostel is women only and you can have male visitors between 1pm and 6pm	*Need for a range of provision* *Haven* *Rules & regulations*

Emma Wincup	What are your thoughts on mixed hostels?	
Residential worker 2	I think I have reservations about the mixed hostels where there are a small number of women. I think that creates pressures. I can't see how the women who are in mixed hostels are going to be less vulnerable than the ones in here. In which case they can't offer the same kind of respite, which can be beneficial, from men who have been abusive. I think that sometimes we have women who haven't done well in a mixed hostel who come here and do much better and that says something.	*Needs of female offenders* *Haven* *Evidence of success*

Interpretation of data

Having interrogated the data and categorized it in line with the areas of thematic interest the researcher moves into the final stage in the analytic process, that of interpretation. At this point the focus will be on examining the data for embedded meanings and understandings that the researcher's meticulous indexing of the data will enable them to identify. It will sometimes be important for the researcher to allow themselves space from the data collection phase when tackling this interpretative stage. May (2001: 164) suggests this is particularly important when analysing data that derives from ethnographic work. Faced with a large volume of field notes and other forms of qualitative data the researcher will at times need to stand back from the field to effectively tackle the interpretation of their data. So while we have encouraged attention to analysis as an ongoing exercise we would recommend that the researcher allows sufficient time for a reflective focus on interpretation in the latter stages of research projects This, of course, does not preclude the researcher from returning to the field and sharing or checking out their interpretations with the research participants.

The act of writing in itself should be seen as central to the analytic process, a point made strongly by Coffey and Atkinson (1996: 109).

> Writing and representing is a vital way of thinking about one's data. Writing makes us think about data in new and different ways. Thinking about how to represent our data also forces us to think about the meanings and understandings, voices and experiences present in the data. As such, writing actually deepens our level of academic endeavour.

While we discuss writing as an analytic tool at a relatively late stage in this section that does not reflect the importance that we attach to it. In practice we would encourage all researchers to begin writing at an early stage and, as with analysis itself, to see writing as an ongoing process. While some of the earliest efforts at writing may well be discarded, such writings will provide important foundations for the academic enterprise.

It is in the final stages of the analytic process that the data can be used to develop theoretical frameworks and conceptual models that reflect and represent the research output. May (2001: 165) highlights the importance of triangulation of data sources at this stage. This approach will ensure that theoretical conceptualizations are grounded in data which has been compared and cross-checked across a variety of sources.

Concluding comments

This chapter has sought to take the reader through the stages of the analytic process, emphasizing throughout that attention to analysis should begin at the outset of the research project and be revisited throughout. Analysis should be reflexive but not rule bound. This does not however mean that it cannot be rigorous and systematic. Data collected is a precious resource and should be dealt with in an organized manner. On the other hand the researcher should avoid being daunted by what can sometimes seem a voluminous amount of data. We hope that the strategies we have shared will prevent feelings of being overwhelmed by one's data and put students on the road to concurring with Coffey and Atkinson's (1996) view that analysis should be both positive and rewarding.

Exercises

1 Draw up a short interview schedule (maximum time allowed for the interview is 15 minutes) that enables you to ask a fellow student about their fear of crime. Tape record the interview and transcribe a five minute section (you will be surprised how much data you can generate in five minutes). Read through the data and identify four analytic themes. Either mark up the data with coloured pens or colour code using a word-processing package. Be alert to how segments of data can be relevant to different analytic categories. If you have undertaken this exercise as part of a research class share your transcribed accounts with fellow students. Be alert to the different interpretations that individuals bring to the task.

2 Access the Internet and identify two newspaper accounts of either (a) reporting of a crime, (b) reporting of a trial, or (c) reporting of the passage of a possible new piece of legislation. Read the accounts carefully and identify common themes that you can take from them. Compare and contrast any differences in approach in the two accounts.

FURTHER READING

Bottoms, A. (2000) 'The relationship between theory and research in criminology' provides an informed discussion on the challenges of addressing the relationship between theory and research in criminology and the implications for data analysis.

- Coffey, A. and Atkinson, P. (1996) *Making Sense of Qualitative Data* offers an informative and focused account grounded in the authors' extensive experiences of analysing qualitative data.
- Dey, I. (1993) *Qualitative Data Analysis: A User-Friendly Guide for Social Scientists* provides an accessible introductory account.
- Fielding, N. and Lee, R. (1998) *Computer Analysis and Qualitative Research* is an instructive and reflective text on the increasing role played by computers in analysis of qualitative research.
- May, T. (2001) *Social Research: Issues, Methods and Process.* In this text the chapters on individual social research methods include a discussion of appropriate data analysis techniques.

Part III

Reflections on the Research Process: Two Criminological Case Studies

9

Researching Substance Use Among Young Homeless People[1]

Introduction

My first foray into qualitative research was as a doctoral student in the School of Social and Administrative Studies, Cardiff University. Now known as the Cardiff School of Social Sciences, this school has come to be associated with a particular style of qualitative research leading some sociologists to identify it as a 'Cardiff School of Ethnography' (Delamont and Atkinson, 2002). Its key characteristics have been explored elsewhere in detail (Delamont et al., 2001), and personally the most important aspects of this approach are that research should be fun, it should be conducted in a reflexive manner and that it should be accomplished in an open, exploratory way, thus allowing theories to be developed from careful analysis of rich and detailed data. Successful completion of my PhD, an ethnographic study of three bail hostels for women, owes a great deal to training in this approach.

My post-doctoral research career has not stayed true to this tradition. While I continue to conduct qualitative research it has been difficult to sustain a full commitment to the methodological approach in which I was trained. In part that has been personal choice as I have opted to pursue different types of research, for example, evaluative research, but equally it reflects the difficulties of securing research funding for ethnographic work and finding sufficient time to do it. Research is still fun, although equally it can lead to disquiet and discomfort as I have explored elsewhere (Wincup, 2001). Reflexivity continues to inform my approach and while the methodology section of the research report inevitably presents a sanitized account, it is possible to explore methodological issues in separate publications such as book chapters and journal articles. What is more difficult within the constraints of research timetables is to find sufficient time to conduct participant observation and explore the data collected in a meticulous way. Although this is frustrating I have been fortunate enough to secure funding to explore some of the issues I developed an interest in during my doctoral research, particularly issues relating to substance use and youth homelessness, and to continue to conduct qualitative research.

The principal aim of this chapter is to highlight a number of methodological issues encountered while conducting funded research on substance use among young homeless people by offering a personal reflexive account of the fieldwork experience. In July 2000, the Home Office invited calls for proposals for a research programme specifically focused on problem drug use among vulnerable groups. The programme had a total budget of up to £700,000 to be spent on studies lasting up to 18 months. There were two strands to the programme. The first comprised research studies examining groups of young people[2] vulnerable to problematic drug use[3], and the second involved estimating the number of problematic drug users in large urban centres with a high prevalence of drug use. In contrast to many studies funded by the Home Office that invite responses to tenders, which can offer only limited scope for research innovation (see Chapter 2), this research programme provided researchers with opportunities to set their own research questions, and suggests suitable methods for collecting data to answer them. Researchers were not given a totally free rein but the guidance offered outlined areas of interest rather than specifying a particular research design. Outline bids were invited, a shortlist drawn up and shortly afterwards we were invited to submit a more detailed bid. In collaboration with Rhianon Bayliss of Cardiff University, I was fortunate enough to secure funding under strand one of the programme for a study of problem substance use among young homeless people.[4] Other vulnerable groups included in the programme included young offenders, care leavers and sex workers. The study began in January 2001 and involved a blend of qualitative and quantitative techniques. We were joined by a researcher (Gemma Buckland) in March 2001.

Theoretical background to the research

Morgan (2000) propounds that it is widely contended that most Home Office funded criminological research is almost entirely atheoretical fact-gathering research, narrowly focused and designed to be policy-friendly. There are undoubtedly examples of research funded by the Home Office which can be aptly characterized in this way (see for example the analysis of the duties performed by police officers in a typical shift (PA Consulting 2001). However, as Morgan notes, this is not the whole story. It is possible to conduct theoretically interesting policy-related research and this is what I have always endeavoured to do.

In a chapter that sets out to explore the relationship between theory and research in criminology, Bottoms (2000) argues for a 'culture of openness' that encourages empirical researchers to be open to a range of theoretical insights and to create a synthesis that welds together theory and data. He suggests that rather than adopting wholesale a general social theory such as structuration theory, selective adoption of concepts can be used as a way of seeking to enrich the theoretical exploration of the topic being studied. In this instance selective adoption of the theoretical work on risk and youth transitions provided an agenda with which to enter the field. This influenced what is seen as problematic, what data are to be collected in relation to that problem, how they are categorized and how they are subsequently analysed.

There has been a rapid growth in recent years in social science research into risk and society (Lupton, 1999). Criminologists have begun to address issues as diverse as fear of crime (Girling et al., 2000) and the management of sex offenders (Kemshall and Maguire (2000) using this analytic concept. Risk is now perceived as concerned with anxiety-provoking danger and thus viewed negatively. This contrasts sharply with the seventeenth century where risk was equated with probability (Douglas, 1990). Social scientists have been influential in highlighting the contested nature of the concept of risk, and have argued that in practice risk offers many attractions to individuals by providing opportunities for excitement, challenge and personal fulfilment. This is explored by Ettorre (1992) in her book on women and substance use. She suggests it is important to ask questions such as whether women experience their substance use[5] as pleasurable and whether or not the use of substances can contribute to women's sense of well-being.

Since the 1950s epidemiologists have identified a range of risks and harmful consequences associated with different forms of substance use. Smoking, drug use and alcohol consumption have come to be regarded as forms of risky behaviours. Traditionally such behaviours were analysed in terms of individual psychology, with individuals perceived as rational actors who could be persuaded to make alternative decisions if convinced of the benefits of adopting less risky behaviours. However, despite increasing health promotion efforts large numbers of young people continue to engage in these behaviours. To understand why we need to explore the social and cultural context that shapes and sustains such behaviours. In the post-Second World War period, drug use was typically associated with atypical sub-cultural groups (South, 2002). More recently researchers have suggested that there is widespread drug use among very large numbers of ordinary, conventional young people. The British Crime Survey (Ramsay et al., 2001) found that approximately half of young people aged 16–24 had tried at least one illegal drug. Coffield and Gofton (1994) go as far as to suggest that drug taking is part and parcel of the process of growing up in contemporary Britain, and is one of a number of ordinary, unremarkable activities. Drug use by young people relates to a new social order in which identity is formed through consumption. Other researchers have also emphasized the normalization of drug use in young people's lives, and highlight the availability of drugs, high levels of drug experimentation, and point to how 'drugwise' young people are (Measham et al., 1994; Parker et al., 1998). There is some evidence to support this view but it is important to stress that for most young people drug use is uncommon or short lived (Ramsay et al., 2001). For these reasons, the normalization thesis has been strongly criticized (see for example Shiner and Newburn, 1999). Since drug experimentation and recreational drug use is so widespread it is not possible to identify groups who are particularly at risk of using drugs in this way. However, it is possible to explore the characteristics of young people who go on to become problem drug users, and to consider the peculiarities of their social and cultural milieu that shapes and sustains such behaviours.

A growing body of research has sought to identify the risk factors associated with problem drug use, and this has included some analysis of social, as well as individual, factors. A useful definition of a risk factor is offered by Clayton (1992). He defines it as an individual attribute, individual characteristic, situational condition, or environmental context that increases the probability of drug use or abuse or a transition in the level of involvement with drugs. Conversely a protective factor is something similar which inhibits, reduces, or buffers drug use. Retrospective studies of substance users and prospective, longitudinal studies of young people have been utilized to identify risk and protective factors related to substance use. Risk factors can relate to the family (for example, parental or sibling drug use, family disruption, poor attachment or communication with parents and child abuse); school (for example, poor education performance, truancy and exclusion); involvement in crime and other conduct disorders such as truancy; mental disorder; social deprivation, and young age of onset (Lloyd, 1998). Lloyd suggests that one key feature of the risk literature is its interconnectedness and thus risk factors are best viewed as a 'web of causation' (Lloyd, 1998: 217). On the basis of research findings it is possible to identify high risk or vulnerable groups such as homeless people, and this has led to an increasing practice focus on prevention and early intervention work with such groups (see for example, Health Advisory Service, 2001). While it is useful to target such groups it is important to be mindful of the fine line between targeting and labelling, and it should not be assumed that vulnerability always implies drug use (Dale-Perera, 1998).

The literature on youth transitions was also pertinent to our interests in youth homelessness. This term is used frequently to refer to empirically and policy-oriented studies of the school-to-work transition which came to dominate youth sociology in the 1980s (MacDonald et al., 2001). The focus of these studies has been on social problems such as youth unemployment and they have explored the changing structural position of young people. More recently youth sociology has enjoyed a revival of theoretically-driven, ethnographic studies of youth sub-cultural style and resistance, reinvigorating a tradition of youth sociology that was dominant in the 1970s. It is possible to link these two strands of work, as others have done (see for example MacDonald et al., 2001), and to look at transitions in a broader way and include transitions to independent living

Given the overall focus on homelessness our research was concerned with social exclusion and its impact on the lives of the young people we met, yet at the same time we wanted to move away from overly deterministic accounts which fail to consider the significance of individual agency. The use of qualitative methods was particularly suited to this theoretical approach.

Research questions and design

Learning more about the substance use of young homeless people is an important area of concern, pragmatically in terms of developing effective prevention and treatment policy which addresses their needs, and sociologically in terms of studying a vulnerable population and the ways in which they may manage this vulnerability through substance use. The overall aim of the research was to provide a detailed account of substance use among young homeless people that could be used to inform future prevention and treatment activity. This was then broken down into a number of objectives:

1 to map out patterns of substance use among young homeless people;
2 to analyse their involvement in risky behaviours which impact on health;
3 to explore the backgrounds of young homeless people and in particular to highlight other risk factors which make them vulnerable to problem substance use; and
4 to examine young homeless people's access to drugs information, drug services and health services, to consider actual and potential barriers and suggest ways of overcoming them.

The research involved a range of research methods leading to the collection of qualitative and quantitative data. Over an 18-month period beginning in January 2001, data were gathered in four case study areas in England and Wales: Cardiff, Brighton and Hove, Canterbury and Birmingham. These areas are not claimed to be representative of all cities in England and Wales but were selected to incorporate a broad cross-section in terms of size and known homelessness and drug problems. We deliberately avoided focusing on London because as other researchers have noted (Fitzpatrick and Klinker, 2000) it is atypical in many respects because of its high levels of homelessness compared to other cities and its wide range of service provision for homeless people. The main methods used were interviews with young homeless people and professionals who work with them, and ethnographic observation.

Interviews

Interviews were conducted with 160 young people aged 25 and under, divided equally across the four case studies. It is difficult to define the characteristics of a population such as the young homeless people who may be hidden, and thus difficult to construct a sample that would reflect the wider young homeless population. Consequently the sample was not recruited in a statistically random way but opportunistically in order to gain access to different experiences of homelessness, for example, rough sleeping, living in hostels and staying with friends on a temporary basis, and to explore the different experiences of young people of different ages, genders and ethnic origins. Young people were contacted through organizations, both in the voluntary and statutory sector that provide services for the young people. We deliberately avoided drug and alcohol services as a route for securing interviews with young people to avoid skewing the data collected on patterns of substance use.

The process of negotiating access to homelessness agencies began with an initial letter, followed by a telephone call and then a face-to-face meeting with at least one member of the research team. None of the agencies refused to participate by explicitly saying no, but other strategies were used to make it difficult, if not impossible, to gain access. For instance, one agency requested that we sought approval through a local social services department ethics committee. The amount of work this would entail to secure only a handful of interviews and the likelihood that this process would be protracted was a considerable barrier and hence we decided to approach other agencies in the area instead. We successfully negotiated access to 28 agencies. Other studies have recognized that enthusiastic and committed workers can play a key role as gatekeepers (Goode, 2000). For the most part this was our experience. All the research respondents were recruited via gatekeepers hence the relationship between the research team and the gatekeepers became a key aspect of the research. We were fortunate that the vast majority of them were supportive of our task. Gatekeepers have a clear responsibility to protect respondents from exploitation by unscrupulous researchers, or from direct or indirect harm, and in negotiating access we carefully explained the research process. This was repeated to all respondents so they were able to give informed consent.

The interviews investigated a wide range of issues and used a schedule that included both closed and open-ended questions. The interview was divided into seven sections covering personal characteristics, experiences of homelessness, health issues (general health, health care, mental health), substance use (tobacco, alcohol and drugs), risky behaviours (for example, injecting drugs) experiences of crime and victimization, and finally a self-assessment of their current needs. While some of the closed questions were essential in order to obtain data on patterns of drug use, as qualitative researchers we were dissatisfied with some of the limitations of these question types. For example, we included in the interview schedule the Drug Attitudes Scale (DAS) devised by Howard Parker and his colleagues (Parker et al., 1998). This consists of 13 statements and interviewees were asked to indicate their level of agreement on a Likert-type scale that ranged from 'agree strongly' to 'disagree strongly'. This was included as a source of data in its own right but also as a 'warm-up' question before we moved on to the more sensitive questions about the interviewee's own use of drugs. During the pilot we became aware that we were potentially missing out on a mass of data by only recording their level of agreement with the question, and consequently began to note the qualitative comments made by the young people when answering the questions. Frequently they would think out loud or talk through with us why they had selected the choice they had. This provided us with some rich data on their attitudes towards different types of drugs and helped to explain some of the apparent contradictions in their attitudes.

Interviews were selected over self-completion questionnaires to overcome problems such as low levels of literacy. There were other advantages too. Interviews provide an opportunity to probe beyond the answers given and to seek elaboration and clarification. They allow the young person to answer more on their own terms and raise issues pertinent to their lives which may have been overlooked when designing the interview schedule. This is especially important for previously neglected areas of research and more so when the interviewee lives a very different lifestyle to the researcher.

The interviews took place in a variety of settings, mainly hostels and day centres, and lasted between one and two-and-a-half hours. This substantial variation can be explained in a number of ways, for example, the extent the young person was willing to open up to the interviewer but predominantly it relates to the extent that the young person had been involved in substance use, whether he or she had been in contact with substance use services, and whether he or she felt they needed help or treatment. These settings were often noisy and bustling places and as a result tape-recording was ruled out. Instead detailed notes were taken and all three members of the research team became adept at recording rich and detailed data offered by our interviews. This also had the advantage that tapes did not have to be transcribed, an extremely time-consuming task. The quantitative data were coded and put into SPSS for Windows. There was insufficient time to use one of the dedicated software packages designed to assist with the management of qualitative data and the data were sorted manually under key analytic themes.

The majority of respondents I interviewed appeared to find it a comfortable rather than daunting experience. They visibly relaxed after a few moments and conversation usually flowed in response to the questions asked. Having carefully constructed the interview schedule to avoid asking sensitive questions about drug use at the outset I was often surprised at the rapidity at which intimate details of the young people's lives were disclosed. Several young people commented that they valued the opportunity to talk and be heard. It is of course important to remember that the young people selected themselves into the research process and only those who were comfortable being interviewed were likely to volunteer.

In addition, 22 semi-structured interviews were conducted with professionals who work with young homeless people. The sample was selected to comprise professionals working in a variety of settings in both managerial and 'hands on' practitioner roles. The following types of workers were included: project workers in drop-in housing advice and young people advice centres, hostel staff, outreach workers, day centre staff, supported housing workers, and nurses (including one community psychiatric nurse) who work with homeless people. The interview schedule was divided into four sections, commencing with questions about their personal characteristics, current post and previous work experience. The following three sections covered their general experiences of working with young homeless people, managing substance use issues and dealing with health problems.

Ethnographic observation

The use of ethnographic observation to explore homelessness has a long history, dating back to the work of the Chicago School. For example, Anderson's (1923) work developed an exhaustive and sensitive account of the complexities and intricacies of hobo life. This was just one of more than 150 studies published about Skid Row, 'a real yet symbolic location that came to epitomize marginality, deviance and social exclusion' (Wardhaugh, 2000: 316). These studies relied solely on the use of ethnographic observation as a source of data. As a result the published findings constitute the product of several years of academic endeavour. The research discussed here had to be completed within 18 months, ruling out the use of ethnographic observation alone. In any case this method was not appropriate on its own to answer all our research questions. Nonetheless ethnographic observation did have a small role to play within the project. We spent some time in settings used by young homeless people, particularly day centres and hostels. The observation took many forms and included watching TV with hostel residents, chatting to Big Issue vendors as they came in and out of the office and observing activities in a day centre. Spending time with the homeless people allowed informal interviews and group discussions to be conducted that generated data in their own right, as well as serving to establish rapport with the young people. The more sensitive or threatening the topic under examination the more difficult sampling is likely to be because potential participants have a greater need to hide their involvement. Given the sensitive nature of illegal drug use, it was important to try to build up rapport in order to obtain rich and detailed data through interviews.

Research issues

In common with all qualitative research projects, numerous research issues arose during the 18 months of the study. I have selected three here: the impact of the political context on the research, managing risk and danger and the use of incentive payments to research participants. All three issues pick up on themes explored elsewhere in the book in Chapters 2, 6 and 3 respectively.

Understanding the political context

Immediately prior to the commencement of the research the links between drug use and homelessness received unprecedented media and political attention. In December 1999 Ruth Wyner and John Brock were sentenced to custody for five and four years respectively for failing to take 'every reasonable step' (according to Judge Haworth) to prevent the supply of heroin within an open access day centre, the Wintercomfort project, for the homeless in Cambridge. They were imprisoned for 'knowingly permitting the use of heroin on the premises' in contravention to Section 8 of the 1971 Misuse of Drugs Act. They appealed and their convictions were not quashed but their sentences were reduced. The implications of the case were far reaching. Homelessness agencies could no longer turn a blind eye to drug use and felt the need to take decisive action but equally it was problematic to assume that those working with the homeless in day centres or hostels could have control over behaviours which are inevitably performed covertly. Faced with such dilemmas there have been moves taken to exclude drug users (Buckland et al., 2002).

High levels of media and political attention on homelessness continued throughout the project, typically focused on rough sleepers rather than other forms of homelessness. A report by the Social Exclusion Unit published in 1998 (Social Exclusion Unit, 1998) gave what purported to be 'a clear picture of the extent of the rough sleeping problem and what was causing it' (Rough Sleepers Unit, 2000: 4). A ministerial committee was set up and in April 1999 the Rough Sleepers Unit (RSU) was established led by Louise Casey. It set a target of reducing the number of people sleeping rough by at least two thirds by 2002, and launched a strategy entitled *Coming in from the Cold* which detailed plans to meet this target. In December 2001 it was announced that the government had already met this target. However, this achievement has not gone unchallenged. Some homelessness organizations such as Crisis expressed concern about whether resources to support rough sleepers would continue in the long term, and highlighted the need to work with the 'hidden homeless'[6] (Perkins, 2001). More controversially other homelessness agencies accused the RSU of fixing its twice-yearly count of the street homeless population (Branigan, 2001). Allegations that the RSU falsified results, moved rough sleepers off the streets for a single night, arrested some and threatened others with arrest if they refused to go into hostels, were made. These allegations were described by Louise Casey as 'unfounded' and made by people with 'an axe to grind' (Branigan, 2001).

The highly publicized clashes between the RSU and homelessness organizations in winter 2001 emulated quarrels from the previous year. On November 6 2000 the Government launched 'Change a Life', a scheme led by the Rough Sleepers Unit (RSU) that aimed to promote alternatives to giving to people begging on the streets. The Government's pre-Christmas £250,000 national advertising campaign asked the public to give time, gifts in kind such as blankets or clothes and money to homelessness charities taking part. Louise Casey, the homelessness 'Tsar', argued that giving money to beggars was misplaced goodwill. One of the driving principles behind the campaign was that homeless people may spend donations from the public on illegal drugs or alcohol. The controversial nature of the campaign was heightened when it was announced that Government funding could be withdrawn from charities that refused to back the RSU campaign. The campaign received a great deal of media attention and was represented (the RSU suggested it has been misrepresented) as an anti-begging campaign. It was widely perceived as contributing little to preventing begging or the underlying problems of which it is a symptom. Its critics also argued that it was simplistic and could stigmatize further an already vulnerable and socially excluded group.

The political context impacted on the research in a number of ways. For the most part it was advantageous. Staff in homelessness agencies were generally supportive of attempts to inject more resources into work with homeless people but were highly critical of some aspects of recent policies. As a result they welcomed input from academics who could produce research evidence to add to their professional experiences of the lived realities of working with young homeless people, and hoped that this work would be fed back into the policy-making process. In particular, virtually all our interviewees who worked with homeless people talked about the difficulties of working with drug users following the Wintercomfort case. However, the heightened political attention had disadvantages too. For instance in Brighton and Hove, where there had been a number of new initiatives established, there was a feeling among some agencies that they were over-researched and thus they were less enthusiastic than they might have been about the research. When we explored this further we realized that agencies were confusing research with other forms of information gathering such as consultations with service users, and these were part of a process of bidding for additional resources.

Given the difficult political context we encountered surprisingly few problems at the publication stage of the research. The draft report was sent out to two academics for review, and was widely circulated for comment within the Home Office Drug and Alcohol Unit. It was also sent to policy-makers in other government departments. We responded to the suggestions made as far as we felt able and the report was published approximately just over six months after the date we had first submitted our draft. In this instance, the political context speeded up rather than delayed the publication of the report. An important conference held in February 2003 on young people and drug use provided the ideal opportunity for the Home Office to announce the publication of the report (Wincup, et al., 2003), and this served as a deadline that had to be adhered to.

Managing risk and danger

As Lee-Treweek and Linkogle (2000b) note the nature of qualitative inquiry means that researchers constantly have to deal with the unexpected, and all too often this includes coping with the presence of danger or risk. When conducting criminological research this risk is heightened. Danger can refer to physical, emotional, ethical and professional danger, and Lee-Treweek and Linkogle suggest that this is an ideal-type scheme because it simplifies and separates out experiences of serious danger. It is vital to appreciate the interconnectedness between the different forms of danger. All are relevant to the study being discussed here but the focus in this section is on physical danger. Physical danger has featured in research accounts in criminology since the work of the Chicago School. Such researchers set themselves the task of enduring physical danger for long periods of time. Contemporary ethnographic work on crime and deviance mirrors this (see Chapter 6).

As researchers we find ourselves doing things we would not normally dream of doing in the name of research. As Wardhaugh (2000: 324) describes 'I cannot think of any circumstances in which I would agree to wander through the city with a group of young men that I had only just met'. I found myself talking to people that, if I am honest, I would normally avoid. When researching young homeless people I found myself anxious and alone in unfamiliar settings such as hostels and day centres. Although I have conducted research in prisons and bail hostels previously and have interviewed offenders convicted of very serious offences, I found hostels for the homeless and day centres to be more risky places in some respects. This is because sometimes little is known about the service users and security measures are often minimal. In contrast, criminal justice agencies conduct detailed risk assessments on offenders and put in place a range of measures to manage potential risk. Day centres for homeless people are largely open access, although sometimes people are excluded for unacceptable behaviour. In hostels for the homeless more is known about the potential risks posed by residents, and admissions policies may exclude working with particularly risky groups. Often a lack of resources imposes constraints on adherence to safety procedures. For instance, some hostels had minimal staff cover, particularly out of office hours. Fortunately, serious incidents are rare, but the murder of a day centre user by another shortly after we had completed our interviews then focused our attention on the possible risks involved. Being known as 'people asking questions about drugs' also had the potential to create problems. We were fortunate that there was only one incident at a day centre which involved some drug dealers becoming suspicious of our motives. This was quickly resolved by the other day centre users who had been interviewed who reassured them that we were not the police and were not gathering intelligence. Situations such as these are potentially explosive and had the problem not been resolved our only alternative would have been to cease conducting interviews in that day centre. Research does not have to be pursued at all costs!

For researchers choosing interviews as their preferred method there is always a difficult choice to be made between ensuring that the discussion cannot be overheard (and hence looking for a quiet and private place to talk) and guaranteeing personal safety. We conducted interviews where we could: in staff offices, in resident lounges, in quiet corners of day centres and so forth. Most of the agencies were desperately short of space and we simply had to use whatever space was available. Practical constraints sometimes overrode safety concerns. On one occasion I found myself interviewing a young man in his bedsit within a hostel because there was no other space available. Once I finished the interview I discovered that the hostel worker on duty had left. While I did not feel particularly unsafe during the interview (although I would have done had I known I was alone in the building) the situation was not ideal and it highlights the need for greater attention to be paid to managing risk and danger when designing research projects.

The use of incentives

The use of payments is frequently seen as essential to successful recruitment of participants in research studies on drug use. For this project a sum of £10 in cash was given to participants once the interview had ended. Non-pecuniary incentives such as vouchers are sometimes suggested for research purposes. However, when determining what to use, a common consideration is the convertibility of such incentives to cash. This payment method does little more than camouflage a cash payment that has to be increased because of the way that vouchers may be discounted if exchanged for cash, thus increasing study costs and perhaps sending out an implicit message to the interviewee that they cannot be trusted. There is of course a risk that payments made may be used to procure drugs as there is when state benefits are paid to drug users. However, payments may equally be used to pay for food, rent or clothing according to the needs of the respondent. Such moral judgements should not influence a decision that in essence concerns the payment of a suitable fee for a service, in other words, the provision of a drug users' knowledge. Using cash minimizes the study costs and maximizes the chance of fulfilling study objectives.

While the use of incentives is widespread in research on drug use (see for example, Edmunds et al., 1999; McKeganey and Barnard, 1996; Turnbull et al. 2000) and this creates its own problems about creating a culture of expectation (McKeganey, 2001), there are relatively few published pieces of work on the matter. A recent exception is a paper published in *Addiction* which presents the results of a study examining why injecting drug users (IDUs) are motivated to participate in research (Fry and Dwyer, 2001). They concluded that IDUs motivations for research participation are often multi-dimensional, rarely to do with economic gain alone, and not necessarily defined by direct benefits or gains to themselves. While economic gain was reported as one of the main reasons for participation (46% of respondents), the study found that the reasons given were frequently consistent with the themes of citizenship (for example to provide information, to help find solutions to drug problems), altruism (perceived as helping), personal satisfaction (for example curiosity, interest) and drug-user activism (for example to improve services). The authors argued that many respondents were cognisant of their role as research stakeholders, their status as 'experts', and the value they could add to drug policy processes through participation.

In the same edition of the journal, *Addiction*, the appropriateness of paying research participants is explored in the editorial. In this McKeganey (2001) argues that there is a tendency for researchers to worry that by paying respondents the risk is increased that they may present an account that the researcher may want to hear, and thus reduce the quality of the information obtained. Dismissing this argument for not using incentive payments, McKeganey devotes the remainder of the article to examining related ethical issues. He notes that ethical committees hone in on the issue of payment and attempt to decide whether the level of payment is appropriate. There is a danger that offering large sums of money to participants might lead them to agree to participate even though they would personally prefer to avoid involvement. In Australia, the National Health and Medical Research Council's statement of ethical conduct declares that where the financial incentive offered is sufficient to render consent involuntary this is deemed to constitute a breach of ethics (Fry and Dwyer, 2001). While this guards against the inappropriate use of large incentives to secure participation at all costs, the difficulty for members of ethics committees is judging when a payment constitutes an unfair incentive.

We were fortunate that the Home Office Drug and Alcohol Research Unit were willing to provide funding for incentive payments. In fact we had not included this in our initial bid, fearing that it might jeopardize our chances of being funded and were pleased when the contract manager at the time suggested we include an additional £1,600 in our costings for incentive payments. Other funders have been more sceptical about such payments. The Three Cities Project, which explored youth homelessness, lawbreaking and criminalization in Manchester, Birmingham and Stoke-on Trent, also involved making payments to interviewees (Wardhaugh, 2000). The application to the Economic and Social research Council (ESRC) included £1,000 in this respect that was rejected on the grounds of lack of precedent even though one member of the research team had made such payments in a study funded by the ESRC. In a chapter reflecting the methodological issues raised by this research, Wardhaugh (2000) states that the research team had a strong political and ethical belief that socially and economically vulnerable participants should be paid for their time. She also recognizes the criticism that they were 'buying' people's stories and counters this by pointing out that they were able to ensure willing participation on the part of potential interviewees before the question of money was raised. She argues that paying homeless people for their time helped to reverse the more usual emphasis on the researcher entering the world of the researched by bringing them a little way into 'our' world with its emphasis on the dignity of employment and economic reward for labour. We might add to this that the payment serves more as a 'thank you' for their time, knowledge and experience rather than an incentive, although undoubtedly it fulfils both objectives.

Offering payment to research participants can produce a host of practical problems too. Risk of theft is the obvious one. The interviews we conducted were lengthy and only a small number could be conducted in one day, therefore there was no need for us to carry around large sums of money. We also introduced a system of receipts, largely to meet the needs of our university finance office, and this served as a record of who had received payment thus avoiding potential disputes. Where possible we ensured that the money was handed over in the presence of staff. Additionally at our initial meetings with homelessness agencies the issue of payment to interviewees was explored. Only one day centre did not allow us to pay respondents in cash and suggested instead that we pre-paid for meals for interviewees[7]. This was in response to a previous research project where she felt some of her clients were willing to create fictional accounts in order to seek payment to purchase drugs. We did not have rigid criteria, apart from being aged 25 or under (and this was checked with staff in homelessness agencies), and this mitigated against possible problems because we had to exclude very few individuals. The only group that was excluded were those who were not sufficiently fluent in English. If the young people obviously appeared to be under the influence of alcohol or drugs we would not interview them at that point but agreed to talk to them at a later date. This was rarely the case and a more common experience was attempting to interview young people suffering from withdrawal symptoms. To cope with this we devised a strategy whereby we prioritized the most important questions to ask and so that the interview could be completed as quickly as possible.

Other researchers have reported more difficulties than we experienced. Wardhaugh (2000) describes how she was approached by two drunk and abusive men aggressively demanding to be interviewed for payment. She was able to defuse the situation by offering cigarettes and a small amount of money to the men and comments that while 'payments to interviewees undoubtedly eased the making of contacts on the streets, but at the same time money proved to be a potentially explosive ingredient when introduced from outside into street homeless culture' (Wardhaugh, 2000: 324).

Concluding comments

In this chapter I have traced my experiences of designing, obtaining funding for, and carrying out one example of a quantitative and qualitative criminological study. In so doing I hope I have portrayed that conducting research is far less straightforward than typically portrayed in research methods texts or the heroic confessional tales of researchers. Whatever the research project, and irrespective of how meticulously it has been designed and carried out, numerous methodological dilemmas appear and are often unresolved. It is never possibl to anticipate all possible problems but time spent thinking through possible dilemmas and how you might resolve them can be highly productive.

Exercises

1   What are the arguments for and against the use of incentive payments in qualitative research studies?
2   What can researchers do to minimize the risks they face when conducting criminological research? You might find it useful to look at the Social Research Association's Code of Practice for the Safety of Social Researchers: www.the-sra.org.uk

FURTHER READING

The literature on youth homelessness is plentiful but there are few recent reflexive accounts of conducting research with this group. The following is one of the few examples:

• Julia Wardhaugh's chapter in R. King and E. Wincup (eds) (2000) *Doing Research on Crime and Justice.*

However, much can be gleaned about qualitative research from reading research monographs based on classic ethnographic studies. Readers are directed to:

• Elliot Liebow's (1993) text entitled *Tell Them Who I Am: The Lives of Homeless Women* and
• Nels Anderson's (1923) research monograph, *The Hobo: The Sociology of the Homeless Man.*

Notes

1   This research was conducted in conjunction with Rhianon Bayliss (Cardiff University) and Gemma Buckland (University of Kent).
2   Researchers were allowed to specify the age ranges of the young people who would be included in the study although it was generally noted that the Government's Drug Strategy uses the term 'young people' to refer to those individuals aged up to 25 years.
3   The Advisory Council on the Misuse of Drugs' (1988) definition was adopted which defined a problem drug user as: any person who experiences social, psychological,

physical or legal problems related to intoxication and/or regular excessive consumption and/or dependence as a consequence of his/her own use of drugs or other chemical substances; and anyone whose drug misuse involves, or may lead to, the sharing of injecting equipment.

4   Substance use is defined as the use of alcohol, illegal drugs and tobacco, and the illicit use of prescribed medication, over-the-counter remedies and solvents. Young people in this context refers to those aged 25 or under. Homelessness was under-stood as a continuum, varying from 'rooflessness' or sleeping rough, to living in bed and breakfast accommodation and hostels, to an inability to leave unsatisfactory housing conditions.

5   As well as the substances included in Note 4, Ettorre also includes smoking and food dependence.

6   This term refers to homeless people who are not accessing homelessness services but are still living in unsuitable accommodation such as sleeping on friends' floors or staying in bed and breakfast accommodation.

7   While this was a satisfactory compromise we did not interview young people at this day centre as we discovered that young homeless people were more likely to access a dedicated young people's centre in the same city.

10

Researching Private Policing

Introduction

This chapter provides a case study of the use of qualitative research methods to explore the activities of a private security group working in a residential community. It will review the methods used to investigate private policing as an emerging but under researched phenomenon. It offers an account of doing criminological research, intended to inform the reader through problematizing the research task. The research, which was my doctoral project, deployed a combination of qualitative and quantitative methods, including a neighbourhood survey, interviews with public police personnel and ethnographic observation within a private security firm. The chapter will focus on issues of access, the role of the informants who acted as a key source of data for this study, related ethical dilemmas in using informants and adopting covert roles, and data analysis.

Background to the research project

Few research studies have focused on the occupational culture of private policing. In contrast, considerable research attention has been paid to the culture of public policing, with much of the work of a qualitative, especially ethnographic, nature and including attention to ethical considerations (Holdaway, 1983; Norris, 1993). The rationale for this project was that the increasing prominence of private police on the criminal justice stage required a similar focus on their role and the general impact of this form of privatization of social control. Johnston (1992) pointed to the need for empirical studies to consider the experiences of residents in areas where policing is 'shared' by public and private bodies.

Establishing strategies to research private policing

In researching the role of private police in a residential community a multi-method strategy was adopted combining qualitative and quantitative methods. The research design involved a methodological triangulation of different interpretative methods and strategies intended to diversify the routes by which data were gathered and maximize the cross-checking of interpretations. This strategy was not adopted in the belief that combining methods will necessarily enhance the validity of data but rather as Maynard and Purvis (1994: 4) propose 'that the differences generated from different research techniques are likely to be as illuminating as the similarities'.

Fieldwork was undertaken with a range of interconnected groups including the private security company (ethnographic observation and interviews); residents in the area who were members of the scheme and those who had elected not to join (ethnographic observation, survey and interviews); and public police managers responsible for strategic decision-making in the locality (interviews and ethnographic observation). As well as the research strategies indicated above, the research drew on informants' accounts and analysis of documentation produced by the private security group and other community groups. Two key informants who were not part of the private security group but provided important information about the company were an important data source. Linked to this some of the challenges and ethical dilemmas encountered in working with informants will be discussed below.

The aim of the research was to explore the perspective and culture of the private guards in providing a policing function to the community. Alongside this, attention was given to how their input was received and evaluated by both their customers and those community members outside the scheme. This included the views of those with legal responsibility for policing the community, and one of the Assistant Chief Constables for the force area and the divisional commander were interviewed.

The security company

The research was undertaken with a security company that at the outset of the research in 1996 had been operating in 'Merryville' for five years. The locality serviced by the private security firm consisted of a mixture of public and private housing, mostly built since the early 1980s, on the outer perimeter of a large city in Southern Britain. The estate constituted a large and expanding development with over 4,300 homes and a population approaching 12,000. The layout of the neighbourhood was such that the two types of accommodation were clearly physically demarcated with the private developments built around the perimeter of the public housing. Although there was only the width of a road between the public and private parts of the estate this main thoroughfare provided a clear boundary line separating the two elements. Until the summer of 1997 the private guards worked exclusively in the private sector but at the request of some public housing residents they extended their services into their area. The company consisted of a director (who had managed the company for the past five years) and five security guards. The director was a previous employee of the company with an employment background in the military. Foot and vehicle patrols were provided between 11 pm and 6 am and an on-call service was available to subscribers at other times of the day. Those residents who chose to join the scheme contributed a weekly charge of £2, with pensioners charged £1. This was collected on a weekly basis by the company director or one of the guards. The area had received local and national media attention regarding its crime problems. This drew on the fact that the local crime audit, undertaken by the city council as a requirement of the 1998 Crime and Disorder Act, identified the area as having the highest rate of burglary of dwellings per head of population. Additionally police beat figures for the city placed the area in the highest bracket for incidents of crime per head of population. The area had also experienced spasmodic periods of violent disorder in the form of riots.

The theoretical background

The theoretical framework underpinning the research was eclectic but drew significantly on a symbolic interactionist approach. The starting point for the research was the ethnographic observation with the private security company. The focus of the observations was the organization of private policing and the value systems and beliefs which underpinned how private guards performed their role. Knowledge derived from that experience informed the survey with residents in the community and subsequent interviews with police managers. The ordering of the research process was important, with the ethnography preceding the survey and analysis of the survey findings preceding the formal interviews with police managers. The research strategy was deliberately cumulative, with the intention of developing social theory from observations of everyday life (Glaser and Strauss, 1967). In developing the research strategy I sought to follow May's perspective that:

As researchers, we should seek to render the attachment between theory and data as close as possible (unlike grand theory which is stated at such a general level we could not possibly match data to theory). Instead of descending upon the social world armed with a body of theoretical propositions about how and why social relations exist and work as they do, we should first observe those relations, collect data on them, and then proceed to generate our theoretical propositions. (May, 2001: 31)

Following this approach lessons learned from the ethnographic observations of the security company influenced the focus of the survey undertaken with residents and how the sample was constructed. Outcomes from both the ethnographic observations and the survey were followed up in interviews with police managers. Recognizing the significance of the sequencing of the research tasks, I will now outline the phases of the research process.

Gaining access

Gaining access for the purposes of the research study was not a single event and required renegotiation with the various populations included in the project. Many researchers have recorded the critical nature of access negotiations (Carter, 1995; Green, 1993, see also Chapter 4 of this volume) as a vital first stage in the research process. In my case I was placed in what appeared to be a uniquely advantageous position in being invited by the director of the private security company to undertake research in relation to his business. My gatekeeper, who undertook an important role as go-between between myself and the company director, was a former student for whom I shall use the pseudonym Martin. Martin's initial relationship to the researcher was as a former mature student in the social science department where I teach criminology. In May 1996 he rang me to discuss a private security company that had begun operating in an area near his home and with whom he had made contact. Martin was involved with the company on a voluntary basis, helping with paperwork and voluntarily accompanying the guards on neighbourhood patrols. Aware of my interest in policing, he offered to introduce me to the company director and facilitate any research that I might be interested in undertaking. Coffey (1993: 94) has acknowledged the importance of informal sponsorship in introducing the researcher to an organization, describing it as 'the ethnographer's best ticket into the community'. She cites Fetterman's view that:

> an intermediary or go-between can open doors otherwise locked to outsiders. The facilitator may be a chief, principal, director, teacher, tramp or gang member, and should have some credibility with the group, either as a member or as an acknowledged friend or associate. (Fetterman, 1989: 43–4)

Martin's links with the security company afforded him an insider status and as such he played a pivotal role in the research project, acting as a gatekeeper and introducing me to James (pseudonym), the company director. Access to the research setting was opportunistic. The setting was presented to me in such a way that:

> the setting itself comes first – an opportunity arises to investigate an interesting setting; and foreshadowed problems spring from the nature of that setting. (Hammersley and Atkinson, 1995: 36)

While Martin facilitated my access to the company and cushioned me from some of the problems others have encountered in researching organizations (Bryman 1988b) his sponsorship did bring the possibility that James would seek to impose his agenda on my research as a condition of allowing me into the company. Other researchers have experienced difficulties in remaining autonomous and independent within organizational settings (Bryman, 1988b) and there had to be a concern that James' commercial agenda would be at odds with my academic interest. The concern was that coming from a commercial focus James would look to the research to emphasize positive features and might only facilitate access to satisfied customers. In practice James proved to have an open mind on what would come from the research. He had no prior experience of academic research and as such no preconceived ideas of what I might contribute. He saw his customers, rather than his company, as the focus of my research interests but never tried to influence the questions that were asked of them.

On first meeting with James I kept my own agenda vague referring to 'a general academic interest' in the role of private security companies as my cover for 'casing the joint' (Hammersley and Atkinson, 1995: 38). On initial contact I was uncertain whether there was sufficient scope in the project for it to become the basis of my doctoral research and I saw the early meetings as a feasibility study to further test this out. In the light of this I made no firm commitments to James, stressing my flexibility regarding company interests and highlighting possible trade-offs and mutual benefits. This lack of openness later contributed to some ethical difficulties in my relationships with both Martin and James as related to my failure to tell the whole story at this point in time.

Diverse agendas

In negotiating access to James' company it was evident that the three parties, James, Martin and myself all came with different agendas and investments in the outcomes of the research. James saw the academic links as raising the professional profile and image of the company. The firm was small scale and relatively local in its operations. At the outset, the company operated from James' home and covered the residential area in which he lived. He had plans to expand the company and saw an academic research input as supporting that expansion. Martin saw introducing me to the company as enhancing his own credibility and position. He came with some academic knowledge and expertise and took every opportunity to reinforce his own links with the university. My own agenda was that at an early stage I saw this research area as having potential as my doctoral thesis. While I saw real potential in this research topic, I elected to bide my time and observe how the research possibilities developed. Unlike Fountain's (1993) ethnography with drug dealers, I was not completely candid at the outset with either of my gatekeepers regarding my personal motivation for my interest in the research topic.

My somewhat vague agenda proved sufficient for James to agree that I could conduct research in relation to the company without any formal agreement as to what the deliverables from the project would consist of or how the research would be conducted. At an early stage I did, however, alert him to the fact that any findings from his customers could be negative and that he should not assume that they would reflect positively on the company. The justification given for the ethnographic study of the company was that I needed to be familiar with their working practices in order to effectively undertake research with his customers.

There was no formal agreement regarding the nature of the feedback that I would provide for the company or its ownership, only an understanding that this would take place in due course. Partial written feedback on the survey results was eventually provided to James and Martin in the summer of 1998. James did not pressure for such an account but I felt that he was owed this in the light of the access he had provided. The summary of survey results pertained only to his company and no data were included relating to residents' fear of crime or assessments of public policing.

Field relations

From the outset in my relations with the company I was able to adopt the role of overt researcher. I was introduced by my gatekeeper as an experienced police researcher and this expertise served to facilitate my access to the organization. While my research agenda was not totally explicit it never proved necessary for me to adopt covert strategies to carry out the research. However, while my research strategy was initially unstructured it soon became necessary to establish parameters and ground rules for my role and the research I was undertaking. This defining of roles was important for external audiences with whom there were real dangers that my role would be identified as acting on behalf of the company rather than that of independent researcher. As I will describe later, provision of access to the company was interpreted with suspicion by some key community figures as employment by a commercial concern to undertake research on their behalf. Attribution of such affiliation jeopardized the independence of the community survey that I eventually intended to conduct. In my consequent negotiation of access to a sample of residents it was important that the project was not over identified with any specific interest group in a manner that would influence responses. Also, for those elements of the research undertaken with the public police it was crucial to avoid over identification with the commercial company. In ongoing negotiations for access with both residents and the police it was important to be able to focus on my independent status, stressing that because my research had used the commercial company as a starting point this did not mean that I acted on their behalf (see Chapter 2).

Presentation of self

My access to the security company was intrinsically bound up with my representation by Martin as an experienced academic researcher. My status as an 'expert' was used by my gatekeeper to facilitate getting me accepted. My personal biography as a researcher facilitated access into the world of the commercial security company. It was evident at the first meeting with James and his staff that Martin had invested time before the face-to-face meeting in establishing my credentials as a 'card carrying' researcher with a track record in police research. He talked openly about the police research projects that he was aware I had been involved with and enquired about the personal well-being of senior academic colleagues. While we had not engineered a formal strategy, his enquiries at the first access meeting enabled me to demonstrate knowledge of key local police personnel, also known to James and to thereby substantiate my claim to be a credible police researcher who should be given access to his company. James appeared flattered by my interest in his company. It was evident that he saw my interest in his business as bestowing kudos and legitimizing the company as a quasi-policing organization. His positive stance was reflected in the fact that his 'co-operation' with the research was prominently advertised, at a very early stage, in the newsletter that he produced and regularly distributed to his customers.

In common with other ethnographic studies I was aware of the need for 'a high degree of awareness about self-presentation' (Hammersley and Atkinson, 1995: 87). In meetings with James, the public police and related community meetings I was able to present myself as a smartly turned out mature researcher. In such contexts my presentation of self reinforced a professional identity. How to dress for shadowing of guards during night-time patrols was more problematic. Other academic colleagues have commented on the need to dress up for visits into the field (Coffey, 1993), although Adams (2000: 391) questions the 'authenticity and integrity' of such actions. In my case night-time patrols called for a dressing down and a casual but warm attire. Previous experience of shadowing of police officers informed my decision (Christopher et al., 1989), although in such contexts there was always the option of being taken for a female plain-clothed detective. On this occasion I opted for leggings, trainers and an anorak but my field notes record that I was immediately struck by the disparity in mine and James' appearances:

> I parked in the street and James strode out to meet me. My first impression is of his uniform. He has close cropped hair and a beard. He looks like a hard man, a bit thuggish and one immediately feels he would know how to handle himself. As we go into the house I comment on the fact that I feel a bit scruffy ... As James makes coffee a second guard, John arrives, along with Martin. I am relieved that Martin like me is casually dressed but John looks smart – white shirt, a tie, a navy blue padded waistcoat. It looks like a uniform and he could be taken for a police or prison officer.

While casual dress was acceptable for patrol duties, as I moved through the different stages of the research process it was necessary for me to adapt the image that I sought to present in accord with Hammersley and Atkinson's view that, 'impression management is unlikely to be a unitary affair ... There may be different categories of participants, and different social contexts, which demand the construction of different "selves"' (Hammersley and Atkinson, 1995: 87).

As well as public and private police, I had an additional audience in the form of the residents whom I sought to interview in my community survey. With that group I highlighted my academic interest in private policing and sought to represent myself as a member of the academic staff at the local university. Cold-calling and regularly interviewing people on their doorsteps required that I present a competent, if somewhat bland, image designed to encourage individuals to talk to me. The link between the project and the university were enhanced by my decision to employ two recent graduate students to help with interviewing residents. The students, one male and one female, were carefully selected with the view of how they would be received by potential respondents in mind. Both students were known to me personally and were what a colleague described as 'head over the parapet students'. Their manner was naturally warm and outgoing. They presented themselves as confident people with good social skills. In a training session they were encouraged to dress casually but not too garishly. We agreed that their attire should not be overly formal.

An ethnography of private policing

A major strand of the research was a qualitative study of the occupational culture of private policing, achieved by means of ethnographic observation, in the form of shadowing of private guards and use of key informants. The ethnographic observations lasted for over two years, facilitating attention to the evolution of the company and any change in its status over time. As an extended period of fieldwork, particular research strategies were adopted to facilitate the researcher remaining in the field for the necessary time period. In particular the project placed a significant reliance on the use of key informants and some of the issues related to this will be discussed below.

Hammersley and Atkinson (1995: 104) discuss the roles adopted by ethnographers as a continuum from complete participation to complete observation. My own role with the company laid major emphasis on unstructured observations. In the research setting I chose to cement early relationships with informants by means of direct participation in patrols and face-to-face encounters and subsequently to maintain such relationships by more sporadic contact, typically by telephone. My initial role in relation to the company and key informants evolved with the time invested in cultivating the informant facilitating the subsequent flow of information via more indirect methods. This research strategy best fitted the aims of the research which were to explore patterns of change over time in the operation of the private security company. I was not interested in a snapshot, which an intensive but brief period of fieldwork would have provided, but rather the evolution of the company and its relationship to other key agencies over an extended period of time. The fact that I was a part-time PhD student gave me the flexibility and time to adopt such an approach. In that regard researchers need to adapt their strategy to what is feasible within their own circumstances.

Having agreed access, the first data collection stage to the research was familiarization with the working of the company. Gaining an understanding of the organization of the company involved analysis of paperwork and documentary evidence including publicity materials, work logs and newsletters distributed to customers (see Chapter 7 on use of documentary sources). Ethnographic observation entailed accompanying the guards on night-time patrols and joining James in his early evening walkabouts collecting payments from customers. During this period, I met key players in the company including James' wife who played a significant administrative role in the firm. An ongoing feature of this period was the continuing presence and influence of Martin. He was regularly present when face-to-face meetings took place and he and I had regular independent contact by telephone on how the research was progressing. His role evolved beyond that of gatekeeper to informant and the information he acquired and passed on to me was an important element in my understandings of the day-to-day running of the organization. As an informant, Martin had been self-selecting in promoting the project idea. His insider position within the company gave him access to a range of information which he was prepared to share with me. This insider knowledge was important in researching a commercial company with an investment in putting a positive gloss on how well the firm was functioning. In addition to talking with Martin I also made contact with a range of key community figures in this period, gaining their perspective on how the company was functioning. One of these was a Neighbourhood Watch co-ordinator, whom I will call Judy. Her knowledge related to the expansion of the company into her locality, a development to which she was strongly opposed. Judy had well-developed links with the public police and was an important source of data on their response to the actions of the private police.

In drawing up my research strategy I had made an explicit decision not to formally interview local police managers until the final phase of the work, when I would be in a position to explore their reactions to my findings. However, as the project proceeded, I was made aware of the attitudes of the police through various routes. James and my other community informants would talk about their perceptions of police attitudes towards the private police. James in particular tended to differentiate between operational officers 'on the ground' and managers:

> We don't feel accepted by the community officer or management. They won't officially acknowledge us. We have good relations with police on the ground. We can help with arrests and share information. They sometimes ask us to keep a check on car numbers in the area. We feel appreciated. They love us.

I had some direct contact with the public police in this period. I attended community meetings where they were participants and from that was able to gather my own evidence on their perspective. When I attended community liaison meetings as an observer, I always informed the police in advance that I would be present, even though in some cases this meant talking to an answer phone. The police were fully aware of my community survey and I offered them a copy of my questionnaire. The inspector at the time did not feel it was necessary to see the questionnaire, although she expressed an interest in hearing in due course about the results of the survey. In the early stages of the research I also exploited my own network of past and present students who were police officers to check out informally the attitudes to privatization of policing. I was aware that they were giving me an individual perspective rather than an organizational line but such discussions were important in building an overall context to the project and as a means of extending an understanding of police responses beyond officially sanctioned accounts. Notes from an informal discussion with a uniformed sergeant record him as saying:

> Unofficially police officers don't like private security. They are suspicious of them and see them as crooks. They will routinely investigate for any links with offenders.

While the use of informants proved an effective strategy for this project, this method is not without its potential pitfalls and dilemmas (Johnson, 1990). I will now review some of the problems encountered in this piece of work.

Problems in handling informants

Checks on the validity of data

Fountain (1993: 162) highlights the dangers of relying exclusively on informants' accounts and the potential for distortion. As informants' accounts provided a core element in the data collated regarding the operation of the security firm, alternative strategies by which accounts could be validated were particularly crucial. The three major informants, James, Martin and Judy, held unique and distinct positions in relation to the company and while their perspective on events reflected that position, some checking out of their accounts against each other's was feasible.

On an insider/outsider continuum James, as director of the company, was a clear insider whose representations were premised on that position. Martin's position bridged the insider/outsider role. As an interested volunteer, he was given access to important inside information but his affiliation to the company was not that of a paid employee and as such he was willing to divulge information that provided a more objective stance on how the business was progressing. As I will discuss below, Martin's position in the company shifted, becoming increasingly marginal as the research progressed, which impacted on the perspectives he was able to provide. In contrast, Judy's position was one of complete outsider. Her interest reflected her position as an active Neighbourhood Watch co-ordinator with established links to the public police. She became an important source of information on how the public police viewed the infiltration of private groups into their patch.

Each of the key informants regularly provided information reflecting their structural position in relation to the organization, with the researcher positioned to check accounts against other core perspectives. The regularity of contacts also allowed for a checking of internal consistencies in accounts given over time. For example, during the two years of fieldwork, Martin typically spoke with me several times a week regarding how things were progressing with the company, increasing to several times a day at critical periods. As part of the cultivation of what I recognized to be important data I went out of my way to be available and receptive to such calls, even at those times when they felt intrusive and did not fit with my research timetable. While it was not feasible for me to be permanently in the field, I was alert to making myself as available as possible to informants. If I was really too busy to speak to my informant at the point when they called I was conscientious about calling them back as soon as possible. Prioritizing the maintenance of contact and availability to informants proved important and effective strategies in maintaining the flow of information over an extended period of time. Other methods deployed in the research, alongside the informants' accounts, have also proved to be important means of validating such data. The perspectives provided by the neighbourhood survey and formal and informal interviews with the public police have supplemented in important ways the informants' accounts.

Shifting roles

A reliance on a small number of informants can be a dangerous strategy as changes in their status or position can directly impact on the researcher's access. My experience with this project is that Martin's position shifted substantially during the period of fieldwork from insider gatekeeper to excluded outsider. This was a gradual process but one which could have adversely affected researcher access. James' changing attitude to Martin developed out of his perceived over-identification with groups opposed to the expansion of the company. He developed his own links with Judy and Neighbourhood Watch groups, which in James' eyes put in to question his reliability and loyalty. As a consequence his access to organizational information was curtailed. His exclusion was confirmed when James rang me to provide the new phone number that the company was operating from and specifically requested that I did not share the number with Martin. At that point James was aware that I had continuing contact with Martin and his ostracizing of him could have put my own access in jeopardy. This scenario was prevented by the timescale of events, with Martin's expulsion occurring some 18 months into the fieldwork period. At that stage in fieldwork relations I had developed a significant direct relationship with James and had moved well beyond using Martin as a go-between. The fact that I had had the opportunity to develop a direct role with the company prevented me being excluded with my personal gatekeeper and enabled me to retain access. Once Martin had been excluded, a strategic decision had to be made regarding retaining him as an informant. In practice, even as an outsider, he had important contributions to make regarding information he was able to share from significant others. The information he provided from groups in opposition to privatized security, including some public police officers, proved valuable. It was important, however, to understand the changing context of the data provided by a key informant (Hammersley and Atkinson, 1995).

Overt and covert roles

Adler (1985) acknowledges that frequently ethnographers are required to deal with the 'delicate combination of overt and covert roles' (Adler, 1985: 27) and my role as the researcher in this study was no exception. My decision to retain contact with Martin once he had forfeited his position in the security company was not something that I highlighted with James. While my own access had survived Martin's exclusion, I was aware that continuing contact with him was likely to be seen by James as threatening to the positive image of the company that he sought to convey. I was also aware of behaving covertly at an early stage in the project in 'selling' my original research idea to James and convincing him that I should be given access to his organization. Supported by Martin, my rationale for the research was an interest in evaluating the impact of private policing on the local community. While this is part of what the research is about and it is not untrue it does not tell the complete story. Following Norris (1993: 128) it provides a 'serviceable account' of what the research was about, obscuring other more covert objectives. In practice, I was interested in the culture of private policing and how the occupational role compared with public police officers. I was interested in the viability of private security in residential areas as a commercial enterprise and the implications of such developments for the delivery of law and order. My cover story of researching the residents rather than the security company constructed the research role in a way that made it 'understandable and acceptable to the researched' (Norris, 1993: 129).

Dangerous and secret knowledge

As the period of fieldwork progressed and Martin's structural position in the company became more marginal, he increasingly provided me with confidential information which demonstrated the uncertain commercial viability of the business. As a researcher I was faced with a situation where key informants were providing markedly different constructions on how the company was developing. James' representation focused on what he perceived as positive developments, including the expansion of the business into new residential areas and his ability to move the business premises out of his home and into a nearby commercial location. In contrast, Martin's accounts increasingly highlighted a range of problems which suggested that the future of the company might be in jeopardy, including problems regarding financial insecurities. While on the face of things it appeared that the company was expanding and transferring its location into commercial premises, there were ongoing cash flow problems with established clients.

The image presented by Martin was much more one of financial instability and uncertainty. Much of the information provided by him was gleaned from his established contacts with the public police. From this source it became evident that there were a series of problematic issues in relation to the operations of the company. Martin indicated that there were problems regarding the adequacy of insurance cover with which the company were operating which involved external enquiries by trading standards officials. Questions were raised as to whether the company staff had criminal records and the related accuracy of publicity materials distributed by the firm. The public police had concerns about some of the operational methods being deployed, including, allegedly, that private guards were listening into police messages in order to arrive at incidents ahead of the police and more seriously encouraging young people to instigate disorder incidents as a means of encouraging residents to sign up for the private policing scheme. My own contacts with the police confirmed that the firm and its operations were the subject of close scrutiny and investigation. I became aware that some of the information that was being passed to me was unknown to the company and knowledge of it could have been valuable to the future survival of the firm.

Martin, part of whose allegiance was to the success of the research project, became increasingly concerned that I complete my neighbourhood surveys before any official action was taken against the company. It was evident to me that on several fronts the company might face official action which would push it over the edge and out of business. The ethical dilemma for myself was that I was a party to such knowledge and was in a potentially exploitative position in not sharing such awareness with James. He had allowed me access to research his company and at the same time I was withholding information from him that might help him secure the future of the business or at least protect himself from possible investigation. On the other hand, the information shared with me by Martin was confidential with my disclosure potentially damaging his relationship with the public police. I was conscious that the covert activities and related knowledge that I had acquired placed in jeopardy the rapport I had established with the informants and the security company and the continuation of the fieldwork.

Dangers of over identification at the research site

The dilemmas for a researcher regarding covert activities and knowledge are intensified when there has been an extended period of fieldwork with a relatively few individuals. I was in the field for two and a half years on this project and came to know the key players as individuals. Familiarization with a small commercial company also involved direct relations with the wife and child of the company director and an awareness of the extent to which the success of the business was critical for the whole family. As the fieldwork progressed, and particularly as the research revealed a range of problems in the operations of the company, I encountered increasing challenges to my construction of the research role as objective researcher. I was conscious of feelings of loyalty to the company and individuals connected to it and the risk that such a position would detract from the broader research perspective. Feelings of identification premised on my level of knowledge of the research subjects and their support for the project, including their ready acceptance that this would constitute my PhD, once this intention was revealed to them. Fountain (1993: 165) recognizes the related guilt which can emerge from the 'ethical compromises made by covert researchers' and the fieldwork relations of this project support that position.

In the context of the work as a whole, I was aware that over identification with the security company had to be avoided to protect other strands of the research, particularly work being undertaken with the police and the general community. Presentation of my research role to external audiences required an emphasis on the objectivity of my status to achieve the necessary access. There were real dangers in me being depicted as acting on behalf of the company, a factor which I was made aware of in the early stages of negotiating my community research. I had attended a community meeting to inform them of my intention to do a household survey of members and non-members of the private policing scheme. The group was made up of residents representing community groups and professionals from a range of agencies working in the locality. My rationale for attending was that this was a useful forum through which to inform the community about the research and to explain my presence and approaches to residents in the area. I was open to answering questions about the research, but had not anticipated the level of resistance that the project attracted from a key political figure attending the meeting. He fundamentally questioned the motivation for the research and was openly sceptical regarding the objectivity of the project. His direct questions as to who was funding the research were seriously undermining in an open community meeting. Convincing key community players, both inside and outside of that meeting, of the academic rigour of the project depended heavily on my being able to confirm the neutrality of the project and the lack of any allegiance to a particular interest group. In a project which sought to establish multiple access to a range of groups the separation of the researcher's interests from any particular group becomes highly significant. For this project, that factor was also pertinent for the research components that involved the public police. The research was structured so that the majority of the work with the public police occurred toward the end of the fieldwork period. While informal contacts with the police were ongoing, the formal interviews with senior police personnel were scheduled to follow the private police fieldwork and the neighbourhood surveys. The research schedule was such that in the latter stages of the fieldwork, I negotiated a fine line between staying in and retaining access with the security company, while being perceived as a neutral academic in order to retain credibility with the police. At the same time the company, facing the commercial difficulties outlined above, had an increasing investment in the outcomes of the neighbourhood survey as a core element in promoting a positive image of the business. Two years into the fieldwork tensions about how best to construct the research role for diverse groups had increased.

Groundwork for the survey

One year into the project I felt I had done sufficient background investigation with the private police and other key community figures to move to the neighbourhood survey of local attitudes to public and private policing. The interconnection between the qualitative and quantitative methods was significant here. The qualitative work undertaken with the private police and members of the community informed the development of the quantitative research tool. This background work included ethnographic observation of the private police, contact with customers of the security company and other community figures. I have explained in detail my reception at a community forum meeting where my research came under attack from a key political figure in the local community. At the end of that meeting I left distributing my business card and inviting any of those who were present to contact me further. That produced one written response from the local vicar, who was then chair of the forum, thanking me for the 'vigorous discussion' I had 'provoked' and making other general points about the research project. At none of the community meetings that I attended was James present. Initially that was a chance event but after some of those at the community meeting were openly sceptical that I was acting on behalf of the company I fielded and resisted requests from James that I attend certain meetings with him. This applied particularly to his meetings with the public police because I saw real dangers of identifying too much with his interests. I was also concerned that James continue to see me as an ally, a position that I might have found it difficult to maintain in an open meeting. As the research progressed, I deliberately avoided meetings that brought together my different research audiences, thereby I hoped avoiding conflicts between my distinct representations of self. I also made a decision at this point not to attend further meetings of the community forum while my research was ongoing. I felt I had been naïve in not being sufficiently prepared for the antagonism from some quarters to my project. However, I had survived the encounter to the point that the local MP finally conceded that the research could be useful 'if done properly'. While I made a verbal agreement that I would eventually come back and share my research findings with the Forum, I chose not to risk ongoing antagonism by attending the meetings as I conducted the research.

The neighbourhood survey

The decision to undertake a community survey was influenced by my previous work in this area. The social survey has become common currency in the criminological field as a means of addressing the inadequacy of official crime statistics (Maguire, 2002; Mayhew, 2000). Victimization surveys have taken an international, national and local perspective (Mayhew, 2000). For the purposes of this study a local survey was adopted as a means of capturing the responses of a range of residents to the crime picture in their locality, including the role played by private security. With the objective of acquiring the views of a significant number of 250 local residents the survey instrument was favoured over the interview or focus group. In adopting this approach it was recognized that while the data might provide less in-depth information this needed to be balanced against the opportunity provided to undertake research with more residents. The triangulation of methods was crucial in addressing some of the limitations of quantitative approaches, and I was alert to May's argument that:

> In the quest to compartmentalize surveys within a positivist orientation and to produce a dichotomy between qualitative and quantitative methods of social research, their broad appeal can be easily overlooked. (2001: 115)

Interviewing

All of the interviews for the survey were face-to-face. Other methods of collecting data were considered but rejected. Self-completion questionnaires were rejected on the grounds of low response rate and the lack of opportunity for probing in open-ended questions (Moser and Kalton, 1985). The appropriateness of this decision was confirmed by the efforts of the local police to subsequently undertake their own postal survey of residents. This attempt failed dramatically with only a tiny percentage of forms returned. For my purposes, a telephone survey would have excluded some groups (for example, households without telephone access and those reliant on mobile phones) and not allowed for the depth of coverage that could be achieved in a face-to-face encounter.

Police Interviews

In accessing the public police I elected to adopt a top-down strategy. During the ongoing fieldwork I had several encounters with the local police, which left me with some concern that they identified my research with the commercial company and as such, might well be resistant to talking to me. With this in mind I made use of a contact with a former student at a senior management level in the local force. He arranged for me to have lunch with one of the Assistant Chief Constables. I used this meeting to sound him out at a general level regarding force policy on privatization and more importantly to facilitate my access to local managers. The meeting closed with him agreeing to ensure that the local commander at divisional level would speak to me. As originally planned I elected not to take up this opportunity until after finalizing my analysis of survey results. An interview with the divisional police commander constituted the final stage of the data collection.

Data collection and analysis

As with other research involving an ethnographic approach 'the processes of data collection, analysis and writing are intricately bound' (Taraborelli, 1996). With regard to the qualitative elements of the research, I kept field notes from the beginning of the project, including the early period when I was uncertain how the research would develop. The field notes were kept in chronological order and provided a running record of my experiences in relation to the company. They were written reflexively to include a description of the event, my own feelings and responses to it and linkages to potential research themes. As analytical memos they also contain my thoughts regarding connections to the literature and prompts for future research and investigation. Notes taken in the field consisted of handwritten jottings later expanded into fuller field notes. As discussed above, as a pragmatic solution to remaining in the field for an extended period as a full-time academic, I deployed a 'distance learning' strategy, regularly communicating with my informants by telephone. Such contacts were supported by regular face-to-face meetings but proved an effective means of maintaining day-to-day contact with the company's activities. The telephone also proved to be an advantageous tool for taking notes. In that scenario there was no need for a covert strategy and I was able to make full notes as we talked. Hammersley and Atkinson (1995: 48) note the disadvantages of a time delay between observation and recording in terms of recall. In this case there was no delay and recording was virtually immediate. While this strategy had the disadvantage of not allowing me access to non-verbal communication, James' frequent use of a mobile allowed me to get immediate feedback on what was occurring. As an example, one of my field notes refers to James talking to me from a city centre shopping precinct as he patrolled during the Christmas period. He had to break off from our conversation to deal with an incident. All the field notes were subsequently organized into emerging themes and these themes informed the survey with residents.

During survey interviews, responses to the open questions were taken down verbatim. Where the respondent had a lot to contribute this sometimes involved use of short hand, immediately expanded into a full account at the close of the interview. Qualitative data from the survey was organized thematically. At this stage of the analysis, generation of themes increased and diversified and organization of the material was computerized, although not by use of a qualitative package. Quantitative data gathered from the survey were analysed using SPSS and similarly linked to the key themes.

Concluding comments

The research project provided a unique insight into both the activities of a private security company operating in a residential setting and the impact of such an input on criminal justice processes in the locality. Evidence emerging in relation to the Merryville security company facilitated reflection on the possible future status of private policing in residential contexts. Even though England and Wales may not have gone as far as other countries in terms of the balance of public/private provision or in levels of partnership and integration of service delivery, important lessons can be learnt from an analysis of the developments that have occurred. Manning (Forst and Manning, 1999: 97) highlights the importance of attention to 'little theaters of policing' and this in-depth account, drawing on triangulated research strategies, forms an important contribution in an area that has received limited empirical enquiry (Jones and Newburn, 1998; Mopas and Stenning, 1999). Most importantly as an exemplar of application of a multi-method strategy the level of understanding unearthed by the research points to effective ways in which qualitative and quantitative methods can be combined.

Exercise

You are invited by either (1) a residents' group concerned about sex offenders operating in Brighton or (2) a residents' group concerned about prostitution in Birmingham, to undertake research with their group. List the ethical dilemmas that such access would entail and write a 500 word statement for an ethics committee providing a rationale for the research.

FURTHER READING

- Fielding, N.G. and Fielding, J. (1986) *Linking Data* provides an important account in relation to using a research strategy that involves a combination of qualitative and quantitative methods.
- Hammersley, M. and Atkinson, P. (1995) *Ethnography: Principles in Practice* is a seminal text on conducting ethnographic research.
- Johnson, J. (1990) *Selecting Ethnographic Informants* gives particular attention to issues relating to the use of informants in an ethnographic approach.
- Norris, C. (1993) 'Some ethical consideration on field-work with the police' highlights some of the ethical issues that can be encountered in conducting fieldwork with the police.
- King, R. and Wincup, E. (eds) (2000) *Doing Research on Crime and Justice* contains a series of pertinent first-hand accounts of the challenges of conducting qualitative research.

11

Looking Forward: the Future of Qualitative Research in Criminology

Reflecting on the future of their topic of interest is a favourite activity of criminologists. Students of criminology are likely to encounter a multitude of these reflections as they dip into the burgeoning criminological literature. For instance, Home Office statisticians attempt to estimate the size of the prison population in the future (Council and Simes, 2002), criminologists devote whole chapters or even books to predicting the future of policing (Johnston, 2000; Morgan and Newburn, 1997) and criminological theorists attempt to forecast the future health of the discipline (see for example Walklate, 1998). In this chapter we follow in this tradition, and deliberate upon the future role of qualitative research within criminology. The chapter consists of three sections. The first pulls together the discussions in previous chapters of the book concerning challenges and controversies in contemporary qualitative research but also reflects briefly on some of the new opportunities which qualitative researchers can enjoy. In the second section we reflect upon the differential employment of qualitative techniques by criminologists and argue that greater use of the full range of qualitative methods could enhance the discipline of criminology. Finally, we end the book by offering words of encouragement to criminologists contemplating using qualitative methods.

Qualitative research: challenges, controversies and opportunities

In the preceding chapters we introduced a number of research traditions which used qualitative methods. These include both interpretive and critical traditions. The former includes the work of the Chicago School, symbolic interactionism, grounded theory, ethnomethodology and conversation analysis (Travers, 2001).

We focus on the critical tradition here because these critical traditions have led to a fundamental questioning of qualitative research methods and methodology. In particular, we focused in previous chapters upon the impact of feminism, particularly in relation to interviewing (Chapter 5) and ethnography (Chapter 6). It would be wrong to give the impression that the development of feminism has transformed the qualitative research tradition without any resistance. On the contrary, as Delamont (2003: 60) notes, 'the controversies aroused by "feminist methods" have been angry, far-reaching and long-lasting'. Despite this, she argues there is 'much less sexism in the ordinary, non-feminist project than there was in 1980' (2003: 61), and this is an important achievement. The controversies referred to above relate also to debates within feminism. As Delamont makes explicit in her account of British feminist sociology, feminism is not a unified theoretical perspective. Instead, within feminism there have been considerable debates on issues of research methods and methodology. An illustrative example here is the debate about whether a feminist ethnography is a contradiction in terms (see Chapter 6). From our point of view, debates within feminism and debates between 'feminist' and 'non-feminist' researchers have contributed to the health and well-being of the qualitative research tradition because they encourage ongoing reflection on the nature of qualitative research.

Similarly, the more recent debates about the impact of postmodernism provide both challenges and opportunities for qualitative researchers. We follow in the footsteps of Delamont (2003) and subsume poststructuralism within postmodernism. The term postmodernism is used here to refer to social and cultural theories which challenge the modernist view that 'universal, objective scientific truths can be reached by scientific methods' (Delamont, 2003: 137). Postmodernism has had the greatest implication for ethnography. Coupled with the impact of globalization which challenges the relevance of research which is both local and small scale (see Chapter 6), ethnography has faced fierce criticism. Brewer (2000) goes as far as to describe the literature on ethnography as a 'battleground' (back cover), and uses this metaphor to describe internal and external critiques of ethnography. Ethnography, and indeed all qualitative methods, have always been subject to criticism from proponents of the natural science model, and has defended itself. Of greater concern are the attacks from within ethnography and attempts by postmodernists to deconstruct it. The effects of this are described by Denzin and Lincoln (1998: 21–2) as a 'double crisis' of 'representation' and 'legitimation', referring to the construction and evaluation of ethnographic accounts. These attacks questioned the ability of ethnography to offer a privileged description of the social world in a way that represented the reality of the 'field'. Postmodern critiques have not led to the abandonment of ethnographic work. Instead, a number of ethnographers have responded to the critique by developing alternatives to the methodological stance of naturalistic realism (see Brewer, 2000 for an overview). The challenge of globalization has also been thwarted by the instance that global processes are always mediated locally.

Further key developments within the qualitative research tradition are the possibilities created by technological advances. In earlier chapters in this book we have noted that new forms of technology offer opportunities for collecting, recording and analysing data. Arguably the growth of the Internet provides one of the most exciting prospects for researchers. The Internet affords researchers the chance to study new forms of behaviour, for instance social interaction in chatrooms, but also offers the possibility of conducting qualitative research in this virtual environment.

Reflection on the future of qualitative research in criminology

In Chapters 5, 6 and 7 we reflected upon the ways in which criminologists have made use of three qualitative research strategies: interviewing, ethnography and documentary analysis. We note here that criminologists have made the greatest use of the interview. The criminological community has been slow to realize the full potential of conducting research using the ever-increasing number of documentary sources available to them. We also highlighted, and attempted to explain, the apparent reluctance of many criminologists to use ethnographic approaches in their criminological studies. Hence, our central argument here is to suggest that criminologists should make full use of the range of qualitative methods afforded to them. In advancing this argument we are cognizant of the difficulties faced by criminologists who attempt to do this. Some of the difficulties relate to the political context (see Chapter 2). For example, while the Home Office have in some respects accommodated qualitative research, typically as an integrated package of research methods, they are unlikely to support purely ethnographic projects or those involving a critical discourse analysis of official documents. Other difficulties relate to resources. There is often pressure from funders to produce research findings quickly or to keep costs to a minimum. Those conducting unfunded research still face the difficulty of finding sufficient time to undertake some forms of qualitative research, particularly ethnography. Given these pressures, the one-off interview frequently becomes the method of choice. To end this section on a positive note we are pleased to note that within British criminology there is at least some evidence of a criminological future in which the qualitative tradition, in all its forms, is alive and well. For example, the growth of interest in cultural criminology brings with it an interest in ethnography as its research strategy of choice (Ferrell, 2001).

Concluding comments

In this text we have explored and celebrated the achievement of qualitative researchers within criminology. We have drawn upon studies on a wide range of topics to illustrate both the depth and vitality of the qualitative research tradition. Unsurprisingly, given our commitment to qualitative research, we recommend it to criminological researchers as an approach which is particularly suited to the study of crime and criminal justice. However, we are neither evangelical in our commitment to qualitative methods nor anti-statistical. As we have argued elsewhere in this book, the most appropriate methods should be used to answer the research question, and this may involve using a combination of methods including quantitative ones. Criminologists using qualitative techniques will find their experiences of conducting research both challenging and rewarding. There are many academic rewards for criminologists who select a qualitative approach and these are described in Chapter 1. In addition, conducting qualitative research on criminological topics has personal rewards for the researcher. Of course, criminological research also has a 'bleak side' (Baldwin, 2000: 254) and we have been keen to portray an honest account of conducting criminological research by exploring the political sensitivities, ethical dilemmas, access difficulties and encounters with risk, vulnerability and danger faced by criminologists. Any negative aspects are easily outweighed by the academic and personal rewards.

We hope in this text that we have conveyed a little of the experiences of conducting qualitative research by grounding our discussion of the research process and methodological issues in our own experiences and those of the wider criminological community. We deliberately use the words 'a little' because it has been our intention to demonstrate that the true learning experience comes from *doing* research. In this respect, one of our main aims was to inspire criminologists to conduct qualitative research, and to equip them with the necessary 'tools' to undertake high-quality studies. We hope we have been successful.

References

Adler, P. (1985) *Wheeling and Dealing: An Ethnography of an Upper-Level Drug Dealing and Smuggling Community*. Washington DC: Columbia University Press.

Adler, P. and Adler, P. (1995) 'The demography of ethnography', *Journal of Contemporary Ethnography*, 24: 3–29.

Adams, C. (2000) 'Suspect data: arresting research', in R. King and E. Wincup (eds), *Doing Research on Crime and Justice*. Oxford: Oxford University Press.

Advisory Council on the Misuse of Drugs (1988) *Aids and Drug Misuse Part 1*. London: HMSO.

Anderson, N. (1923) *The Hobo: The Sociology of Homeless Men*. Chicago, IL: University of Chicago Press.

Arksey, H. and Knight, P. (1999) *Interviewing for Social Scientists*. London: Sage.

Armstrong, G. (1998) *Football Hooliganism: Knowing the Score*. Oxford: Berg.

Atkinson, P. (1990) *The Ethnographic Imagination: Textual Constructions of Reality*. London: Routledge.

Atkinson, P. (1992) *Understanding Ethnographic Texts*. London: Sage.

Atkinson, P., Coffey, A., Delamont, S., Lofland, J. and Lofland, L. (eds) (2001) *Handbook of Ethnography*. London: Sage.

Back, L. (2002) 'Dancing and wrestling with scholarship: things to do and things to avoid in a PhD career', *Sociological Research Online*, 7 (4).

Baldwin, J. (2000) 'Research on the criminal courts', in R. King and E. Wincup (eds), *Doing Research on Crime and Justice*. Oxford: Oxford University Press.

Ballinger, A. (2000) *Dead Woman Walking*. Dartmouth: Ashgate.

Beck, R. (1999) 'Rape from afar: men exposing to women and children', in F. Brookman, L. Noaks and E. Wincup (eds), *Qualitative Research in Criminology*. Aldershot: Ashgate.

Beck, R. (2002) 'Integration or exclusion? Perceptions of gender equality in policing'. Unpublished PhD thesis, Cardiff University.

Becker, H. (1963) *Outsiders: Studies in the Sociology of Deviance*. New York: Free Press.

Becker, H. (1967) 'Whose side are we on?' *Social Problems*, 14: 239–47.

Bell, J. (1999) *Doing Your Research Project: A Guide for First Time Researchers in Education and the Social Sciences*. Buckingham: Open University Press.

Bennett, T. and Wright, R. (1984) *Burglars on Burglary*. Aldershot: Gower.

Bittner, E. (1967) 'The police on Skid Row: a study in peace-keeping', *American Sociological Review*, 32: 699–715.

Blaxter, L., Hughes, C. and Tight, M. (1996) *How to Research*. Buckingham: Open University Press.

Bloor, M., Frankland, K., Thomas, M. and Robson, K. (2001) *Focus Groups in Social Research*. London: Sage.

Blumer, H. (1969) *Symbolic Interactionism*. Englewood Cliffs, NJ: Prentice-Hall.

Bonger, W. (1916) 'Criminality and economic conditions', abridged extract in E. McLaughlin, J. Muncie and G. Hughes (eds) (2003), *Criminological Perspectives: A Reader*. London: Sage.

Bottomley, K. and Pease, K. (1986) *Crime and Punishment: Interpreting the Data*. Milton Keynes: Open University Press.

Bottoms, A. (2000) 'The relationship between theory and research in criminology', in R. King and E. Wincup (eds), *Doing Research on Crime and Justice*. Oxford: Oxford University Press.

Branigan, T. (2001) 'Rough sleepers unit "is fixing figures"', *The Guardian*, 24 November.

Brannen, J. (ed.) (1992) *Mixing Methods: Qualitative and Quantitative Research*. Aldershot: Ashgate.

Brewer, J. (2000) *Ethnography*. Buckingham: Open University Press.

British Journal of Criminology (2001) 41 (3).

British Psychological Society (2000) *Code of Conduct: Ethical Principles and Guidelines*. British Psychological Society.

British Society of Criminology (2003) *Code of Ethics for Researchers in the Field of Criminology*. British Society of Criminology.

British Sociological Association (2002) *Statement of Ethical Practice for the British Sociological Association*. British Sociological Association.

Brookman, F. (1999) 'Accessing and analysing police murder files', in F. Brookman, L. Noaks and E. Wincup (eds), *Qualitative Research in Criminology*. Aldershot: Ashgate.

Brookman, F. (2000) *Dying for Control: Men, Murder and Sub-lethal Violence in England and Wales*. Unpublished PhD thesis, Cardiff University.

Brookman, F., Noaks, L. and Wincup, E. (eds) (1999) *Qualitative Research in Criminology*. Aldershot: Ashgate.

Brookman, F., Noaks, L. and Wincup, E. (2001) 'Access to justice, remand issues and the Human Rights Act', *Probation Journal*, 48: 195–202.

Brown, J. (1996) 'Police research: some critical issues', in F. Leishmann, B. Loveday and S. Savage (eds), *Core Issues in Policing*. London: Longman.

Brown, J. and Heidensohn, F. (2000) *Gender and Policing: Comparative Perspectives*. London: Macmillan.

Bryman, A. (1988a) *Quantity and Quality in Social Research*. London: Routledge.

Bryman, A. (ed.) (1988b) *Doing Research in Organisations*, London: Routledge.

Buckland, G., Wincup, E. and Bayliss, R. (2002) 'Excluding the excluded: working with homeless drug users', *Criminal Justice Matters*, 47: 12–13.

Burgess, R. (1984) *In the Field: An Introduction to Field Research*. London: Allen and Unwin.

Burman, M., Batchelor, S. and Brown, J. (2001) 'Researching girls and violence', *British Journal of Criminology*, 41: 472–84.

Butler, I. and Williamson, H. (1994) *Children Speak: Children, Trauma and Social Work*. London: Longman.

Calvey, D. (2000) 'Getting on the door and staying there: a covert participant observation study of bouncers', in G. Lee-Treweek and S. Linkogle (eds), *Danger in the Field*. London: Routledge.

Campbell, A. (1984) *The Girls in the Gang*. Blackwell: Oxford.

Campbell, B. (1993) *Goliath: Britain's Dangerous Places*. London: Methuen.

Campbell, D. and Fiske, D. (1959) 'Convergent and discriminant validation by the multitrait-multimethod matrix', *Psychological Bulletin*, 56: 81–105.

Carlen, P. (1985) *Criminal Women*. Cambridge: Polity Press.

Carter, K. (1994) 'Access: my flexible friend', *Prison Service Journal*, 93: 30–5.

Carter, K. (1995) 'The Occupational Socialisation of Prison Officers: an Ethnography'. Unpublished PhD thesis, Cardiff University.

Cavadino, M. and Dignan, J. (2002) *The Penal System: An Introduction*. London: Sage.

Chambliss, W. (1975) 'Towards a political economy of crime', abridged extract in E. McLaughlin, J. Muncie and G. Hughes (eds) (1996) *Criminological Perspectives: A Reader*. London: Sage.

Christensen, P. and James, A. (1999) *Research with Children: Perspectives and Practices*. London: Routledge.

Christopher, S., Noaks, L. and Levi, M. (1989) *Assaults Against the Police*. Unpublished research report, Cardiff University.

Clayton, R. (1992) 'Transitions into drug use: risk and protective factors', in M. Glantz and R. Pickens (eds), *Vulnerability to Drug Abuse*. Washington, DC: American Psychological Association.

Clough, P. (1992) *The Ends of Ethnography*. Newbury Park, CA: Sage.

Cockcroft, T. (1999) 'Oral history and the cultures of the police', in F. Brookman, L. Noaks and E. Wincup (eds), *Qualitative Research in Criminology*. Aldershot: Ashgate.

Coffey, A. (1993) 'Double Entry: the Professional and Organizational Socialization of Graduate Accountants'. Unpublished PhD thesis, Cardiff University.

Coffey, A. and Atkinson, P. (1996) *Making Sense of Qualitative Data*. Sage: London.

Coffield, F. and Gofton, L. (1994) *Drugs and Young People*. London: Institute of Public Policy Research.

Cohen, S. (1973) *Folk Devils and Moral Panics*. London: Paladin.

Cohen, S. and Taylor, I. (1972) *Psychological Survival*. Harmondsworth: Penguin.

Cohen, S. and Taylor, I. (1977) 'Talking about prison blues', in C. Bell and H. Newby (eds), *Doing Sociological Research*. London: George Allen and Unwin.

Cohen, S. and Young, J. (eds) (1973) *The Manufacture of News*. London: Constable.

Coleman, C. and Moynihan, J. (1996) *Understanding Crime Data*. Buckingham: Open University Press.

Coleman, C. and Norris, C. (2000) *Introducing Criminology*. Cullompton: Willan Publishing.

Council, R. and Simes, J. (2002) *Projection of Long Term Trends in the Prison Population to 2009*. London: Home Office.

Crace, J. and Plomin, J. (2001) 'Grant aid', *The Guardian*, 17 July.

Crawley, E. (2003) *Doing Prison Work: The Public and Private Lives of Prison Officers*. Cullompton: Willan Publishing.

Croall, H. (1998) *Crime and Society in Britain*. Harlow: Addison Wesley Longman.

Croall, H. (2001) *Understanding White Collar Crime*. Buckingham: Open University Press.

Dale-Perera, A. (1998) 'Education, education, education', *Druglink*, May/June: 6.

Davies, C. (2002) 'The dictionary, the reader and the handbook', *Qualitative Research*, 2: 417–21.

Davies, P. (2000) 'Doing interviews with female offenders', in V. Jupp, P. Davies and P. Francis (eds), *Doing Criminological Research*. London: Sage.

Deegan, M. (2001) 'The Chicago School of ethnography', in P. Atkinson, A. Coffey, S. Delamont, J. Lofland and L. Lofland (eds), *Handbook of Ethnography*. London: Sage.

Delamont, S. (2002) 'Whose side are we on? Revisiting Becker's classic ethical question at the *fin de siecle?*, in T. Welland and L. Pugsley (eds), *Ethical Dilemmas in Qualitative Research*. Aldershot: Ashgate.

Delamont, S. (2003) *Feminist Sociology*. London: Sage.

Delamont, S. and Atkinson, P. (2002) 'Editorial', *Qualitative Research*, 2: 139–42.

Delamont, S., Atkinson, P., Coffey, A. and Burgess, R. (2001) *An Open Exploratory Spirit? Ethnography at Cardiff 1974–2001*, Working Paper Series Paper 20, Cardiff: School of Social Sciences.

Denscombe, M. (1998) *The Good Research Guide*. Buckingham: Open University Press.

Denzin, N. (1970) *The Research Act in Sociology*. London: Butterworths.

Denzin, N. (1990) 'Researching alcoholics and alcoholism in American society', in N. Denzin (ed.), *Studies in Symbolic Interactionism*, 11: 81–107.

Denzin, N. (1994) 'Postmodernism and deconstructionism', in D. Dickens and A. Fontana (eds), *Postmodernism and Social Inquiry*. London: UCL Press.

Denzin, N. (1997) *Interpretive Ethnography*. Thousand Oaks, CA: Sage.

Denzin, N. and Lincoln, Y. (1998) 'Entering the field of qualitative research', in N. Denzin and Y. Lincoln (eds), *Strategies of qualitative Inquiry*. London: Sage.

Dey, I. (1993) *Qualitative Data Analysis: A User-friendly Guide for Social Scientists*. London: Routledge.

Ditton, J. (1977) *Part-time Crime: An Ethnography of Fiddling and Pilferage*. London: Macmillan.

Ditton, J. and Duffy, J. (1983) 'Bias in the newspaper reporting of crime news', *British Journal of Criminology*, 23: 159–65.

Douglas, M. (1990) 'Risk as a forensic resource', *Daedalus: Journal of the American Academy for Arts and Science*, 119: 1–16.

Downes, D. and Morgan, R. (1994) 'Hostages to fortune? The politics of law and order in post-war Britain', in M. Maguire, R. Morgan and R. Reiner (eds), *The Oxford Handbook of Criminology*. Oxford: Oxford University Press.

Downes, D. and Morgan, R. (1997) 'Dumping the hostages to fortune? The politics of law and order in post-war Britain', in M. Maguire, R. Morgan and R. Reiner (eds), *The Oxford Handbook of Criminology*. Oxford: Oxford University Press.

Downes, D. and Morgan, R. (2002) 'The skeletons in the cupboard: the politics of law and order at the turn of the millennium', in M. Maguire, R. Morgan and R. Reiner (eds), *The Oxford Handbook of Criminology*. Oxford: Oxford University Press.

Downes, D. and Rock, P. (2003) *Understanding Deviance*. Oxford: Oxford University Press.

Drakeford, M. (1999) 'The Public Order Act 1936 and the Greenshirt Movement for Social Credit', in F. Brookman, L. Noaks and E. Wincup (eds), *Qualitative Research in Criminology*. Aldershot: Ashgate.

Durkheim, E. (1895) 'The normal and the pathological', abridged extract in E. McLaughlin, J. Muncie and G. Hughes (eds) (2003), *Criminological Perspectives: A Reader*. London: Sage.

Eaton, M. (1993) *Women After Prison*. Buckingham: Open University Press.

Edmunds, M., May, T., Hearnden, I. and Hough, M. (1998) *Arrest Referral: Emerging Lessons from Research*, Drugs Prevention Initiative Paper 23. London: Home Office.

Eisner, E. (1991) *The Enlightened Eye: Qualitative Enquiry And the Enhancement of Educational Practice*. New York: Macmillan.

Ericson, R. and Carriere, K. (1994) 'The fragmentation of criminology', abridged extract in J. Muncie, E. McLaughlin and M. Langan (eds) (1996), *Criminological Perspectives: A Reader*. London: Sage.

Ettorre, E. (1992) *Women and Substance Use*. London: Macmillan.

Feeley, M. and Simon, J. (1992) 'The new penology', abridged extract in J. Muncie, E. McLaughlin (eds) (2003), *Criminological Perspectives: A Reader*. London: Sage.

Feenan, D. (2002) 'Legal issues in acquiring information about illegal behaviour through criminological research', *British Journal of Criminology*, 42: 762–81.

Ferrell, J. (2001) 'Cultural criminology', in E. McLaughlin and J. Muncie (eds), *The Sage Dictionary of Criminology*. London: Sage.

Ferrell, J. and Hamm, M. (1998) *Ethnography at the Edge: Crime, Deviance and Field Research*. Boston, MA: Northeastern University Press.

Fetterman, M. (1989) *Ethnography: Step-by-Step*. Newbury Park, CA: Sage.

Fielding, N. (1982) 'Observational research on the National Front', in M. Bulmer (ed.), *Social Research Ethics: An Examination of the Merits of Covert Participant Observation*. London: Macmillan.

Fielding, N. and Fielding, J. (1986) *Linking Data*. London: Sage.

Fielding, N. and Lee, R. (1998) *Computer Analysis and Qualitative Research*. London: Sage.

Finch, J. (1986) *Research and Policy: The Uses of Qualitative Methods in Social and Educational Research*. Lewes: Falmer Press.

Fine, G. (ed.) (1995) *A Second Chicago School? The Development of a Post-war American Sociology*. Chicago: University of Chicago Press.

Flick, U. (1998) *An Introduction to Qualitative Research*. London: Sage.

Flood-Page, C., Campbell, S., Harrington, J. and Miller, J. (2000) *Youth Crime: Findings from the 1998/99 Youth Lifestyles Survey*, Home Office Research Study 209. London: Home Office.

Forst, B. and Manning, P. (1999) *The Privatization of Policing: Two Views*. Washington, DC: Georgetown University Press.

Foster, J. (1990) *Villains: Crime and Community in the Inner City*. London: Routledge.

Fountain, J. (1993) 'Dealing with data', in D. Hobbs and T. May (eds), *Interpreting the Field: Accounts of Ethnography*. Oxford: Oxford University Press.

Fry, C. and Dwyer, R. (2001) 'For love or money? An exploratory study of why injecting drug users participate in research', *Addiction*, 96: 1319–25.

Fuller, R. and Petch, A. (1995) *Practitioner Research: The Reflexive Social Worker*. Buckingham: Open University Press.

Furedi, F. (2002) 'Don't rock the research boat', *The Times Higher Education Supplement*, 11 January.

Garland, D. (2002) 'Of crimes and criminals: the development of criminology in Britain', in M. Maguire, R. Morgan and R. Reiner (eds), *The Oxford Handbook of Criminology*. Oxford: Oxford University Press.

Geertz, C. (1973) 'Thick description', in C. Geertz (ed.), *The Interpretation of Cultures*. New York: Basic Books.

Gelsthorpe, L. (1990) 'Feminist methodologies in criminology: a new approach or old wine in new bottles?, in L. Gelsthorpe and A. Morris (eds), *Feminist Perspectives in Criminology*. Buckingham: Open University Press.

Gelsthorpe, L. (1992) 'Response to Martyn Hammersley's paper "On Feminist Methodology"', *Sociology*, 26: 213–18.

Gelsthorpe, L. (ed.) (1993) *Minority Ethnic Groups in the Criminal Justice System*. Papers presented to the 21st Cropwood Roundtable Conference 1992. Cambridge: Institute of Criminology.

Girling, E., Loader, I. and Sparks, R. (2000) *Crime and Social Change in Middle England*. London: Routledge.

Glaser, A. and Strauss, A. (1967) *The Discovery of Grounded Theory*. Chicago: IL: Aldine.

Gomez-Cespedes, A. (1999) 'Organised crime in Mexico', in F. Brookman, L. Noaks and E. Wincup (eds), *Qualitative Research in Criminology*. Aldershot: Ashgate.

Goode, S. (2000) 'Researching a hard-to-access and vulnerable population: some considerations on researching drug and alcohol-using mothers', *Sociological Research Online*, 5 (1).

Goodey, J. (2000) Biographical lessons for criminology, *Theoretical Criminology*, 4: 473–98.

Gouldner, A. (1975) 'The sociologist as partisan', in A. Gouldner (ed.), *For Sociology*. Harmondsworth. Penguin.

Green, P. (1993) 'Taking sides: partisan research on the 1984–85 miners' strike', in D. Hobbs and T. May (eds), *Interpreting the Field: Accounts of Ethnography*. Oxford: Oxford University Press.

Greene, J. (1994) 'Qualitative program evaluation: practice and promise', in N. Denzin and Y. Lincoln (eds), *Handbook of Qualitative Research*. Newbury Park, CA: Sage.

Hale, C. (1996) 'Fear of crime: a review of the literature', *International Review of Victimology*, 4: 79–150.

Hale, C. (1999) 'The labour market and post-war crime trends in England and Wales', in P. Carlen and R. Morgan (eds), *Crime Unlimited: Questions for the 21st Century*. Basingstoke: Macmillan.

Hall, S., Critcher, C., Jefferson, T., Clarke, J. and Roberts, B. (1978) *Policing the Crisis: Mugging, the State and Law and Order*. London: Macmillan.

Hall, S. (1979) *Drifting into a Law and Order Society*. London: Cobden Trust.

Hall, T. (2000) 'At home with the homeless', *International Journal of Social Research Methodology*, 3: 121–33.

Hammersley, M. (1995) *The Politics of Social Research*. London: Sage.

Hammersley, M. and Atkinson, P. (1995) *Ethnography: Principles in Practice*. London: Routledge.

Hancock, L. (2000) 'Going around the houses: researching in high crime areas', in R. King and E. Wincup (eds), *Doing Research on Crime and Justice*. Oxford: Oxford University Press.

Health Advisory Service (2001) *The Substance of Young Need*. London: Health Advisory Service.

Heidensohn, F. (2000) *Sexual Politics and Social Control*. Buckingham: Open University Press.

Hester, S. and Eglin, P. (1992) *A Sociology of Crime*. London: Routledge.

HM Chief Inspector of Prisons (1997) *Women in Prison: A Thematic Review by HM Chief Inspector of Prisons*. London: Home Office.

Hobbs, D. (1988) *Doing the Business*. Oxford: Oxford University Press.

Hobbs, D. (1994) 'Professional and organized crime in Britain', in M. Maguire, R. Morgan and R. Reiner (eds), *The Oxford Handbook of Criminology*. Oxford: Oxford University Press.

Hobbs, D. (1995) *Professional Criminals in Modern Britain*. Oxford: Oxford University Press.

Hobbs, D. (2000) 'Researching serious crime', in R. King and E. Wincup (eds), *Doing Research on Crime and Justice*. Oxford: Oxford University Press.

Hobbs, D. (2001) 'Ethnography and the study of deviance', in P. Atkinson, A. Coffey, S. Delamont, J. Lofland and L. Lofland (eds), *Handbook of Ethnography*. London: Sage.

Hobbs, D. and May, T. (1993) *Interpreting the Field: Accounts of Ethnography*. Oxford: Oxford University Press.

Hobbs, D., Hadfield, P., Listers, S. and Winlow, S. (2003) *Bouncers: Violence and Governance in the Night-time Economy*. Oxford: Oxford University Press.

Hollway, W. and Jefferson, T. (1998) 'The risk society in an age of anxiety: situating the fear of crime', *British Journal of Sociology*, 48: 255–66.

Holdaway, S. (1983) *Inside the British Police: A Force at Work*. Oxford: Blackwell.

Holdaway, S. (1992) 'An inside job: a case study of covert research on the police', in M. Bulmer (ed.), *Social Research Ethics: An Examination of the Merits of Covert Participant Observation*. London: Macmillan.

Home Office (2000) *National Standards for the Supervision of Offenders in the Community*. London: Home Office.

Hood, R. (1992) *Race and Sentencing*. Oxford: Oxford University Press.

House, E. (1993) *Professional Evaluation*. Newbury Park, CA: Sage.

Hoyle, C. (2000) 'Being a "nosy bloody cow": ethical and methodological issues in researching domestic violence', in R. King and E. Wincup (eds), *Doing Research on Crime and Justice*. Oxford: Oxford University Press.

Hudson, B. (2000) 'Critical reflection as research methodology', in V. Jupp, P. Davies and P. Francis (eds), *Doing Criminological Research*. London: Sage.

Hudson, K. (2003) 'The Treatment and Management of Sex Offenders: Sex Offenders' Perspectives'. Unpublished PhD thesis, Cardiff University.

Hughes, G. (1998) *Understanding Crime Prevention: Social Control, Risk and Late Modernity*. Buckingham: Open University Press.

Hughes, G. (2000) 'Understanding the politics of criminological research'. in V. Jupp, P. Davies and P. Francis (eds), *Doing Criminological Research*. London: Sage.

Janowitz, M. (1972) *Sociological Models and Social Policy*. Morriston, NJ: General Learning Systems.

Johnson, J. (1990) *Selecting Ethnographic Informants*. London: Sage.

Johnston, L. (1992) *The Rebirth of Private Policing*. London: Routledge.

Johnston, L. (2000) *Policing Britain: Risk, Security and Governance*. London: Longman.

Jones, D. (1996) *Crime and Policing in the Twentieth Century*. Cardiff: University of Wales Press.

Jones, T. and Newburn, T. (1998) *Private Security and Public Policing*. Oxford: Clarendon Press.

Jones, T. and Newburn, T. (2002) 'Learning from Uncle Sam? Exploring US influences on British crime control policy', *Governance*, 15: 97–119.

Jupp, V. (2001) 'Triangulation', in E. McLaughlin and J. Muncie (eds), *The Sage Dictionary of Criminology*. London: Sage.

Jupp, V., Davies, P. and Francis, P. (eds) (2000) *Doing Criminological Research*. London: Sage.

Kelly, L., Regan, L. and Burton, S. (1991) *An Exploratory Study of the Prevalence of Sexual Abuse in a Sample of 16–21 Year Olds*. London: Child Abuse Studies Unit, Polytechnic of North London.

Kemshall, H. and Maguire, M. (2000) 'Public protection, partnership and risk penality', *Punishment and Society*, 3: 237–64.

King, R. (2000) 'Doing research in prison', in R. King and E. Wincup (eds), *Doing Research on Crime and Justice*. Oxford: Oxford University Press.

King, R. and Wincup, E. (2000) (eds) *Doing Research on Crime and Justice*. Oxford: Oxford University Press.

Kvale, S. (1996) *InterViews: An Introduction to Qualitative Research Interviewing*. London: Sage.

LeCompte, M. (2002) 'The transformation of.ethnographic practice: past and current challenges', *Qualitative Research*, 2: 283–99.

Lee, R. (1993) *Doing Research on Sensitive Topics*. London: Sage.

Lee-Treweek, G. and Linkogle, S. (2000a) 'Putting danger in the frame', in G. Lee-Treweek and S. Linkogle (eds), *Danger in the Field: Risk and Ethics in Social Research*. London: Routledge.

Lee-Treweek, G. and Linkogle, S. (eds) (2000b) *Danger in the Field: Risk and Ethics in Social Research*. London: Routledge.

Lewis, A. and Lindsay, G. (ed.) (1999) *Researching Children's Perspectives*. Buckingham: Open University Press.

Lewis, D. (1997) *Hidden Agendas*. London: Hamish Hamilton.

Levi, M. (1981) *The Phantom Capitalists: The Organisation and Control of Long-Firm Fraud*. London: Heineman.

Levi, M. and Noaks, L. (1999) 'Social constructions of violence against the police', in F. Brookman, L. Noaks and E. Wincup (eds), *Qualitative Research in Criminology*. Aldershot: Ashgate.

Liazos, A. (1972) 'The poverty of the sociology of deviance: nuts, sluts and perverts', *Social Problems*, 20: 103–20.

Liebow, E. (1993) *Tell Them Who I Am: The Lives of Homeless Women*. New York: Free Press.

Liebling, A. (1992) *Suicides in Prison*. London: Routledge.

Liebling, A. (2001) 'Whose side are we on? Theory, practice and allegiance in prisons research', *British Journal of Criminology*, 41: 472–84.

Liebling, A. and Stanko, E. (2001) 'Allegiance and Ambivalence', *British Journal of Criminology*, 41: 421–30.

Lilly, R., Cullen, F. and Ball, R. (2002) *Criminological Theory: Context and Consequences*. Thousand Oaks, CA: Sage.

Lloyd, C. (1998) 'Risk factors for problem drug use: identifying vulnerable groups', *Drugs: Education, Prevention and Policy*, 5: 217–32.

Loader, I., Girling, E. and Sparks, R. (1998) 'Narratives of decline: youth, dis/order and community in an English "Middletown"', *British Journal of Criminology*, 38: 388–403.

Lofland, J. (1987) 'Reflections on a thrice named journal', *Journal of Contemporary Ethnography*, 18: 202–33.

Lofland, J. and Lofland, L. (1984) *Analysing Social Settings*. Belmont, CA: Wadsworth.

Lupton, D. (1999) *Risk*. London: Routledge.

MacDonald, R., Mason, P., Shildrick, T., Webster, C., Johnston, L. and Ridley, L. (2001) 'Snakes and ladders: in defence of studies of youth transition', *Sociological Research Online*, 5 (4).

Maher, L. (1995) 'In the name of love: women and initiation to illicit drugs', in R. Dobash, R. Dobash and L. Noaks (eds), *Gender and Crime*. Cardiff: University of Wales Press.

Maguire, M. (2000) 'Researching "street" criminals', in R. King and E. Wincup (eds), *Doing Research on Crime and Justice*. Oxford: Oxford University Press.

Maguire, M. (2002) 'Crime statistics: the "data" explosion and its implications', in M. Maguire, R. Morgan and R. Reiner (eds), *The Oxford Handbook of Criminology*. Oxford: Oxford University Press.

Maguire, M., Kemshall, H., Noaks, L., Wincup, E. and Sharpe, K. (2001) *Risk Management of Sexual and Violent Offenders: The Work of Public Protection Panels*. Police Research Series Papers 139. London: Home Office.

Mair, G. (2000) 'Research on community penalties', in R. King and E. Wincup (eds), *Doing Research on Crime and Justice*. Oxford: Oxford University Press.

Manning, P. (1987) 'The ethnographic conceit', *Journal of Contemporary Ethnography*, 16: 49–68.

Martin, C. (2000) 'Doing research in a prison setting', in V. Jupp, P. Davies and P. Francis (eds), *Doing Criminological Research*. London: Sage.

Matza, D. (1969) *Becoming Deviant*. New Jersey: Prentice Hall.

May, T. (1997) *Social Research: Issues, Methods and Process*. Buckingham: Open University Press.

May, T. (2001) *Social Research: Issues, Methods and Process*. Buckingham: Open University Press.

Mayhew, P. (2000) 'Researching the state of crime: local, national and international victim surveys', in R. King and E. Wincup (eds), *Doing Research on Crime and Justice*. Oxford: Oxford University Press.

Maynard, M. and Purvis, J. (1994) (eds) *Researching Women's Lives from a Feminist Perspective*. London: Taylor and Francis.

McEvoy, K. (2001) *Paramilitary Imprisonment in Northern Ireland: Resistance, Management and Release*. Oxford: Oxford University Press.

McKeganey, N. (2001) 'To pay or not to pay: respondents' motivation for participating in research', *Addiction*, 96: 1237–8.

McKeganey, N. and Barnard, M. (1996) *Sex Work on the Streets: Prostitutes and their Clients*. Buckingham: Open University Press.

Mead, G. (1934) *Mind, Self and Society*. Chicago: University of Chicago Press.

Measham, F., Newcombe, R. and Parker, H. (1994) 'The normalization of recreational drug use amongst young people in north-west England', *British Journal of Sociology*, 45: 287–312.

Mhlanga, B. (1999) *Race and Crown Prosecution Service Decisions*. London: Home Office.

Mhlanga, B. (2000) 'The numbers game: quantitative research on ethnicity', in R. King and E. Wincup (eds), *Doing Research on Crime and Justice*. Oxford: Oxford University Press.

Mienczakowski (2001) 'Ethnodrama: performed research – limitations and potential', in P. Atkinson, A. Coffey, S. Delamont, J. Lofland and L. Lofland (eds), *Handbook of Ethnography*. London: Sage.

Miles, M. and Huberman, A. (1994) *Qualitative Data Analysis: An Expanded Sourcebook*. Thousand Oaks, CA: Sage.

Millman, M. (1975) 'She did it all for love: a feminist view of the sociology of deviance', in M. Millman and R. Kantet (eds), *Another Voice*. New York: Anchor.

Mopas, M. and Stenning, P. (1999) 'Tools of the Trade: The Symbolic Power of Private Security – an Exploratory Study'. Unpublished conference paper, British Society of Criminology, Liverpool.

Morgan, R. (2000) 'The politics of criminological research', in R. King and E. Wincup (eds), *Doing Research on Crime and Justice*. Oxford: Oxford University Press.

Morgan, R. and Newburn, T. (1997) *The Future of Policing*. Oxford: Oxford University Press.

Moser, C. and Kalton, G. (1985) *Survey Methods in Social Investigation*. Aldershot: Gower.

Muncie, J. (2001) 'Positivism', in E. McLaughlin and J. Muncie (eds), *The Sage Dictionary of Criminology*. London: Sage.

National Audit Office (2003) *Getting the Evidence: Using Research in Policy-making.* London: National Audit Office.

National Opinion Poll (2000) Personal communication with the researchers.

Naylor, B. (1995) 'Women's crime and media coverage', in R. Dobash, R. Dobash and L. Noaks (eds), *Gender and Crime.* Cardiff: University of Wales Press.

Newburn, T., Crawford, A., Earle, R., Goldie, S., Hale, C., Masters, G. Netten, A., Saunders, R., Hallam, A., Sharpe, K. and Uglow, S. (2002) *The Introduction of Referral Orders into the Youth Justice System,* Home Office Research Study 242. London: Home Office.

Noaks, L. (1988) 'The Perception and Fear of Crime and Its Implications for Residents in the Bettws Community'. Unpublished MSc (Econ) thesis, Cardiff University.

Noaks, L. (2000) 'Private Cops on the Block: a Review of Private Security in a residential Area'. Unpublished PhD thesis, Cardiff University.

Noaks, L. and Christopher, S. (1990) 'Why police are assaulted', *Policing,* 6: 625–38.

Noaks, L. and Butler, I (1995) 'Silence in court? Language interpreters in the courts of England and Wales'. *Howard Journal* 34 (2): 124–35.

Norris, C. (1993) 'Some ethical considerations on field-work with the police', in D. Hobbs and T. May (eds), *Interpreting the Field: Accounts of Ethnography.* Oxford: Oxford University Press.

Oakley, A. (1981) 'Interviewing women: a contradiction in terms', in H. Roberts (ed.), *Doing Feminist Research.* London: Routledge.

O'Connell Davidson, J. and Layder, D. (1993) *Methods, Sex and Madness.* London: Routledge.

Olesen, V. (1994) 'Feminism and models of qualitative research', in N. Denzin and Y. Lincoln (eds), *Handbook of Qualitative Research.* Thousand Oaks, CA: Sage.

Owen, J. (1995) 'Women-talk and men-talk: defining and resisting victim status', in R. Dobash, R. Dobash and L. Noaks (eds), *Gender and Crime.* Cardiff: University of Wales Press.

PA Consulting Group (2001) *Diary of a Police Officer,* Police Research Series Paper 149. London: Home Office.

Parker, H. (1996) 'Young adult offenders, alcohol and criminological cul-de-sacs', *British Journal of Criminology,* 36: 282–98.

Parker, H., Aldridge, J. and Measham, F. (1998) *Illegal Leisure: The Normalization of Adolescent Recreational Drug Use.* London: Routledge.

Pearson, G. (1983) *Hooligan: A History of Respectable Fears.* Basingstoke: Macmillan.

Pearson, G. (1993) 'Talking a good fight: authenticity and distance in the ethnographer's craft', in D. Hobbs and T. May (eds), *Interpreting the Field: Accounts of Ethnography.* Oxford: Oxford University Press.

Peckham, A. (1985) *A Woman in Custody.* London: Fontana.

Perkins, A. (2001) 'Homeless target "in sight" as 3,000 are taken off streets', *The Guardian,* 4 August.

Plummer, K. (2001) *Documents of Life 2.* London: Sage.

Polsky, N. (1971) *Hustlers, Beats and Others.* Harmondsworth. Pelican.

Prior, L. (2003) *Using Documents in Social Research.* London: Sage.

Punch, M. (1979) *Policing the Inner City.* London: Macmillan.

Quetelet, A. (1842) 'Of the development of the propensity to crime', abridged extract in E. McLaughlin, J. Muncie and G. Hughes (eds) (2003), *Criminological Perspectives: A Reader.* London: Sage.

Quinn, J. (2001) 'Stuck in Traffick: The Trafficking of Human Beings, Organisation and Context'. Unpublished MSc thesis: Cardiff University.

Radford, J. (1989) 'Women and policing: contradictions old and new', in J. Hanmer, J. Radford and E. Stanko (eds), *Women, Policing and Male Violence: International Perspectives*. London: Routledge.

Ramsay, M., Baker, P., Goulden, C., Sharp, C. and Sondhi, A. (2001) *Drug Misuse Declared in 2000: Results from the British Crime Survey*, Home Office Research Study 224. London: Home Office.

Rappert, B. (1997) 'Users and social science research: policy, problems and possibilities', *Sociological Research Online*, 2 (3).

Rawlinson, P. (2000) 'Mafia, methodology and "alien" culture', in R. King and E. Wincup (eds), *Doing Research on Crime and Justice*. Oxford: Oxford University Press.

Reiner, R. (1997) 'Media made criminality: the representation of crime', in M. Maguire, R. Morgan and R. Reiner (eds), *The Oxford Handbook of Criminology*. Oxford: Oxford University Press.

Reiner, R. (1991) *Chief Constables*. Oxford University Press.

Reiner, R. (2000a) *The Politics of the Police*. Oxford: Oxford University Press.

Reiner, R. (2000b) 'Police research', in R. King and E. Wincup (eds), *Doing Research on Crime and Justice*. Oxford: Oxford University Press.

Reinharz, S. (1992) *Feminist Methods in Social Research*. New York: Oxford University Press.

Robson, C. (2001) *Real World Research*. Oxford: Blackwell.

Rock, P. (1993) *The Social World of an English Crown Court: Witness and Professionals in the Crown Court Centre at Wood Green*. Oxford: Oxford University Press.

Rock, P. (1994) 'The social organisation of British criminology', in M. Maguire, R. Morgan and R. Reiner (eds), *The Oxford Handbook of Criminology*. Oxford: Oxford University Press.

Roseneil, S. (1993) 'Greenham revisited: researching myself and my sisters', in D. Hobbs and T. May (eds), *Interpreting the Field: Accounts of Ethnography*. Oxford: Oxford University Press.

Rough Sleepers Unit (2000) *Coming in from the Cold: Progress Report on the Government's Strategy on Rough Sleeping*. London: DETR.

Scott, J. (1990) *A Matter of Record*. Cambridge: Polity Press.

Shaffir, W. (1991) 'Managing a convincing self-presentation: some personal reflection on entering the field', in W. Shaffir and R. Stebbins (eds), *Experiencing Fieldwork: An Insider View of Qualitative Research*. Newbury Park, CA: Sage.

Shaffir, W. and Stebbins, R. (eds) (1991) *Experiencing Fieldwork: An Insider View of Qualitative Research*. Newbury Park, CA: Sage.

Shaffir, W., Stebbins, R. and Turowetz, A. (eds) (1980) *Fieldwork Experience: Qualitative Approaches to Social Research*. New York: St. Martin's Press.

Sharpe, K. (1998) *Red Light, Blue Light: Prostitutes, Punters and the Police*. Aldershot: Ashgate.

Sharpe, K. (2000) 'Mad, bad and (sometimes) dangerous to know: street corner research with prostitutes, punters and the police', in R. King and E. Wincup (eds), *Doing Research on Crime and Justice*. Oxford: Oxford University Press.

Shaw, C. (1930) *The Jack-roller: A Delinquent Boy's Own Story*. Chicago: University of Chicago Press.

Shaw, C. and McKay, H. (1942) *Juvenile Delinquency and Urban Areas*. Chicago: University of Chicago Press.

Shaw, I. (2003) 'Ethics in qualitative research and evaluation', *British Journal of Social Work*, 33: 107–20.

Shiner, M. and Newburn, T. (1999) 'Taking tea with Noel', in N. South (ed.), *Drugs: Cultures, Controls and Everyday Life*. London: Sage.

Silvestri, M. (2003) *Women in Charge: Policing, Gender and Leadership*. Cullompton: Willan Publishing.

Silverman, D, (1985) *Qualitative Methodology and Sociology*. Aldershot: Gower.

Silverman, D. (1998) 'Qualitative/Quantitative', in C. Jenks (ed.), *Core Sociological Dichotomies*. London: Sage.

Silverman, D. (2001) *Interpreting Qualitative Data: Methods for Analysing Talk, Text and Interaction*. London: Sage.

Skeggs, B. (2001) 'Feminist ethnography', in P. Atkinson, A. Coffey, S. Delamont, J. Lofland and L. Lofland (eds), *Handbook of Ethnography*. London: Sage.

Smith, C. (1996) 'The Imprisoned Body: Women, Health and Imprisonment'. Unpublished PhD thesis, University of Wales, Bangor.

Smith, C. and Wincup, E. (2000) 'Breaking in: researching criminal justice institutions for women', in R. King and E. Wincup (eds), *Doing Research on Crime and Justice*. Oxford: Oxford University Press.

Smith, M. (2003) *Developing Crime Prevention Techniques for Taxi Drivers: A Study of Taxi Drivers and Crime Prevention in Cardiff*. Report to the National Assembly for Wales.

Snow, D. (1980) 'The disengagement process: a neglected problem in participant observation research', *Qualitative Sociology*, 3: 100–22.

Social Exclusion Unit (1998) *Rough Sleeping*. London: The Stationery Office.

Socio-Legal Studies Association (1993) *Statement of Ethical Practice*. Socio-Legal Studies Association.

Soothill, K. (1999) *Criminal Conversations: An Anthology of the Work of Tony Parker*. London: Routledge.

South, N. (2002) 'Drugs, alcohol and crime', in M. Maguire, R. Morgan and R. Reiner (eds), *The Oxford Handbook of Criminology*. Oxford: Oxford University Press.

Spradley, J. (1979) *The Ethnographic Interview*. New York: Holt, Rinehart and Winston.

Spradley, J. (1980) *Participant Observation*. New York: Holt, Rinehart and Winston.

Stacey, J. (1988) 'Can there be a feminist ethnography?', *Women's Studies International Forum*, 17: 417–19.

Stanley, L. and Wise, S. (1993) *Breaking Out: Feminist Consciousness and Feminist Research*. London: Routledge and Kegan Paul.

Strauss, A. (1987) *Qualitative Analysis for Social Scientists*. Cambridge: Cambridge University Press.

Sumner, C. (1994) *The Sociology of Deviance: An Obituary*. Buckingham: Open University Press.

Sutherland, E. H. (1949) *White-collar Crime*. New York: Holt, Rinehart and Winston.

Taraborelli, P. (1996) 'Tapestries of Dementia: Exploring Caregiving Biographies', unpublished PhD thesis, Cardiff University.

Taylor, A. (1993) *Women Drug Users: An Ethnography of a Female Injecting Community*. Oxford: Oxford University Press.

Taylor, S. (1991) 'Leaving the field: research, relationships, and responsibilities', in W. Shaffir and R. Stebbins (eds), *Experiencing Fieldwork: An Insider View of Qualitative Research*. Newbury Park, CA: Sage.

Taylor, I., Walton, P. and Young, I. (1973) *The New Criminology: For a Social Theory of Deviance*. London: Routledge and Kegan Paul.

Tesch, R. (1990) *Qualitative Research: Analysis Types and Software Tools*. London: Falmer.

Toch, H. (1969) *Violent Men*. Chicago: Aldine.

Tombs, S. and Whyte, D. (2001) 'White collar crime', in E. McLaughlin and J. Muncie (eds), *The Sage Dictionary of Criminology*. London: Sage.

Tonkiss, (1998) 'Civil/political', in C. Jenks (ed.), *Core Sociological Dichotomies*. London: Sage.

Toor, S. (2001) 'Understanding the Criminality of Ethnic Minority Girls'. Unpublished PhD thesis, University of Leeds.

Travers, M. (2001) *Qualitative Research Through Case Studies*. London: Sage.

Turnbull, P., MacSweeney, I., Webster, R., Edmunds, M. and Hough, M. (2000) *Drug Treatment and Testing Orders: Final Evaluation Report*, Home Office Research Study 212. London: Home Office.

Walklate, S. (1998) *Understanding Criminology: Current Theoretical Debates*. Buckingham: Open University Press.

Walklate, S. (2000) 'Researching victims', in R. King and E. Wincup (eds), *Doing Research on Crime and Justice*. Oxford: Oxford University Press.

Wardhaugh, J. (2000) 'Down and outers: fieldwork amongst street homeless people', in R. King and E. Wincup (eds), *Doing Research on Crime and Justice*. Oxford: Oxford University Press.

Watson, D. (1990) 'Some features of the elicitation of confessions in murder investigations' in G. Psathas (ed.), *Interaction Competence*. Washington DC: International Institute for Ethnomethodology and Conversation Analysis, and University Press of America.

Wax, R. (1971) *Doing Fieldwork: Warnings and Advice*. Chicago: University of Chicago Press.

Webb, E., Campbell, D., Schwartz, R. and Sechrest, L. (1966) *Unobtrusive Measures: Nonreactive Research in the Social Sciences*. Chicago: Rand McNally College Publishing Company.

Weber, M. (1949) *The Methodology of the Social Sciences*. Glencoe, IL: The Free Press.

Westmarland (2000) 'Taking the flak: operational policing, fear and violence', in G. Lee-Treweek and S. Linkogle (eds), *Danger in the Field*, London: Routledge.

Westmarland (2001a) 'Blowing the whistle on police violence: gender, ethnography and ethics', *British Journal of Criminology*, 41: 523–35.

Westmarland (2001b) *Gender and Policing: Sex, Power and Police Culture*. Cullompton: Willan Publishing.

Whyte, D. (2000) 'Researching the powerful: towards a political economy of method', in R. King and E. Wincup (eds), *Doing Research on Crime and Justice*. Oxford: Oxford University Press.

Whyte, W. (1943) *Street Corner Society: The Social Structure of an Italian Slum*. Chicago: University of Chicago Press. Reprinted 1981.

Wilby, E. (forthcoming) 'A Comparative Study of English and American Children's Perception of the Police'. Unpublished PhD thesis, Cardiff University.

Wilczynski, A. (1995) 'Child-killing by parents: social, legal and gender issues', in R. Dobash, R. Dobash and L. Noaks (eds), *Gender and Crime*. Cardiff: University of Wales Press.

Williams, M. and Robson, K. (2003) 'Re-engineering focus group methodology for the online environment' in S. Sarina Chen and J. Hall (eds), *Online Social Research: Methods, Issues and Ethics*. New York: Peter Lang.

Williams, P. and Dickinson, J. (1993) 'Fear of crime: read all about it? The relationship between newspaper crime reporting and fear of crime', *British Journal of Criminology*, 33: 33–56.

Wincup, E. (1997) 'Waiting for Trial: Living and Working in a Bail Hostel'. Unpublished PhD thesis, Cardiff University.

Wincup, E. (2001) 'Feminist research with women awaiting trial', in K. Gilbert (ed.), *The Emotional Nature of Qualitative Research*. Boca Raton, FL: CRC Press.

Wincup, E. (2002) *Residential Work with Offenders: Reflexive Accounts of Practice*. Aldershot: Ashgate.

Wincup, E., Buckland, G. and Bayliss, R. (2003) *Youth Homelessness and Substance Use*. Home Office Research Study 258. London: Home Office.

Winlow, S. (2000) *Badfellas: Crime, Tradition and New Masculinities*. Oxford: Berg.

Wolf, D. (1991) 'High risk methodology: reflections on leaving an outlaw society', in W. Shaffir and R. Stebbins (eds), *Experiencing Fieldwork: An Insider View of Qualitative Research*. Newbury Park, CA: Sage.

Wolf, M. (1992) *A Thrice-told Tale: Feminism, Postmodernism and Ethnographic Responsibility*. Stanford, CA: Stanford University Press.

Worrall, A. (1997) *Punishment in the Community: The Future of Criminal Justice*. Harlow: Addison Wesley Longman.

Worrall, A. (1990) *Offending Women*. London: Routledge.

Wykes, M. (1995) 'Passion, marriage and murder', in *Gender and Crime*, in R. Dobash, R. Dobash and L. Noaks (eds), *Gender and Crime*. Cardiff: University of Wales Press.

Wykes, M. (2001) *Crime, News and Culture*. London: Pluto Press.

Zedner, L. (1991) *Women, Crime and Custody in Victorian England*. Oxford: Clarendon Press.

Zedner, L. (2002) 'Victims', in M. Maguire, R. Morgan and R. Reiner (eds), *The Oxford Handbook of Criminology*. Oxford: Oxford University Press.

Index